Charles Seale-Hayne Library
University of Plymouth
(01752) 588 588
LibraryandITenquiries@plymouth.ac.uk

Participation, Citizenship and Trust in Children's Lives

Studies in Childhood and Youth

Series Editors: **Allison James**, University of Sheffield, UK, and **Adrian James**, University of Sheffield, UK.

Titles include:

Kate Bacon
TWINS IN SOCIETY
Parents, Bodies, Space and Talk

David Buckingham and Vebjørg Tingstad (*editors*)
CHILDHOOD AND CONSUMER CULTURE

Tom Cockburn
RETHINKING CHILDREN'S CITIZENSHIP

Sam Frankel
CHILDREN, MORALITY AND SOCIETY

Allison James, Anne Trine Kjørholt and Vebjørg Tingstad (*editors*)
CHILDREN, FOOD AND IDENTITY IN EVERYDAY LIFE

Manfred Liebel, Karl Hanson, Iven Saadi and Wouter Vandenhole (*editors*)
CHILDREN'S RIGHTS FROM BELOW
Cross-Cultural Perspectives

Helen Stapleton
SURVIVING TEENAGE MOTHERHOOD
Myths and Realities

Afua Twum-Danso Imoh, Robert Ame
CHILDHOODS AT THE INTERSECTION OF THE LOCAL AND THE GLOBAL

Hanne Warming
PARTICIPATION, CITIZENSHIP AND TRUST IN CHILDREN'S LIVES

Studies in Childhood and Youth
Series Standing Order ISBN 978-0-230-21686-0 hardback
(*outside North America only*)

You can receive future titles in this series as they are published by placing a standing order. Please contact your bookseller or, in case of difficulty, write to us at the address below with your name and address, the title of the series and the ISBN quoted above.

Customer Services Department, Macmillan Distribution Ltd, Houndmills, Basingstoke, Hampshire RG21 6XS, England

Participation, Citizenship and Trust in Children's Lives

Edited by

Hanne Warming
Roskilde University, Denmark

palgrave
macmillan

First published 2013 by
PALGRAVE MACMILLAN

Palgrave Macmillan in the UK is an imprint of Macmillan Publishers Limited, registered in England, company number 785998, of Houndmills, Basingstoke, Hampshire RG21 6XS.

Palgrave Macmillan in the US is a division of St Martin's Press LLC, 175 Fifth Avenue, New York, NY 10010.

Palgrave Macmillan is the global academic imprint of the above companies and has companies and representatives throughout the world.

Palgrave® and Macmillan® are registered trademarks in the United States, the United Kingdom, Europe and other countries

ISBN 978-0-230-30264-8

This book is printed on paper suitable for recycling and made from fully managed and sustained forest sources. Logging, pulping and manufacturing processes are expected to conform to the environmental regulations of the country of origin.

A catalogue record for this book is available from the British Library.

A catalog record for this book is available from the Library of Congress.

10   9   8   7   6   5   4   3   2   1
22   21   20   19   18   17   16   15   14   13

Printed and bound in Great Britain by
CPI Antony Rowe, Chippenham and Eastbourne

Contents

Notes on Contributors   vii

Introduction   1
    Hanne Warming

Chapter 1   Theorising Trust – Citizenship Dynamics   10
               Conceptualisation of the Relationship Between
               Trust and Children's Participation and
               Citizenship in Globalised Societies
               Hanne Warming

Chapter 2   Adult Trust and Children's Democratic   32
               Participation
               Jo Moran-Ellis and Heinz Sünker

Chapter 3   Trust Building and Violation During Childhood   52
               Consequences for Children's Wellbeing and
               Dispositions for Trust in Later Life
               Julia Grosse and Hanne Warming

Chapter 4   Betrayal of Trust: Victims of Maternal Incest   73
               Jackie Turton

Chapter 5   Trust Relationships Between Children, Social   93
               Welfare Professionals and the Organisations
               of Welfare
               Sharon Pinkney

Chapter 6   Trust, Social Work and Care Ethics   114
               An Exploration of the Luhmannian Concept
               of Trust and Social Work with Children
               at Risk: Relating Luhmann's Concept of
               Trust to the Ethics of Care
               Michael Christensen

Chapter 7   Trust and Facilitation in Educational Interactions 132
               Claudio Baraldi and Federico Farini

Chapter 8   Negotiating 'Children's Best Interests' in the   154
               Context of Parental Migration
               Maria-Carmen Pantea

Chapter 9   'I trust my mom the most': Trust Patterns of   174
             Contemporary Youth
             Mirjana Ule

Conclusion: Potentials, Challenges and Limitations of the   194
             Trust Approach
             Hanne Warming

Index   210

Notes on Contributors

Claudio Baraldi is Professor of Sociology of Cultural and Communicative Processes, Department of Language and Cultural Sciences, University of Modena and Reggio Emilia, Italy. His research includes work on interactions between adults and children in institutional settings, promotion of children's citizenship and social participation and the development of methodologies and techniques for conflict management and dialogue.

Michael Christensen holds a Master's in Social Science and Social Geography from Roskilde University, Denmark, and is currently a doctoral student at the same university at the Department of Society and Globalisation. Michael's main field of interest is the everyday life of children and young people, and, for some, their contact with social welfare institutions and social workers. Moreover, Michael has worked in two Danish organisations, researching in the social welfare institutions' perspectives on their contact with children and young people.

Federico Farini is a contracted researcher at the Department of Language and Culture Sciences, University of Modena and Reggio Emilia, Italy, where he received his PhD in 2008. He participates in research teams about children and young people's participation, inter-linguistic and intercultural mediation. His field of expertise covers the topics of educational interaction, healthcare interaction, intercultural communication, mass media and methodology of social research.

Julia Grosse has been affiliated to the Institute for Civil Society Research at Ersta Sköndal University College and the Department of Social Work at Stockholm University, Sweden. She recently finished her PhD thesis on trust from a life course perspective. In her earlier works she dealt with young people's engagement in civil society and is also interested in mixed methods approaches.

Jo Moran-Ellis is Senior Lecturer in the Department of Sociology, University of Surrey, UK. Her two main areas of childhood research are children as social actors and the implications of this for everyday life, and considerations of research issues in empirical studies of children's lives. Her other key area of work looks at methodological questions in integrating multiple research methods.

Maria-Carmen Pantea holds a PhD in Sociology (BBU, Romania), an MSc in Evidence Based Social Interventions (Oxford) and a MA with Merit in Gender Studies (CEU). She has conducted research on the impact of migration on children and young people, on volunteering and the Roma minority. She is a member of the Pool of European Youth Researchers and holds a teaching position at the 'Babes Bolyai' University, Romania.

Sharon Pinkney is Senior Lecturer in Social Policy at the Open University, UK, and is currently the Faculty's Associate Dean (Nations, Regions and External Relations). She is engaged in research on children and young people's 'participation' in decision-making about their lives and how this constructs, produces and reproduces children as 'new subjects' within social-welfare formations.

Heinz Sünker is Professor in Social Pedagogy and Social Politics in the Faculty of Educational and Social Science at Wuppertal University, Germany. He is engaged in research and publications on critical social theory, history and theory of social pedagogy and social politics, childhood studies and child and youth welfare, German fascism and resistance.

Jackie Turton is Senior Lecturer in the Department of Sociology at the University of Essex, UK. She is an experienced qualitative researcher with both national and international publications. Her research activities include social and health needs of marginalised groups, child protection and women as offenders. Jackie has completed projects for the Home Office, Department of Health and the Royal College of Paediatrics and Child Health in the UK as well as the Ministry of Integration in Ireland. The subsequent reports have been used to influence both policy and practice.

Mirjana Ule is Professor of Social Psychology at the University of Ljubljana, Faculty of Social Sciences, Slovenia. She is the head of the Center for Social Psychology and the coordinator of the graduate programme 'Sociology of everyday life'. Her main topics of research are youth studies, life course (from youth to adulthood), identity studies and gender studies.

Hanne Warming is Professor of Sociology, Childhood and Social Work at the Department of Society and Globalisation, Roskilde University, Denmark. For many years, she has been doing research on childhood and children's everyday lives, perspectives, participation and lived citizenship. Currently she leads a research project on 'Trust in social work with children at risk', financed by the Danish Research Council. Further she holds the position as appointed member of the National Council of Children's Affairs (until Oct. 2012), as coordinator of the ESA research network on children and childhood, and as head of the international research network TRUDY (Trust dynamics in the governance of childhood), which was created in relation to this book project.

Introduction

Hanne Warming

This book is a pioneering work addressing trust dynamics in children's lives from the perspective of the new sociological studies of childhood. It aims to enhance our understanding of children's wellbeing, citizenship and participation, and offers new theoretical angles which we hope will inform future research into these pressing issues.

Over 30 years ago, Niklas Luhmann pointed out the lack of studies about trust in the sociological literature (Luhmann, 1979). Today, this no longer holds true. Quite the contrary, trust is nowadays widely recognised as highly pertinent to social life and individual agency in highly complex societies. Trust as a central concept is today deployed in theoretical and empirical analyses in various fields, as evident from literature reviews of trust studies carried out by Misztal (1996), Blomqvist (1997) and Grosse (2009). These reviews identify no less than 15 overarching fields of trust research covering a myriad of subcategories and subthemes (Christensen, forthcoming). Although the large number of overarching fields recorded is partly attributable to the different categorisation strategies used (e.g. according to scientific discipline or the relationship of trust to other concepts), it is striking that in this literature trust only appears once in connection with childhood and children, namely in Grosse's review (Grosse, 2009). Here, childhood is linked to one of the five categories of scientific discipline that she lists under trust research, namely psychology. The other disciplines listed are sociology, political science, economy, philosophy, theology and the sociology of religion (Grosse, 2009; Christensen, forthcoming). It seems that childhood has been largely overseen in trust research in most disciplines, even sociology, with the single exception of psychology. And even here, childhood tends to be approached from a traditional developmental psychological perspective which regards children as objects and 'becomings' rather than as active agents and 'beings'. None of these studies draw on insights from the new social studies of childhood, nor do they contribute significantly to this paradigm.

In 2010, Michael Christensen conducted a review on trust in childhood research as part of a Danish research project on trust in social work with children at risk (see www.tillid.ruc.dk). The review is based on 1.258 articles from peer reviewed childhood research journals, which include the words 'trust', 'mistrust' or 'distrust' in their title, abstract or keywords. This review reveals an interesting paradox: although trust is considered very important in these articles, it is vaguely defined and often not explicitly conceptualised. Only very few articles pay attention to the diversity of meanings of trust, or discuss how trust differs from related concepts such as confidence, faith and trustworthiness. These articles include Tranter and Skrbis (2009), Raamat et al. (2008), Salmi et al. (2007), Paton (2007) and Harlow and Shardlow (2006) (Christensen, forthcoming). Finally, the book *Violations of Trust: How Social and Welfare Institutions Fail Children and Young People* (Bessant et al., 2005) deserves mention as a more extensive piece of work; however, it refers solely to the Australian context and focuses on the dynamics of trust violation at the expense of the dynamics of trust building.

In sum, trust and mistrust typically figure in sociological research on childhood as significant, but under-theorised and very seldom systematically explored factors which shape children's participation, citizenship and wellbeing. There is a dearth of in-depth sociological studies on the dynamics of trust building and violation which take into account the interplay of micro, meso and macro dynamics. This book is intended as a first step towards filling these gaps. We hope that it will be a source of inspiration for further research and publication within this important field.

Trust, participation and citizenship in complex globalised societies

In sociological literature on life conditions in globalised societies characterised by increasing risk, complexity and unpredictability, trust is regarded not only as an essential human need, but as crucial to individuals' agency and their ability to cooperate with others (Luhmann, 2005). Following this line of thought, the concept of trust can help us to understand the challenges to, and opportunities for, individual and collective agency, and thus also for children's and young people's participation and citizenship in globalised societies. Not surprisingly, therefore, researchers from many different disciplines have shown increasing interest in the role played by trust in social cohesion, social capital and citizenship (e.g. Warren, 1999; Uslaner, 1999 and Misztal, 2001), deliberative democracy (see Harré, 1999 and Inglehart, 1999), and responsivity in social work (see Howe, 1998; Smith, 2001 and Ruch, 2005). Giddens (1990, 1991), for his part, analyses how the disembedding processes of modernity change and challenge trust. Likewise, in their research on social work, Parton (1998), Smith (2001) and Ruch (2005) point out that processes of bureaucratisation, contractualisation and standardisation undermine trust, making it a 'scarce resource' (Smith, 2001: 289).

Curiously, however, this important research on trust has not yet really filtered into the field of children's participation and citizenship. Figuratively speaking, the two research fields seem to have inhabited parallel universes. One explanation for this may be that despite the growing number of publications in the field of children's citizenship and participation, the subject is still quite under-theorised, as pointed out by Moosa-Mitha (2005), Tisdall and Liebel (2008) and Thomas and Percy-Smith (2010). Although this is changing – Moosa-Mitha's article, the first part of the collected book *Children and Citizenship* (Williams & Invernizzi, 2007) and the third part of *A Handbook of Children and Young People's Participation* (Percy-Smith & Thomas, 2010) are important examples of that – on the whole this emergent theorising still overlooks the significance of trust for participation and citizenship.

This book arose from my realisation that the trust concept held great potential for research into children's participation and citizenship in particular, and for their wellbeing and agency in general. I hope that the book will go some way towards remedying the absence of a theoretically-based understanding of trust in the new social studies of childhood. The book is based on work carried out within the framework of an international research network on 'Trust dynamics in the governance of children and youth' (TRUDY),[1] which I initiated in 2010.

Content of the book

The book explores trust dynamics in the governance of children and youth as contextualised in specific social arenas (institutions, the local, the national and the global), in time (the global age) and as constructed over time. Thus, in line with Halldén (2005) and Uprichard (2008), we approach childhood from a combined 'becoming' and 'being' perspective. Becoming and being are two intertwined dimensions of childhood, which are both located within what Bronfenbrenner (1979, 1994) has termed the ecological system. The ecological system, that provides the context for children's lives and development, consists of five different types of subsystem: *microsystems*, which are the face-to-face settings in which children participate, for example school, daycare institutions, peer groups and the family; *mesosystems*, which are the linkages and processes between two or more microsystems; *exosystems*, which are the 'linkages and processes between two or more settings, at least one of which does not contain the child but in which events occur that indirectly influence' (Bronfenbrenner, 1994: 39–40) the child's microsystems; *macrosystems*, which are the overarching cultural patterns of discourses and practices; and *chronosystems*, which encompass 'changes and consistency over time' which may affect both the child and the environment in which s/he lives (Ibid.).

Using the concept of *trust dynamics*, we address the causes and consequences of trust building and trust violation processes, which are explored through the combination of theoretical depth and direct application to analyses in different institutional and cultural contexts. The theoretical and empirical exploration of trust dynamics range from a subjective level, to interactions and institutional dynamics, to research examining the discursive and social structural level, and not least linkages between the different levels, covering the entire ecological system (Bronfenbrenner, 1994).

Chapter 1, by Warming, revisits the issues raised in this introduction regarding how to theorise the relationship between trust and children's participation and citizenship. The chapter shows how Luhmann's concept of trust can be developed by reinterpreting it in the light of a difference-centred approach to children's citizenship, and combining it with Delanty's distinction between disciplinary and inclusive citizenship learning processes (identity) and Bourdieu's power sensitive theory of practice for the purpose of a critical rather than functional approach. These theoretical points are illustrated using a case borrowed from a Danish child-led research project on trust in social work. Chapter 2, by Moran-Ellis and Sünker, develops the issue of a critical power sensitive approach. Based on the observation that adult support of children's participation is in practice still a contested space, the authors argue that this is related to adults trust and mistrust in children, which is again related to generational power structures. The argument unfolds through analysis of three cases of children as collective agents. The chapter enhances an understanding of trust-power dynamics, and how they shape the social spaces of children as collective agents.

The next two chapters offer empirical analyses of trust dynamics on a subjective level. Chapter 3, by Grosse and Warming, examines the impact of childhood trust experiences for children's wellbeing and trust dispositions throughout the life course. The chapter moves beyond an individual psychological understanding of trust by examining the impact of critical incidents within the framework of institutions such as the family, schools or social work settings, and those of a more inter-personal nature such as relationships with parents and peers, as well as more latent perceptions of early life. The analysis, which is based on qualitative interviews with young and middle aged Swedes and Danish children, shows how institutional practices and logics, the personality of significant others and dominant discourses all shape experiences of confidence and trust, and influence the development of subjective trust attitudes and behaviour dispositions. In Chapter 4, Turton takes an in-depth look at the identity and agency consequences of trust violation by a 'significant other'. Her contribution enhances our knowledge about the micro dynamics of the relationship between trust and children's participation and wellbeing. Her analysis moves beyond an individual psychological understanding, demonstrating how these micro dynamics are shaped by the discursive context. Her empirical focus is the difficulties that victims of maternal incest have in disclosing their abuse, and the dilemmas these children face when considering who to trust. The analysis is based on interviews with adult survivors of female perpetrators.

Picking up key themes from the two previous chapters, the next two chapters examine trust dynamics in social work. In Chapter 5, by Pinkney, the analysis is based on qualitative interviews with British welfare pro-fessionals and consultations held by children's rights organisations with groups of children and young people. The focus is on work with children and young people who are either already in residential or foster care, or who have been deemed to be at risk of significant harm. The analysis assesses the personal and institutional constraints experienced during the trust development process. It further provides examples of good practice in which such constraints are overcome. It is argued that a key task both for individual professionals and child welfare institutions is to recognise the significance of the trust development process, and of trust relations, within the often fraught and contested arena of social work with children and youth. Along similar lines, Christensen's chapter (Chapter 6) on 'Trust, Social Work and Care Ethics' in a Danish context uses a Luh-mannian perspective on trust to explore the situated position of social workers employed within a municipality structure. Taking its point of departure in critiques of the current dominant institutional focus on pro-cedure, cost reduction, cost effectiveness and documentation, the chapter argues that the latter constitute significant constraints in trust building processes between social workers and children at risk. Drawing upon empirical material from an ongoing research project, Christensen shows how, seen from a Luhmannian perspective on trust, social workers may be regarded as situated between the role of a system representative with specific trust signifiers, and that of an individual with personal trust attributes. He explains how social workers struggle to manage these different roles, but that these struggles – if carried out successfully – have the potential to create spaces in which positive, trustful relations between social workers and children at risk can be forged.

Chapter 7, by Baraldi and Farini, explores the dynamics of trust, especially trust building, on an interactional and institutional level. Based on different theoretical conceptualisations of trust (Luhmann, Giddens, Rogers and Kelman) and the possibilities they offer for trust building, combined with empirical analysis of interactions between students and educators, the chapter examines the theoretical consistency and empirical verifiability of presuppositions about trust building. The empirical analysis is based on videotaped interactions recorded during two international peace building summer camps for adolescents held in Italy, that is, videotaped activities of peace education among non-scholastic intercultural cross-national groups, and mediation activities in intercultural classrooms. These cases are strategically chosen for the purpose of examining, identifying and highlighting the types of educational actions that hold potential for trust promotion. The chapter thus offers theoretical development as well as examples of good trust building practice in educational systems.

Exploring the intersection between different discursive constructions of 'wellbeing', 'children's best interest' and 'proper parenting', Chapter 8, by Pantea, studies trust dynamics at the structural discursive level. The chapter situates children whose parents work abroad as under-recognised participants in the globalisation process. It contributes to our understanding of trust dynamics in the governance of children, and to knowledge about how children's participation and citizenship are shaped, by analysing how 'children's best interest' is symbolically negotiated among different actors (children, parents, caretakers, teachers, social workers) and the state of Romania. The empirical basis for the analysis is a literature review, document analysis and qualitative interviews with children and social workers. By exploring the intersection between different meanings of 'wellbeing', the chapter advances our understanding of the dynamics of power, control and trust as they relate to children as a social group, and of how these connect to the national context, in this case a former totalitarian society. The latter point is followed up in Chapter 9, in which

Ule explores trust dynamics in the governance of youth at the structural level in Slovenia, by analysing changes in the relationship between youth and society during the past two decades. This period was characterised by the transition from socialism to neoliberalism, which has accentuated social differences such as class, gender and ethnicity. The analysis, which is based on comparisons of data from youth studies carried out during this period, shows how this transition has transformed the position of young people from being a privileged group to being the 'weakest link'. This is because they are increasingly subject to pressures from social institutions such as the labour market, educational system, social care and protection, social security and health, over which they have very little or no influence. Increasingly, young people in Slovenia perceive the social world as unclear and unpredictable. They display low levels of trust in political institutions and subjects, and show a distinct tendency to turn towards privacy and private life. Thus, this chapter offers important insights into the – in this case negative – dynamic relationship between the general social structure and young people's trust in the society in which they live.

The concluding chapter reflects on the lessons learned across the chapters, arguing that the trust approach poses great potentials for a dynamic understanding of the shaping of children's participation, citizenship and life quality, including of the role of the welfare professionals. However, also limitations and a need for further theoretical development is revealed, which then together with the proven potentials form the basis for pointing out directions for future research.

Note

1 See www.ruc.dk/institutter/isg/forskningen/centre-netvaerk-samarbejder/trudy.

Bibliography

Bessant, J., R. Hill & R. Watts (eds) (2005) *Violations of Trust. How Social and Welfare Institutions Fail Children and Young People*, Hampshire & Burlington: Ashgate.

Blomqvist, K. (1997) 'The many faces of trust', *Scandinavian Journal of Management*, 13(3): 271–86.

Bronfenbrenner, U. (1979) *The Ecology of Human Development*, Cambridge, MA: Harvard University Press.

Bronfenbrenner, U. (1994) 'Ecological models of human development' in T. Husten & T. N. Postlethewaite (eds) *International Encyclopedia of Education*, 2nd ed., Vol. 3, New York: Elsevier Science, pp. 1643–7.

Christensen, M. (forthcoming) *Tillid på trods i socialt arbejde med udsatte børn og unge – om kommunalt baserede institutionelle barrierer og facilitatorer for tillidens udfoldelse*. PhD dissertation. Roskilde University, Department of Society and Globalisation.

Grosse, J. (2009) 'Forskning om Tillit i Norden' in L. Trägård (ed.) *Tillit I det Moderna Sverige*, Stockholm: SNS Forlag.

Inglehart, R. (1999) 'Trust, well-being and democracy' in M. E. Warren (ed.) *Democracy and Trust*, Cambridge: Cambridge University Press, pp. 88–120.

Giddens, A. (1990) *Consequences of Modernity*, Cambridge: Polity Press.

Giddens, A. (1991) *Modernity and Self-Identity: Self and Society in the Late Modern Age*, Cambridge: Polity Press.

Halldén, G. (2005) *The Metaphors of Childhood in a Preschool Context*, paper presented at AARE conference, Sydney, 27 November–1 December, http://www. aare.edu.au/ 05pap/hal05001.pdf.

Harlow, E. & S. M. Shardlow (2006) 'Safeguarding children: Challenges to the effective operation of core groups', *Child and Family Social Work*, 11(1): 65–72.

Harré, R. (1999) 'Trust and its surrogates: Psychological foundations of political process' in M. E. Warren (ed.) *Democracy and Trust*, Cambridge: Cambridge University Press, pp. 249–72.

Howe, D. (1998) 'Relationship-based thinking and practice in social work', *Journal of Social Work Practice*, 12: 45–56.

Luhmann, N. (1979) *Trust and Power*, Chichester: Wiley.

Luhmann, N. (2005) *Tillid – en mekanisme til reduktion af social kompleksitet*, København: Hans Reitzels Forlag.

Misztal, B. A. (1996) *Trust in Modern Societies*, United Kingdom: Polity Press, Blackwell Publishers Ltd.

Misztal, B. A. (2001) 'Trust and cooperation: The democratic public sphere', *Journal of Sociology*, 37(4): 371–86.

Moosa-Mitha, M. (2005) 'A difference-centred alternative to theorization of children's citizenship rights', *Citizenship Studies*, 9(4): 369–88.

Parton, N. (1998) 'Risk, advanced liberalism and child welfare: The need to rediscover uncertainty and ambiguity', *British Journal of Social Work*, 28(1): 5–28.

Paton, G. (2007) 'Working together. Policy and practice in Scottish early childhood centres', *European Early Childhood Education Research Journal*, 15(3): 441–54.

Percy-Smith, B. & N. Thomas (eds) (2010) *A Handbook of Children and Young People's Participation. Perspectives from Theory and Practice*, London & New York: Routledge.

Raamat, R., M. Keller, A. Martesen & B. Tufte (2008) 'Young Estonians and Danes as online shoppers: A comparative study', *Young. Nordic Journal of Youth Research*, 16(3): 303–24.

Ruch, G. (2005) 'Relationship-based practice and reflective practice: Holistic approaches to contemporary child care social work', *Child and Family Social Work*, 10: 111–23.

Salmi, V., M. Smolej & J. Kivivuori (2007) 'Crime victimization, exposure to crime news and social trust among adolescents', *Young*, 15(3): 255–72.

Smith, C. (2001) 'Trust and confidence: Possibilities for social work in "high modernity"', *British Journal of Social Work*, 31: 287–305.

Thomas, N. & B. Percy-Smith (2010) 'Introduction' in B. Percy-Smith & N. Thomas (eds) *A Handbook of Children and Young People's Participation. Perspectives from Theory and Practice*, London & New York: Routledge, pp. 1–7.

Tranter, B. & Z. Skrbis (2009) 'Trust and confidence: A study of young Queens-landers', *Australian Journal of Political Science*, 44(4): 659–78.

Tisdall, K. M. & M. Liebel (2008) *Overview Paper: Theorising Children's Participation in 'Collective' Decision-Making*, paper presented at the European Science Foundation Seminar 'Children's participation in decision-making: Exploring theory, policy and practice across Europe', Berlin, June 2008.

Uprichard, E. (2008) 'Children as "beings and becomings": Children, childhood and temporality', *Children and Society*, 22(4): 303–13.

Uslaner, E. M. (1999) 'Democracy and social capital' in M. E. Warren (ed.) *Democracy and Trust*, Cambridge: Cambridge University Press, pp. 121–50.

Warren, M. E. (1999) 'Introduction' in M. E. Warren (ed.) *Democracy and Trust*, Cambridge: Cambridge University Press, pp. 1–21.

Williams, J. & A. Invernizzi (2007) *Children and Citizenship*, London: Thousand Oaks; New Delhi, Singapore: Sage.

1

Theorising Trust – Citizenship Dynamics Conceptualisation of the Relationship Between Trust and Children's Participation and Citizenship in Globalised Societies

Hanne Warming

This chapter explores how sociological theories of trust can contribute to a dynamic and critical understanding of children's participation and citizenship within the new sociology of childhood paradigm. Critical is understood here as a dialectical approach which is attentive to power relations and that illuminates dynamics of discrimination, disciplining and exclusion. Using the concept of trust for this purpose might seem a bit peculiar, as many sociological approaches to trust are functionalist rather than critical, including Luhmann's perspective which informs this chapter. However, in line with Harré (1999), I will argue that a functionalist concept of trust can underpin a critical agenda and that this can be further reinforced using Bourdieu's relational sociology and Delanty's theory of cultural citizenship.

The chapter opens with a brief discussion of classical trust theorising, which was characterised by universalism and a clear distinction between psychological and sociological conceptualisation of trust. I then turn to the work done on trust by Giddens and Luhmann, who conversely contextualise their theorising of (the conditions, need for and function of) trust in globalised high complex societies and move towards a more dialectical approach through including psychological as well as sociological perspectives. I argue that Luhmann's concept of trust in trust and trustworthiness, compared to Giddens' concept of basic trust, is more successful regarding overcoming the theoretical heritage of universalism and thus more in accordance with the new sociology of childhood. Further, I find his distinction between trust and confidence fruitful for approaching (conditions for) children's active' citizenship in globalised complex societies. Next, I present Bourdieu's theory of practice showing how this framework can contribute to a power-attentive development of Luhmann's trust theorising and Harré's re-reading of Luhmann's trust theorising, which connect dynamics of trust with democracy and active participation. I link this framework with Delanty's quadripartite conceptualisation of citizenship and Moosa-Mitha's argumentation for a difference-centred approach to children's citizenship and go on to explore the relationship between trust, citizenship and the social construction of childhood. I illustrate my argument using an empirical example from an ongoing research project about trust in social work with children. The chapter concludes by pointing to the risk that prevailing societal tendencies, such as the search for evidence-based practice in social work, pedagogic etc. and the neoliberal responsibilisation of the individual, might cause negative spirals of distrust – lacking citizenship.

Trust: The theoretical heritage

Although I agree broadly with Luhmann's point about the absence of trust in the sociological literature until he put it on the agenda (see the introduction of this book), trust has in fact been theorised in sociology since the days of Tönnies, Simmel, Durkheim and Parsons, all of whom acknowledged its role in social life and cohesion. In keeping with this heritage, Lewis and Weigert propose that from a sociological perspective trust 'must be conceived as a property of collective units (ongoing dyads, groups, and collectivities), not of isolated individuals' (Lewis & Weigert, 1985: 986). They thus draw a sharp distinction between the sociological concept of trust and psychological concepts, such as the concept of 'basic trust' developed by Erikson (1950) in development psychology. Whereas the latter addresses individuals' inner psychological capacities and feelings, the former address a characteristic of – or, as the above mentioned classical sociologists would argue, a precondition for – sociality.

However in later theorising, this distinction is neither simple and clear cut nor regarded as appropriate. Thus, in accordance with broader tendencies in social theory, most contemporary sociological and social psychological trust theorising strives to include both the dimension of personality and the social dimension, moving towards a more dialectical conceptualisation of trust. Hence, beyond the sociological heritage, Erikson's developmental psychological concept of basic trust (Erikson, 1950) has proven a significant source of inspiration for later sociological trust theorising. This includes the work of Giddens (1990, 1991), in which the concept of basic trust is more or less adopted, the work of Harré, who emphasises that trust 'constitutes both a pattern of psychological dispositions and beliefs' and 'a pattern of moral obligations' (Harré, 1999: 271), and Luhmann's theorising of system internal conditions for trust formation (Luhmann, 2005: 135–46). Despite these theorists' shared assumption of a dialectic relationship between a personality dimension and a social dimension of trust, the three authors approach this dialectic relationship quite differently as I explain below, starting with Giddens.

Adoption of the concept of basic trust

One of Giddens' important books, in which he also contributes to our understanding of trust, is *The Consequences of Modernity* (Giddens, 1990). Here, he analyses how the late modern life conditions threatens our ontological security, by which he addresses a stable mental state, and changes the social relations such that personal trust must be replaced by abstract (system) trust. According to Giddens (1991), basic trust, understood as a psychological structure developed in early childhood, is the essential and universal condition for trusting one self, other people and systems. Thus in Giddens' analyses of how the life conditions in late modernity threatens our 'ontological security' and changes the social relations, the individual's psychological structure of basic trust (or distrust) developed though early childhood is regarded as decisive for the resilience towards these threats and changes. In this, Giddens' work is typical of much sociological and social psychological trust theorising, which is directly based on Erikson's concept of basic trust. Below I will argue that this concept runs counter to the insights which have emerged from the new sociology of childhood.

The concept of basic trust relies on a model of personality development based on temporally ordered stages, in which passing successfully through earlier stages is a precondition for non-pathological development in subsequent stages. According to this model, the capacity for trust develops through the parents' care for the child during the first years of a child's life. This model has been criticised for being deterministic, universalistic and incompatible with empirical findings and theories about children's development from the new childhood studies (Sommer, 1996). Further, the concept of basic trust relies on a traditional understanding of child socialisation in which the adult care persons are regarded as the agents and the children as passive objects of this agency. This approach is not in accordance with important insights from the new childhood research (Sommer, 1996; James et al., 1998) which emphasise that: 1) the child plays an active role in interaction from the very beginning; 2) other people apart from the mother might be important in the young child's life, depending on the societal organisation and social construction of childhood; and 3) societal, historical and cultural specific features shape the context for interaction and therefore also influence the child's socialisation. While Giddens would probably not disagree on the latter point, as this is in accordance with his structuration theory about human action, it is not reflected in his use of the concept of basic trust.

Trust as a communicative act and system internal condition for trust

Luhmann (2005) conceptualises trust as a situated communicative act rather than as an inner feeling or an essential psychological structure. However he does acknowledge the existence of 'system internal conditions for trust'. These are conceptualised as trust in trust. Further, besides trust in trust, Luhmann also addresses the other side of the coin, namely 'system internal conditions for trustworthiness' (being trusted).

The notion of trust in trust is closely connected to the concept of basic trust. But while the latter is a personal competence learned through a successful passage through an early development stage during the first year of a child's life, trust in trust is a relational concept. Hence, trust in trust develops over time throughout life and vary according to the object of trust within a psychic system (a personality). Along similar lines, Luhmann's notion of trustworthiness, which is mainly inspired by Goffman's concepts of self-presentation and impression management, emphasises mutuality and the roles of social norms in the trust building process (Frederiksen, 2009: 9). This dual conceptualisation acknowledges the personality dimension as an important factor, but not as a determining factor in processes of trust building and reproduction. It also suggests that the personality dimensions of trust, that is trust in trust and trustworthiness, are not essential individual abilities, but are built up or damaged in cultural structured communication. Thus, it represents a step towards a dialectical understanding of trust that is in keeping with the new sociology of childhood approach.

Yet this framework is still quite weak when it comes to the genesis of the psychic system including the system internal conditions for trust. Indeed, the psychic system remains something of a black box in Luhmann's theorising, which was not the case regarding Giddens' theorising. Here however, we found the framework too essentialistic and deterministic.

Thus there is a need for the development of a theoretical framework that enables a closer analysis of the role played by the social in the genesis of the personality dimension of trust as well as an account of how it changes over time. For this purpose, I suggest combining Luhmann's work on the system internal conditions for trust with Bourdieu's conceptualisation of the relationship between individual dispositions (habitus) and the social. I introduce this framework in the next section and then develop it further in the subsequent discussion of trust and citizenship.

Combining Bourdieu's concept of habitus with Luhmann's work on system internal conditions for trust

Despite considerable differences between Bourdieu's and Luhmann's theories, at a very basic level they share a dialectic approach to the relationship between the individual and the social, as well as an autopoietic approach to society,[1] addressed through the concept of fields (Bourdieu) and systems (Luhmann) respectively. These shared ontological positions make it feasible to combine the two theories (Almlund, 2008: 9–10), however we also need to acknowledge the disagreements. These include a functionalistic (Luhmann) versus a conflictual (Bourdieu) approach to the dynamics of development and the disagreement concerning the relation between a system/field and the surrounding systems/fields. Whereas Bourdieu emphasises a hierarchy between fields, in which the field of power has an impact on the internal dynamic of all other fields, Luhmann only talks about how the surroundings can irritate a given system (Ibid.; Bourdieu & Wacquant, 1992: 90; Bourdieu, 1987: 6). This chapter is fundamentally based on the Bourdieusian approach, and the Luhmannian conceptualisation of trust is reconstructed through a Bourdieusian re-reading. Within the autopoietic approach, Bourdieu has dedicated his main efforts to illuminating domination and power dynamics such as discipline, discrimination, exclusion and not least reproduction of inequality. Thus, a Bourdieusian re-reading of Luhmann's concept of trust enables a critical analysis of trust dynamics that is attentive to power relations.

Following Bourdieu's thinking, habitus is generated as an internalisation of the social, including societal power structures. Habitus includes dispositions for trusting, which in Luhmann's vocabulary correspond to trust in trust, and the personal attitude that in relation to social norms leads others to see one as trustworthy or not. The societal power structures are theorised through the conceptions of social, cultural, economic and symbolic capital, field, positions and doxa by which we can understand the mechanisms of trustworthiness as a game of symbolic capital. Within this framework, parent's (abilities for) caring for their child is shaped through internalised and external power relations and doxas. Further, the personal capacities for trusting others do not only develop through the early child-parent relation, as it was the case within the developmental psychological approach and the concept of basic trust, but also throughout life through participation in, and incorporation of, the power structures of different fields, experiencing and learning whether others are worthy of your trust or not.

Bourdieu has been criticised for being overly structuralistic and attributing too much importance to habitus as a fixed structure (Jenkins, 1982). Seen in this light, his theory falls into the same trap as the developmental psychological concept of basic trust of assigning too great a role to early childhood in the genesis of capacities for trusting and the genesis of attitudes that promote trustworthiness. I will, however, argue that a more constructivist reading is appropriate, in keeping with Bourdieu's own description of himself as a structuralistic-constructivist and a constructivistic-structuralist (Bourdieu & Wacquant, 1992). Though Bourdieu regards early socialisation as more important than later socialisation, he emphasises that habitus, rather than a fixed determining structure, is a set of dispositions – or more figuratively speaking a vocabulary – that will play out in different ways depending on the field in which it acts and is not a fixed determining structure like in the development stage model. He underlines the creativity of habitus, which is necessary since any given situation is never the same as a previously experienced one, and he points out that habitus develops throughout life (Bourdieu & Wacquant, 1992: 133; Delica, 2011). In response to the critique of determinism, he further points to the sociology of the social determinants, that socioanalysis, 'can help us unearth the *social* unconscious embedded into institutions as well as lodged deep inside us' (Bourdieu & Wacquant, 1992: 49).

It has now been indicated how Bourdieu's concept of habitus can contribute to development of Luhmann's theorising of system internal conditions. In the remainder section of the chapter, which addresses the relation between trust and citizenship and how this relation is shaped in globalised societies, the analytical potentials of combining Luhmann and Bourdieu will be developed based on an elaboration of Luhmann's concept of trust.

Trust, citizenship and societal tendencies

While Giddens, in accordance with the classical sociologist, regards trust as a universal significant condition for social life and social cohesion, Luhmann, conversely, argues that its significance is conditioned by the growing freedom of individuals. In this view, trust becomes increasingly important as the degree of complexity and risk in society increases due to the role played by trust in reducing complexity. Thus, Luhmann argues that trust is far more important – but also a much more prominent phenomenon – in our highly complex societies than it was in the past. Rather than a disagreement in society diagnose, this difference between Giddens and Luhmann is due to Luhmann's stringent distinction between trust and confidence:

> If you do not consider alternatives (every morning you leave the house without a weapon!), you are in a situation of confidence. If you choose one action in preference to others in spite of the possibility of being disappointed by the action of others, you define the situation as one of trust. In the case of confidence you will react to disappointment by external attribution. In the case of trust you will have to consider an internal attribution and eventually regret your trusting choice. Moreover, trust is only possible in a situation where the possible damage may be greater than the advantage you seek (Deutsch, 1958, 1962: 302ff.). Otherwise, it would simply be a question of rational calculation and you would choose your action anyway, because the risks remain within acceptable limits. Trust is only required if a bad outcome would make you regret your action.
>
> (Luhmann, 2000: 97–8)

This narrow and more precise definition of trust does not address the taken for granted attitude nor the pure rational calculation, but describes a way of acting based on reflexive choice and acknowledgement of risk. If you do not trust, you are doomed to be suspicious and 'on guard' all the time, as confidence and rational calculation are increasingly impossible. Such a suspicious attitude is a psychological burden and a barrier to smooth agency, cooperation and active citizenship. This suggests that trust is the attitude needed to cope with risk, unpredictability, contingency and complexity, which characterises today's globalised societies. Thus, trust is a key precondition for smooth agency and cooperation and thereby for active citizenship in globalised highly complex societies, in which confidence and rational calculation are increasingly impossible.

While Luhmann argues that trust – due to the need for trust – is not lacking, but rather more prominent today than before, other theorists claim that it is declining. For instance, Hardin's (1999: 39) data from the United States, Ule's data about declining trust among young people in post-communist countries (see Chapter 9) and Parton (1998) and

Smith's (2001) observations of New Public Management within the field of social work suggest that confidence in for instance evidence-based practice and institutionalised distrust are increasing at the expense of social trust. The latter theorists regard institutional distrust as the opposite of trust and by extension of responsive governance and active citizenship. However, according to Luhmann, 'institutionalised distrust is not in opposition to trust but rather the opposite, it liberates agents from controlling each other, i.e. liberates them to trust' (Mortensen, 2005: 27, my translation). We will return to this difference later in the chapter after an exploration on the dynamics between democratic, inclusive citizenship and trust.

Trust as essential to democratic participation and active citizenship

Luhmann connects participation and trust in two ways. Firstly, by identifying a growing need for trust to be able to act in highly complex societies. Though he in this respect points to institutionalised distrust as a functional equivalent to trust regarding reducing complexity, he emphasises that institutionalised distrust reduces the possible alternatives of action (Luhmann, 2005) that is for participation and influence. Secondly, by pointing to that while confidence makes opportunities for participation available, trust mobilises specific engagement 'extending the range and degree of participation' (Luhmann, 2000: 99). Other theorists such as Harré (1999), Englehart (1999) and Misztal (2001) radicalise this point about trust as significant for engaged participation, identifying trust as a precondition for democratic participation and active citizenship (Misztal, 2001: 271; Harré, 1999: 264; Englehart, 1999: 88). Unfortunately however, without the same clear distinction between trust and confidence. Nevertheless, especially Harré's theorising can contribute to this chapter's theorising of children's participation and citizenship.

Harré differentiates between thin and thick democracies. In both types, an elected assembly establishes laws or rules. However, whereas in the first 'an official or factotum, usually appointed rather than elected, applies the rule regardless of the particularities of individual cases', in the latter 'the officials charged with implementing it negotiate its application with the citizens on a case-by-case basis, the outcomes of which will depend on the situation' (Harré, 1999: 263–4). Thus, the latter type is conditioned by trust relationships on two levels: between the legislative assembly and the officials charged with implementation and between the latter and the citizens. The important difference is that thin democracy consists of 'an overlay of parliamentary democracy over an essentially authoritarian life-form' in opposition to thick democracy, which consists 'of a thin layer of parliamentary democracy over an essential consensual and democratic life-form "below"' (Harré, 1999: 264).

Although Harré is here suggesting that trust relationships constitute the precondition for democratic participation and active citizenship, he doubts that the relationship works the other way around, that is citizens in thick democracies trust officials more than they do in thin democracies (Ibid.). This may be so if we stick to Harré's quite loose definition of trust, but it does not hold within Luhmann's narrower definition with a distinction between trust and confidence. Although, according to Luhmann, trust is a communicative act rather than an inner feeling, he acknowledges that emotional bonds can trigger and sustain trust and that distrust might therefore undermine social bonds (Luhmann, 2005: 140).[2] This relates back to the point about trust depending on an increase in individual freedom: Luhmann emphasises that trust cannot be commanded, but only offered and accepted, and that trust constructed in interaction builds on mutuality and accrues 'when the partner responds one's actions and one acknowledges the good actions of the other' (Jalava, 2001: 3). Keeping to this definition, trust is neither relevant nor possible in a thin democracy. Thus, citizens are more likely to trust officials in thick rather than thin democracies.

By briefly introducing the possibility of a normative interpretation of the concept of trust as a force that shapes citizenship and vice versa, I have outlined the main theme of the remainder of this chapter. Thus, in the following – after an introduction to a difference-centred approach to citizenship based on Moosa-Mitha and Delanty – I elaborate on the combining of Bourdieu's and Luhmann's theorising for the purpose of a normative and power attentive theorising of the trust – citizenship dynamic.

A difference-centred approach to children's citizenship

Based on a critique of traditional theories on citizenship rights for being adultish in their construction of children as not-yet-citizens and for being based on a false assumption of the autonomic self, Moosa-Mitha (2005) suggests a relational difference-centred approach to children's citizenship rights. On a practice level, this adultism is mirrored in that children's citizenship can be conceptualised as a struggle over recognition (Fitzgerald et al., 2010; Warming, 2012; see also Moran-Ellis and Sünker, Chapter 2). The difference-centred approach 'looks beyond formal rights in defining citizenship, emphasising instead the lived experience of citizenship, i.e. the realisation of citizen rights as perceived, and the subjective feeling of belonging as a full member of society' (Warming, 2012: 32). The latter is what Delanty (2003) in his quadripartite conceptualisation of citizenship conceptualises as the identity dimension or as cultural citizenship. The other three dimensions are rights, responsibilities and participation. Like the identity dimension, the participation dimension is also included in Moosa-Mitha's difference-centred conceptualisation of rights as a relational difference-centred re-definition of the right for freedom. She emphasises that the difference-centred conceptualisation implies every child's (and everybody else's) 'right to participate differently in the social institutions and culture of the society' (Moosa-Mitha, 2005: 375), so that their participation and contribution is recognised despite its deviance from a given norm of citizenship in terms of ways of participating, including both competences, habits and duties (Ibid.; Warming, 2012). This important point about recognition is in Delanty's theorising conceptualised in his distinction between disciplinary and inclusive citizenship, in which he points to a dynamic relation between the kind of citizenship (disciplinary or inclusive) and the shaping of identity, including the feeling of belonging (Delanty, 2003).

Trust and its relation to citizenship, rights, responsibilities and participation

The relation between trust and rights from a difference-centred approach – I argue – depends on the kind of society we are talking about: whether it is characterised by codes or costumes (Harré, 1999), and by foundational knowledge or by uncertainty and ambiguity (Parton, 1998; Beck, 1992). Let me illustrate and support this point using an example relating to children's citizenship. According to the UN Convention on the Rights of the Child, Article 20 (OHCHR, 1989), children have the right to special protection and assistance from the state if they are temporarily or permanently deprived of or in their family environment.

In a society characterised by foundational knowledge, the weighing out whether a given child is deprived in his or her family environment and the determination of what is needed to protect and assist that child can be perceived as an objective matter – something you or the professionals know. In such a society, the only risk which has to be overcome is the risk that the professionals will not fulfil their duty. This risk can – if not totally avoided – then be minimised through institutionalised distrust. However, as recognised by Luhmann – and research on social work with children and youth (Howe, 1994; Parton, 1998) – this is not the situation today. Rather, foundational knowledge today is beset with uncertainty and ambiguity, both in the field of social work (Parton, 1998) and in society as a whole (Luhmann, 2000; Beck, 1992). To redress this problem, a combination of system trust, for instance in knowledge and experts, and mutual personal trust – or institutional distrust, which must also rely on system trust however – is needed.

The interesting question then becomes: which difference does it make, whether it is handled through trust or institutional distrust? From a non-normative functionalist perspective the difference appears as a difference in number of possible alternatives of actions with more alternatives if handled through trust (Luhmann, 2005). From a critical perspective that addresses power relations and children's possibilities of influence, the number of possible action is critical to influence and participation. However, whether risk, uncertainty and ambiguity is handled through trust or institutionalised distrust has implications for other dimensions of children's citizenship. I will demonstrate the latter using an example from an ongoing research project on trust in social work[3] and theorise the difference based on Bourdieu's theory of practice. Further, from such a critical perspective neither foundational knowledge nor system trust are 'innocent' but rather a result of – and a tool in reproduction of – power relations and symbolic violation.

The impact of distrust

Liza, a 16-year-old girl, has been placed in foster care and institutions several times during her childhood to protect her from deprivation in her family environment. Today she lives in her own apartment – her own decision, but one that is considered a risky solution by the social services, as well as by Liza herself. The authorities' way of handling this risk is to appoint a social worker, a so-called contact person, to meet regularly with Liza and check if the arrangement lives up to Liza's right to protection and assistance and provides her with the support that she needs. Thus, the contact person can be regarded as one level of institutionalised distrust, in that authorities do not trust Liza's ability to manage in an apartment on her own. Another level of institutionalised distrust is evident in the regular meetings between Liza and her case manager. This time, the distrust is about the entire arrangement, not only Liza's placement in own apartment but also her contact person. Seen from the perspective of the case manager and the social protection system, this institutionalised distrust enables trust, so that they can take the risk of allowing Liza to live in her own home. Yet Liza doesn't want authorities like contact persons or case managers in her life and she doesn't feel that she needs them to be able to cope and to daring to take the risk of moving in her own home. This isn't because she doesn't like or trust the contact person and case manager – she does. But what matters most to her is normalisation and the right to take a risk, not protection against risk. Normalisation means an end to supervision by the authorities and trust in her ability to manage her own (risky) life.

Thus, what is at play is a conflict of interests between containing risk through institutionalised distrust on the one hand and normalisation, inclusion in the ranks of normal people with rights to take risks, through trust on the other. Institutionalised distrust enforces Liza's right to protection, but is a double-edged sword when it comes to her right to participation, the third dimension in Delanty's (2000) citizenship framework. It also fulfils Liza's right to have a say in her protection arrangements, but it does so at the expense of her main goals and priorities, namely normality and independence. From a difference-centred approach, which emphasises rights as perceived, it is question-able whether the institutionalised distrust actually contributed positively to the fulfilment of Liza's rights. Two key points about power are per-tinent to mention in connection with this situation.

Power dynamics

First, institutionalised distrust is not necessarily satisfactory for both parties in a trust relationship, and thus does not enable both sides to trust. Indeed, the opposite is true: institutionalised distrust typically takes the form of control and surveillance of one party by the other. Here, it becomes significant to see who initiates the control and sur-veillance. If a person or a system offers to subject themselves to control and surveillance voluntarily and on their own initiative, this may con-stitute a communicative act of trustworthiness. In that case, I agree with Luhmann that institutionalised distrust can enable the other part to trust, however the offer to subject oneself to control and surveil-lance voluntarily can also be interpreted as an outcome of symbolic violence. If a person or system, conversely, imposes control and sur-veillance on another party, this constitutes a communicative act of dis-trust. The person or system who is subjected to communicative acts of distrust is, according to Luhmann, liable to feel released from earlier moral obligations and therefore act in ways which confirm that distrust (Mortensen, 2005: 26), resulting in a vicious spiral of growing distrust. This has important implications for citizenship. Mutual trust morally obliges both parts, since it supports the fulfilment of citizens' rights and responsibilities. Institutional distrust, on the other hand, can either undermine or support the latter, depending on whether the measures taken are voluntary or enforced.

Second, not all agents are in a position to impose institutionalised distrust on others and others are not in a position to resist this. This has significant implications for the agent's influence on decision-making, and hence for the participation dimension of citizenship, since institutionalised distrust both identifies a certain problem and constructs it as risk, thereby conditioning the person's future space for acting and negotiation. In Liza's case, the social care system was the powerful actor. Liza was forced to accept institutional distrust as a precondition for being allowed to live on her own, even though this undermined her goal of freeing herself from supervision and surveillance by the authorities and managing on her own. Thus, while institutionalised distrust made it possible for Liza to participate in an important decision about her life, it did not allow for any discussion of her wish to manage on her own without supervision and surveillance. This is not a unique case, and neither is it specific to the field of social work. The same mechanism can be identified if we look into more collective forms of children's participation, for example pupils' councils, in which the presence of teachers or a head-teacher as well as a predefined teacher-led agenda are a frequent source of institutionalised distrust (see also Moran-Ellis and Sünker, Chapter 2). Children have to accept this if they want to participate in pupils' councils which they can do either unreflexively based on confidence in the adults, or more reflexively based on system trust in adults' privileged knowledge on how to run pupil's councils and which problems to address, or they can do it because the institutional distrust is enforced on them. Bourdieu has termed this 'the dilemma of the unprivileged', that is being caught between (self-)exclusion and assimilation into the power structure, where both choices confirm their relative powerlessness (Bourdieu, 1996). Thus, institutionalised distrust is usually based on, and re-produces, existing power structures.

The impact of the generational order on trust dynamics and children's citizenship

I mentioned earlier that distrust in relation to Liza's placement in her own apartment could be interpreted as communicative distrust of Liza's capability to manage on her own. However, this distrust is not necessarily directed specifically at Liza, but rather at children and young people under the age of 18 generally. Hence, I suggest that institutionalised distrust on the part of the state and municipalities is, in this case, rooted in 'what Leena Alanen (2001) with inspiration from Bourdieu's relational approach to the social(ly constructed) reality has termed the generational order', in which children are constructed as 'incompetent, irresponsible, vulnerable *becomings* in opposition to adults as competent, responsible, robust *beings*' (Warming, 2012: 32). In everyday life and social work practice with children, the generational order is the socially constructed root of what appears to be a natural and insoluble dilemma between influence and care, in which the former is too often subordinated to the latter (Ibid.). In this case, however, Liza's right to influence (the participation dimension of citizenship) was recognised, but due to the generational order which positioned Liza as incompetent and under age, Liza's own wishes needed extra precautions that may be seen as institutionalised distrust.

The social construction of children as incompetent and irresponsible undermines the possibility of trusting children's capability to make wise decisions, as well as their participation and, in this case, also their chances of managing on their own (see also Moran-Ellis and Sünker, Chapter 2). Further, the social construction of children as vulnerable compared to adults places responsibility on adults to take action to protect and assist children. This responsibility is reflected in the UN Convention on the Rights of the Child. Thus, the generational order constitutes a discursive frame for interaction between children and adults (or adult institutions) that promotes institutionalised distrust imposed by adults (or adult institutions) on children at the expense of mutual trust.

Thus the case illustrates that although social trust, system trust and institutionalised distrust have the same complexity reducing function, the qualitative outcomes with regard to children's citizenship and empowerment may vary greatly. Social trust supports social justice and active citizenship to a much higher degree than system trust and institutionalised distrust, hence while social trust is characterised by mutuality, system trust is based on – and reproduces – power relations. Likewise institutionalised distrust is conditioned by power structures, and thus only satisfies the one side of the relationship, in Liza's case the social protection system through meetings with – and supervision by – authorities that was enforced on Liza. Although this institutionalised distrust is actually instrumental in enabling Liza to fulfil her wish to live in her own apartment, at the same time it defeats her whole purpose for wanting this in the first place, namely her longing for normality and independence.

Trust, conversely, would have made it possible for her dream of independence and normality to come true. In other words, it would have given her access to (perceive) full citizenship and inclusion in the ranks of normal people.

Trust and citizen identity

I will now develop on the relationship between trust and the fourth dimension in Delanty's conceptualisation of citizenship (Delanty, 2000), namely identity or cultural citizenship.[4] Vega and Boele van Hensbroek (2010) posit that this dimension inscribes the notion of citizenship in cultural theory, extending it beyond its traditional political connotations:

> To talk about cultural citizenship means to articulate some kind of link between culture and citizenship. The concept thus broaches a very general problematic, as it is not too difficult to bring several such links to mind. But it also broaches a very specific problematic. It brings citizenship into a new area of concerns, compared to its classic conceptualisations – it infers that citizenship has other than merely political connotations!
>
> (Vega & Boele van Hensbroek, 2010: 245)

Thus, cultural citizenship extends the concept of citizenship beyond a relationship between the individual and the state, encompassing processes of meaning-making and explorations of how these promote or obstruct subjective feelings of belonging (Delanty, 2002; Vega & Boele van Hensbroek, 2010). Hence, the concept of cultural citizenship is normative in that it critically addresses meaning-making processes in relation to social integration/exclusion, recognition/misrecognition and belonging/alienation. Citizen identity, which includes an emotional as well as a cognitive dimension, grows – or is damaged – in the everyday practices in which webs of meaning-making are produced, reproduced, challenged and changed. These practices include interactions between peers and with civil society agents and officials charged with implementation of state policies. It is through these interactions that the subject comes to know and experience his or her identity as a citizen, as belonging, included and recognised – or not – in society. Delanty addresses this as a learning process:

> As a learning process, citizenship takes place in communicative situations arising out of quite ordinary life experiences. It appears that

an essential dimension of the experience of citizenship is the way in which individual life stories are connected with wider cultural discourses.

(Delanty, 2002: 65)

Like trust, citizen identity is build up – or damaged – through communicative acts in a broader web of meaning-making, namely cultural discourses. It is by virtue of these acts that individual life stories are connected with wider cultural discourses.

In accordance with his critical normative aim, Delanty makes a distinction between inclusive learning processes, which take on board experiences of deprivation or disrespect, and discriminative and disciplining learning processes (Delanty, 2003). Inclusive processes produce feelings of belonging and involve citizens becoming 'co-authors of the cultural context or contexts in which they participate' (Vega & Boele van Hensbroek, 2010: 25). Such inclusive processes counter demoralisation and social pathologies (Ibid.). Disciplining and discriminative processes, conversely, produce alienation and the feeling of being a stigmatised outsider (Hart, 2009). In the following, I look into the interplay between communicative acts of trust and the connecting of individual life stories with wider cultural discourses. This interplay works both ways. Nevertheless the mutual influences between the two are hard to distinguish in practice, hence the need for an analytical distinction. Therefore, in the following I address the influence of cultural citizenship on the process of learning trust and vice versa.

The influence of cultural citizenship on trust dynamics

Let us return to Liza's case, and specifically the point about the generational order as the meaning-making pattern that motivated distrust of Liza as capable of managing on her own. Theories of meaning-making and narratives explain how meaning is constructed through the emphasising of some facts at the expense of others, connecting those emphasised facts to each other in a cause-effect relationship and adding values (Frønes, 2001). The generational order meaning-making pattern under discussion here was connected to Liza's life story in a way that emphasised her age, her experience of deprivation in her home environment, her wish to live on her own and her assumed (lack of) competences. These factors were further problematised in relation to a distinction between adults and children, defined as people under the age of 18. First, it was emphasised that Liza would not live in her mother's home and this was constructed as a social problem and a concern for the social authorities because she was below the age of 18. Second, this problem then required a solution that somebody monitor and support Liza. And third, Liza's ability to manage on her own was constructed as impressive and extraordinary compared to what one could expect from a person of her age – though this did not help to mitigate the first and second constructions. Thus, the connection of Liza's individual life story with the discourse on childhood (the generational order meaning-making pattern) resulted in an inclusive process where Liza's experience of deprivation in her home environment and her wish to live on her own were voiced, yet she still found herself trapped in a framework of discrimination and disciplining. She had no choice but to submit to surveillance and guidance by the contact person and case manager.

According to Luhmann, trust is built up 'when the partner responds one's actions and one acknowledges the good actions of the other' (Jalava, 2001: 3; Luhmann, 2005). Thus, we might say that the act of connecting Liza's individual life story with a discourse on childhood enabled trust in Liza as a person, but this trust was caught up in a system of institutionalised distrust of minors, that is agents in a child position. And, as discriminative and disciplining communicative acts make it impossible to acknowledge another's good actions and thereby prevent trust from being built, we can assume that although Liza's experience of being allowed to express her wishes has probably promoted her trust in the social care system, her parallel experience of being trapped within a system of discrimination and disciplining is likely to have damaged this trust.

The influence of trust on citizen identity

The other side of the coin, that is the effect of trust on citizen identity, might by now seem self-evident. Communicative acts of trust where each party responds to the other's actions and acknowledges their good intentions would seem likely to promote inclusive rather than discriminatory and disciplining processes. Not least because communicative acts of trust, according to Luhmann, are conditioned by the freedom of the actors and their mutual commitment (Luhmann, 1979). If, with Luhmann, we differentiate between personal and system trust, this assumption can be substantiated with regard to personal trust, but not entirely with regard to system trust.

Communicative acts of personal trust have to do with a mutual process of constructing narrative identity as a trustworthy person among participants. The first step is that one party offers to trust the other, acknowledging the risk inherent in the act of trust. Thus, this first step can be said to make a non-naïve invitation for co-authoring. The next step is that the other party seizes this offer of trust and confirms, agreeing to be co-author. In other words, communicative acts of personal trust building are closely related to the inclusive building of citizen identity. Conversely, distrust, in the form of construction of one's identity as a non-trustworthy person, promotes disciplining strategies of surveillance and control which impede the construction of inclusive citizen identity, which involves a feeling of being recognised and belonging. Further, since distrust frees the individual of the moral obligations inherent in the trust relationship, it undermines the obligation dimension of citizenship, triggering a spiral of negative citizen identity construction.

System trust is related to generalised communication mediums such as money in the economic subsystem and truth in expert subsystems (Luhmann, 1979). However, as pointed out by Bourdieu and Foucault among others, truth is not only a medium of communication but also of power (Bourdieu & Wacquant, 1992: 90; Foucault, 1998). Trusting an expert subsystem implies accepting that others, for example children and youth, are not experts, with the probable consequence that they are not invited or do not feel qualified to take part in the co-authoring process. Further, trust also means to accept a certain identification of problems and solutions, either in form of demands, discipline and control or as demands for self-governance. These may also be combined. If cooperating partners believe in the same truth, it makes the cooperation smoother; however it does not necessary enable experiences of deprivation or disrespect to be voiced. Rather, it may silence such experiences, and thus prevent inclusive citizen identity. The child expert system truth about the best interest of the child is one example. Another example is the education expert system truth about the competences, for instance in reading and mathematics, which children should have at a given age, combined with a truth about children's responsibility for their own learning. The latter, which is part of a broader neoliberal discourse of responsibilisation, is particularly prone to discrimination, disciplining and the silencing of experiences of deprivation and disrespect (Delanty, 2003; Hart, 2009).

Concluding discussion: Trust dynamics and children's citizenship in globalised societies

In globalised, highly complex societies, trust constitutes a precondition for children's active citizenship. Luhmann's theorising establishes this link between trust and active citizenship, but does not offer a framework for critically analysing the relationship between trust dynamics and the realisation of children's citizenship rights as perceived, and thus not between trust dynamics and the processes of children's learning of citizenship as either democratic and inclusive or discriminative and disciplining. However, combining Luhmann with Bourdieu and Delanty makes it possible to illuminate positive spirals of social trust-inclusive citizenship, as well as the reverse, which is how distrust constitutes a barrier to children's citizenship and participation, since it is constructed through the power dynamics of the generational order. Moran-Ellis and Sünker elaborates on this point with regard to children as collective agents, in Chapter 2.

Luhmann himself suggests that social trust, system trust and institutionalised distrust all play a similar role in reducing complexity, and all enable agency in highly complex societies, however with regard to institutionalised distrust with the consequence of a limited choice of alternatives of action. From a critical perspective, an important addendum is necessary: although social trust, system trust and institutionalised distrust have the same complexity reducing function, the qualitative outcomes with regard to children's citizenship and empowerment can vary greatly. Social trust supports the realisation of citizenship rights as perceived and positive learning of citizenship identity to a much higher degree than system trust and institutionalised distrust, because while social trust as an ideal-type is characterised by mutuality and equality, system trust and institutionalised distrust is based on – and reproduces – power structures.

A prevailing tendency in contemporary society, at least in Europe, Australia and the United States, is a tendency to handle complexity by relying on institutionalised distrust and a search for foundational or evidence-based knowledge. This precludes the possibility of foundational knowledge and of acknowledging the power dynamics at play at the expense of trust and with negative consequences for children's citizenship. Another prevalent tendency is the neoliberal responsibilisation of the individual which, I argue, makes trust relations very vulnerable and worsens the impact of system trust and institutionalised distrust on children's citizen identity through symbolic violence. This claim requires further examination and substantiation, however. Thus, I suggest the impact of the neoliberal responsibilisation of the individual on children's citizenship as an important object for future research.

Notes

1   The concept of autopoietic systems is very often directly correlated with Luhmann's use of the concept. Originally however, it was introduced by Maturana and Varela in 1971. Varela defines autopoietic systems as a unity, organised 'as a network of processes of production (synthesis and destruction) of components such that these components: (i) continuously regenerate and realise the network that produces them, and (ii) constitute the system as a distinguishable unity in the domain in which they exist' (Varela, 1991). Thus, an autopoietic system does not necessarily work through one overall code of communication nor is it characterised by operational closure, such as in Luhmann's system theory.
2   For an elaboration on how emotions and emotional bonds can trigger and sustain trust, see Chapter 7 by Baraldi and Farini.
3   The research project is financed by the Danish research council (FSE), and is planned to be finalised in Denmark in 2012. It is based on fieldwork in two municipalities and includes observations, workshops with children and youth, and qualitative interviews with children/youth, their care persons and case workers (see www.tillid.ruc.dk).
4   Delanty uses both terms for this dimension, see for example Delanty (2002).

Bibliography

Alanen, A. (2001) 'Childhood as a generational condition: Children's daily life in a central Finland town' in L. Alanen & B. Mayall (eds) *Conceptualizing Child – Adult Relations*, London & New York: Routledge Falmer, pp. 129–43.

Almlund, P. (2008) *Når Pierre Bourdieu og Niklas Luhmann spiller duet*, paper presented at the 24th conference of the Nordic Sociological Association, University of Aarhus, Denmark, 14–17 August.

Beck, U. (1992) *Risk Society: Towards a New Modernity*, London: Sage.

Bourdieu, P. (1987) 'The force of law: Toward a sociology of the juridical field', *Hastings Journal of Law*, 38(5): 806–53.

Bourdieu, P. (1996) *Symbolsk Makt*, Oslo: Pax Forlag.

Bourdieu, P & L. Wacquant (1992) *An Invitation to Reflexive Sociology*, Cambridge and Oxford: Polity Press.

Delanty, G. (2000) *Citizenship in a Global Age*, Buckingham: Open University Press.

Delanty, G. (2002) 'Two conceptions of cultural citizenship: A review of recent literature on culture and citizenship', *The Global Review of Ethnopolitics*, 1(3): 60–6.

Delanty, G. (2003) 'Citizenship as a learning process: Disciplinary citizenship versus cultural citizenship', *Lifelong Education*, 22(6): 597–605.

Delica, K. (2011) 'Social innovation og områdebaserede indsatser – mod en kritisk socialvidenskab om innovation' in S. Voxed & C. J. Kristensen (eds) *Innovation og entreprenørskab*, København: Hans Reitzel, pp. 113–30.

Englehart, R. (1999) 'Trust, well-being and democracy' in M. E. Warren (ed.) *Democracy and Trust*, Cambridge: Cambridge University Press, pp. 88–120.

Erikson, E. (1950) *Childhood and Society*, New York: Norton.

Fitzgerald, R., A. Graham, A. Smith & N. Taylor (2010) 'Children's participation as a struggle over recognition: Exploring the promise of dialogue' in B. Percy-Smith & N. Thomas (eds) *A Handbook of Children and Young People's Participation. Perspectives from Theory and Practice*, London and New York: Routledge, pp. 293–305.

Foucault, M. (1998) *Viljen til viden. Seksualitetens histoire 1*, Frederiksberg: DET lille FORLAG.

Frederiksen, M. (2009) *Trusting Relations: Recasting the Sociology of Trust*, paper presented at San Francisco, United States, 7–11 August 2009, http://citation.all-academic.com/meta/p_mla_apa_research_citation/3/0/6/1/1/pages306110/p3061 10-1.php.

Frønes, I. (2001) *Handling, Kultur og Mening*, Oslo: Fagbokforlaget.

Giddens, A. (1990) *Consequences of Modernity*, Cambridge: Polity Press.

Giddens, A. (1991) *Modernity and Self-Identity. Self and Society in Late Modern Age*, Cambridge: Polity Press.

Harré, R. (1999) 'Trust and its surrogates: Psychological foundations of political process' in M. E. Warren (ed.) *Democracy and Trust*, Cambridge: Cambridge University Press, pp. 249–72.

Hardin, R. (1999) 'Do we want trust in government?' in M. E. Warren (ed.) *Democracy and Trust*, Cambridge: Cambridge University Press, pp. 22–41.

Hart, S. (2009) 'The "problem" with youth: Young people, citizenship and the community', *Citizenship Studies*, 13(6): 641–57.

Howe, D. (1994) 'Modernity, postmodernity and social work', *British Journal of Social Work*, 24(5): 513–32.

James, A., C. Jenks & A. Prout (1998) *Theorizing Childhood*, Cambridge and Oxford: Polity Press.

Javala, J. (2001) 'Trust or confidence? – Comparing Luhmann's and Gidden's views of trust'. Paper presented at the 5th Conference of the European Sociological Association, 'Visions and divisions', August 28–September 1, Helsinki, Finland.

Jenkins, R. (1982) 'Pierre Bourdieu and the reproduction of determinism', *Sociology*, 16(2): 270–81.

Lewis, J. D. & A. Weigert (1985) 'Trust as a social reality', *Social Forces*, 63(4): 967–85.

Luhmann, N. (1979) *Trust and Power*, Chichester: Wiley.

Luhmann, N. (2000) 'Familiarity, confidence, trust: Problems and alternatives' in D. Gambetta (ed.) *Trust: Making and Breaking Cooperative Relations*, Department of Sociology, University of Oxford, pp. 94–107.

Luhmann, N. (2005) *Tillid – en mekanisme til reduktion af social kompleksitet*, København: Hans Reitzels Forlag.

Misztal, B. A. (2001) 'Normality and trust in Goffman's theory of interaction order', *Sociological Theory*, 19(3): 312–24.

Moosa-Mitha, M. (2005) 'A difference-centred alternative to theorization of children's citizenship rights', *Citizenship Studies*, 9(4): 369–88.

Mortensen, N. (2005) 'Introduktion. Aktualiteten af Luhmanns tillidsanalyse' in N. Luhmann *Tillid – en mekanisme til reduktion af social kompleksitet*, København: Hans Reitzels Forlag, pp. 7–28.

Office of the United Nations High Commissioner for Human Rights (OHCHR) (1989) *Convention on the Rights of the Child*, www2.ohchr.org/english/law/pdf/crc.pdf.

Parton (1998) 'Risk, advanced liberalism and child welfare: The need to rediscover uncertainty and ambiguity', *British Journal of Social Work*, 28(1): 5–28.

Smith (2001) 'Trust and confidence: Possibilities for social work in high modernity', *British Journal of Social Work*, 31: 287–305.

Sommer (1996) *Barndomspsykologi*, København: Hans Reitzels forlag.

Varela, F. J. (1991) 'Autopoiesis and a biology of intentionality' in R. Whitaker *Autopoiesis and Enaction*, pp. 4–14, http://www.enolagaia.com/Bib.html, date accessed 15 February 2012.

Vega, J. & P. Boele van Hensbroek (2010) 'The agendas of cultural citizenship: A political-theoretical exercise. Introduction', *Citizenship Studies*, 14(3): 245–57.

Warming, H. (2012) 'Theorizing (adult's facilitation of) children's participation and citizenship' in C. Baraldi (ed.) *Facilitation of Children's Participation and Citizenship*, Routledge, pp. 30–48.

2
Adult Trust and Children's Democratic Participation

Jo Moran-Ellis and Heinz Sünker

This chapter considers the role played by adult trust in relation to children's democratic participation. Following an analysis of how discourses of trust in relation to children construct the participating child in different spaces of participation we find a high degree of contingency attends on how trust and distrust are mobilised by adult in relation to children when it comes to including children in decision-making processes. From a participatory perspective we find that where participatory mechanisms are realised through formalised system processes of confidence this can serve in children's favour, but that where adults retain the warrant to override children's views this is often articulated through questions of interpersonal trust and distrust. Finally, we argue that adults deploy or withhold interpersonal trust in relation to children as a class of person in ways which are akin to early Parsonian formulations of trust within familiar situations which suggests children as a category are held in a web of what could be characterised as 'pre-modern' relations to adults as a class.

Introduction

Over the last two decades there have been considerable changes in adult approaches to children's[1] participation in the public processes and institutions which govern their lives. From having little recognition that their views and experiences were of value, since the late 1980s children who come into contact with state institutions such as welfare services and schools can now count on there being opportunities for them to be involved in matters that affect their welfare directly (Hill et al., 2004; Burke, 2010). A requirement to create these spaces of individualised child participation is encoded in civil laws that govern the relationship between the State and the child in most European countries.[2] Many European countries now also have mechanisms through which children can have an input into matters that affect them less directly as individuals but are relevant to the broader category of being a child in general or a child in a specific type of situation. These mechanisms include institutions such as children's parliaments, school councils, and what we term here 'voice groups', that is groups of young people with experiences in common who are brought together as a group that can be consulted by policy-makers in local or national government.[3] However, welcome as these developments are, age-related or competency-related assessments of the child's capacity to have a view or contribute to decision-making tend to persist, especially in relation to individualised participation (Vis et al., 2012; Holland, 2001; Swiderek, 1999).

Developments in individual participation in decision-making about personal circumstances through to participation in wider democratic processes owe much of their impetus to the United Nations Convention on the Rights of the Child, 1989[4] (UNCRC) which includes participation rights alongside rights to certain provision and protections (Alderson, 2008). Other sources for this change to a more participative approach for children include particular country-specific events, such as a child sexual abuse scandal in 1987 in the UK which revealed the extent to which children's voices were absent from the child protection process (Wattam et al., 1989), research which demonstrated that participation was possible and desirable such as that by Thomas and O'Kane (1999a, 1999b), and the political effectiveness of the 'user' movement which has been key in ushering in a politics of voice and citizenship (Beresford & Croft, 1993; Beresford, 2000; Barnes & Cotterell, 2012). Another significant underpinning for children's participation has come from work in the sociology of childhood and childhood studies which has been concerned with theoretical and empirical work on children as social actors with the capacity to be agentic (see for example James & Prout, 1990; Mayall, 1994; James et al., 1998; Hutchby & Moran-Ellis, 1998a).

This is not to say that all such changes have been successful in material terms. As we will discuss later, participation is a problematic concept in practice since it challenges adult constructions of the child and often leaves undisturbed the distribution of intergenerational power which favours adults (Coley, 2007). Lansdown succinctly pointed out that children's participation is '[…] a simple and self-evidently worthy principle which would, if taken seriously, have a revolutionary impact on the nature of adult-child relationships […]' (Lansdown, 1995: 30). Contemporary intergenerational relationships are shaped by ideological assumptions about children which position them primarily as incompetent social actors in relation to the serious matter of their own present and/or future wellbeing. In the light of this, the idea that adults (as parents, carers, guardians or professionals) should make decisions on behalf of children becomes a naturalised and essentialised given (Archard, 1993). This creates an ambiguity between children as participants in processes of decision-making and children as recipients of adult care and control (Lee, 1999).

Another effect of the ambiguous subject position of children in this context is that the range of participatory spaces which have been established are restricted or are unevenly available even in countries where there is wide cultural support for children's participation (Vis et al., 2011). Caught between a politics of child rights which supports participation for children and an ideology of developmentalism, children are not routinely afforded a presence in formal political processes via voting and representation rights, nor in fora in which decisions are made which affect the whole of a community or society rather than only the child members (Wall, 2012). Where participatory rights are granted and facilitated this often follows an adult perception that children have a specific experience which equips them to have an 'insider' view which is of relevance to children in similar circumstances, such as having lived with mental health difficulties (Svanberg & Street, 2003; Worrall-Davies, 2008), having a disability (Burke, 2010), or having experienced particular life circumstances such as having been sexually exploited (Brown, 2006). This sits alongside the legal requirement for the provision of mechanisms for children's participation in processes where decisions are being made which relate to their individual lives (for example Eriksson, 2008; van Nijnatten & Jongen, 2011).

The ambiguities and tensions that emerge around the various forms of children's participation produce a mixed landscape of supported and denied participation. In some contexts children are seen as holding legitimate subjectivities which can, and should be, incorporated into decision-making processes, whilst in other contexts they are deemed too incompetent in experiential and knowledge terms to be able to make informed judgements in their own best interests. The landscape is made more complex by the potential for the same child to be seen to occupy both positions (Eriksson, 2011). Whilst this variation in the configuration of the potentially participating child goes some way towards explaining the existence of conflicting subject positions for children, it does not reveal what lies behind these ambiguities and ambivalences. We propose that the key to these inconsistencies lies within a fundamental, albeit contextually determined, variation in the extent to which adults, on an individual and institutional level, *trust or distrust* children as participative actors within a context of strongly morally and structurally ordered intergenerational relationships.

Adults, children and trust

Understanding how trust works in intergenerational relationships where adults are the trusting party and children are the trusted objects requires recognising that, in general, the power differential between adults and children persists even whilst children's participation has grown. This is contrary to the empirical emphasis placed on inter-personal trust as a mutual event (Gambetta, 2000). In addition, the focus of enquiry into the role of trust in contexts of unequal power relations is usually on why the less powerful (clients) trust the more powerful (professionals) (for example di Luzio, 2006) with prominence placed on the trust that circulates in systems. When it comes to the sit-uation of adults and children two conundra emerge – interpersonal trust is relevant but it is not located in mutuality since there is a power imbalance; and within the power imbalance the question of whether or not the more powerful party trusts the less powerful one becomes more relevant than vice versa. Noting these conundra, our discussion of trust is focused on two questions: what does trust between adults and children look like when children occupy or are admitted to a space of participation, and how do systems of participation configure trust components of intergenerational relationships?

Gambetta defines trust as:

> a particular level of the subjective probability with which an agent assesses that another agent or a group of agents will perform a par-ticular action, both <u>before</u> he can monitor such action (or indepen-dently of his capacity ever to be able to monitor it) <u>and</u> in a context in which it affects <u>his own</u> action.
>
> (2000: 217; original emphasis)

By definition, interpersonal trust seems to be predicated on some degree of mutuality being present in the relationship or interaction in which trust is operant (Smith, 2001). In respect of adults trusting chil-dren, however, the relationship is somewhat different. In the main, the relationship between adults and children is built on unequal power relations, with adults holding more institutionally sanctioned power than children, not least because of the legally governed age restrictions that limit children's institutional ability to be autonomous and self-determining.

Other mechanisms by which power is invested in the hands of adults rely on ideologies of developmentalism, socialisation, and notions of care and governance (James & Prout, 1990; Thomas & O'Kane, 1998; Burman & Stacey, 2010; Burman, 1996; Hutchby & Moran-Ellis, 1998b). The forms these mechanisms take vary by culture and historical period, ranging from authoritarian power such as that wielded within schools and other institutions (Bühler-Niederberger & Sünker, 2008) which regulate children's lives, to power through care and control within child-parent relationships (Bühler-Niederberger & Sünker, 2009).

However, if trust is related to risks, as is argued by Luhmann (2000) and others (Javala, 2003), it only becomes a relevant element in the relationship between adults and children where the child has the option to decide between two or more courses of action and the adult cannot be certain which course of action the child will choose. Conventions and norms of intergenerational orderings tend to situate the adult in the moral and material role of determining whether or not a child has any choice over particular courses of action. 'Allowing' a child to freely decide a course of action requires some trust on the part of the adult since, by definition, the outcome of the child's decision is not pre-determined. Parents and other adults do not easily hand over such decision-making power (Such & Walker, 2004; Kerr et al., 1999; Thomas & O'Kane, 1998) either because they do not 'trust' the child to act in their own best interests or because to do so would require a particular sharing of power which the adult is not willing to do. Trust and power remain intertwined even when intergenerational orderings are loosened through children temporarily occupying spaces of self-determination.

In contrast formal, organised participation by children has systems which support and enable it ranging from civil laws, policies, specific mechanisms, and the practices of professional workers with respect to the children with whom they engage or intervene. Smith (2004) notes, however, that systems cannot act and have no moral agency:

> Systems are designed to be functional and to achieve identified ends – their internal effectiveness depends neither on the moral motivation of those who operate them, nor on the moral nature of their outcomes.
>
> (Smith, 2004: 6)

As such, systems are characterised by confidence in the mechanisms of the system to deliver the expected outcome rather than trust (Smith,

2001). Risk is also putatively absent since the implementation of processes creates the conditions under which particular outcomes are delivered. Smith also notes that system approaches such as standardisation and process-driven, bureaucratically governed activities remove the agent from the picture and replace the person with a set of procedures which, if followed, guarantee the outcome. However, as she notes, this neglects the moral dimensions of those workers whose job it is to enact what the system requires of them and who are the point of delivery of the service or intervention. In this respect, trust re-enters the equation since with human agents (the professional workers for example) comes the risk that they will not follow the system's requirements or that the system's design will not control their autonomous actions. Relating this to child participation, we can see that systems which facilitate the child being included in decision-making meetings ostensibly negate the need for trust of the child since the process of inclusion will 'manage' the outcome of the child's participation, but what the child will say and what the workers will do with that, all entail risk and hence require trust if child participation is to occur. Participation for children then is better understood as the outcome of interplay between system confidence and intergenerational trust. We explore this complexity later in relation to three types of participatory practices.

Paradoxically, the restriction of children's participation can also be the product of interplay between confidence and intergenerational trust, albeit at an individualised and interpersonal level rather than a system level. Taking confidence to generally mean that the outcome is known (Luhmann, 2000; Javala, 2003), it is where adults as individuals and as professionals have confidence, albeit a *negative* confidence, in the ideological positioning of children as generic subjects who are *unable* to choose well for themselves that adults feel entitled (or required) to exercise authority to decide on the child's behalf. Equally, where adults are confident that they know what a child would want if the child had the insight and experience that comes with being an adult or being a professional, then they again understand their role to be one that is warranted to decide and act on behalf of the child without any need for consultation. In a third formulation of the interplay between confidence and intergenerational trust at the interpersonal level, if adults are confident they know what is best for the child, they may consult with the child, but where the child's view does not accord with the adult view a risk is introduced which elevates the significance of the need for trust from the adult for participation to be effective. Without investing in trusting the child or doing so only to a limited extent, the adult retains the authorised capacity to make a decision which is contrary to the wishes of the child, or to reinterpret the child's wishes to coincide with the adult view. In all three of these formulations, trust is not mobilised when the relation in operation is a negative confidence that the child will not act in their own best interests or in the best interests of other stakeholders, possibly including the adult(s). This situation of a negative adult confidence in knowing the child underpins both a paternalistic and authoritarian stance by adults. In the paternalistic mode, adults know what children want, or rather what is wanted for their wellbeing and thus what they need (Woodhead, 1990), anticipate that and make provision on that basis without any consultation. Still operating within a paternalistic model, adults also anticipate children's needs and incorporate their understandings of these (derived from bodies of disciplinary knowledge such as developmental psychology (Luke, 1989) into their own decision-making. Examples of this include 'children need safe places to play' leading to the building of specific outdoor play areas (Elsely, 2004) through to 'children need to be with their mothers' leading to a weighting of decisions in custody cases in favour of children remaining with their mothers (James & James, 1999). The confidence adults have in determining the decisions that need to be made on children's behalf has a long history of a politics of paternalism (see Archard, 1993) and rests on, as well as perpetuates, certain ideological assumptions concerning children as essentially vulnerable and in need of protection (Bühler-Niederberger-Sünker, 2008).

Participation and trust

We turn now to an examination of the role of adult trust in determining children's participatory involvement via a critical examination of three specific cases of participation: children's 'voice groups', children's school councils, and general suffrage and voting rights.

'Voice groups'

'Voice groups' arise out of a particular kind of approach to children's participation in democratic life. They include organisations run by children for children as well as groups of young people who are consulted by services and organisations to shape or steer those services. Examples in the UK range from those operating at a local level (for example Surrey CAMHS Youth Advisors[5]) to the National Advisory Council for children's mental health and psychological wellbeing which was a reference group of young people who have experience of mental health difficulties to 'inform and influence the work of the Council'.[6]

Some 'voice groups' have had notable impacts on policy (Burke, 2010), however they can also be limited in what they are able to achieve on behalf of their (child) constituency. Cashmore points out that young people in formalised voice groups may become co-opted to the agendas of the powerful as there is a tendency for them to be used as a 'convenient means of consultation for agencies without having to do the work themselves of engaging and involving the children and young people in the care of their own agency' (Cashmore, 2002: 842). Co-option essentially means that the voice group members have been repositioned inside the group which has the power to implement changes and no longer function as a critical outsider voice or representative of the interests of a less powerful constituency (de Montigny, 1998). Separate to this, but running alongside it as an outcome of formal involvement, is the potential problem that the processes of producing a 'children's voice' as representatives of a special interest constituency may offset criticality in the processes of translating the views of children into acceptable forms of input. The conventions of participation in policy-setting may have to be actively adopted by the voice group members for them to be sufficiently empowered to participate in unfamiliar mechanisms of committees and planning. However, learning the 'right way' to present a report or formulate a position can mean that children's voices are mediated via processes of system confidence which are already designed to nullify the risk associated with any ungoverned voices and views. Badham (2004) highlights this risk in arguing in favour of children being able to choose the means of mediating their views to maximise their impact. In addition, incorporation of voice within policy-making processes does not mean that the views expressed will be given more weight than the views of any other stakeholder and so again the potential for shifting the balance of power from adults to children is tempered by committee processes, power-holders and forms of democracy which dismiss particular positions if they do not accord with a majority view.

Given the conventions under which voice groups are set up or emerge, their participatory legitimacy generally derives from (contingent) positioning of certain children as 'lay experts' (Wynne, 1992; Irwin, 1995) on the basis of their experiences of non-standard childhoods – whether that be as disabled children, children in state care, or children with particular health conditions. The mode of representing children's voices to (adult) policy-makers or service deliverers is often based on processes of system confidence which do not require any long-term or fundamental re-distributions of power between parties. For the adults involved on the professional/political side of the equation, children's expertise is mediated through system conventions and bureaucratic processes which produce the children as legitimate actors and agents. Uncertainty of outcome is reduced through processes such as the formalisation of meeting, the structuring of the discursive means of contributing opinions and views, and the management of significance of those views. This effectively negates the need for adults to 'trust' children on an interpersonal basis, replacing that with system confidence but at the same time fundamental intergenerational power imbalances are not challenged, leaving adults with the ultimate capacity to decide what, if any actions, will follow specifically from children's participation.

School councils

A second form of participation has been realised through institutional arrangements such as school councils and children's parliaments. Both are examples of children positioned as a special group, but in contrast to voice groups, they are located as such on the basis of being children rather than in relation to the nature of their childhoods. We focus here on school councils as an instance of a particular kind of democratic structure within the wider institutional setting of school.

There has been quite extensive research into how school councils function and what they achieve (see Wyness, 2003, 2005; Cotmore, 2004; Thornberg & Elvstrand, 2012 for example). In general, research suggests that school councils can be effective but that the terms of their remit are limited to matters which teachers are prepared to allow children to have power over (Cotmore, 2004) and there is little general sharing of power and decision-making over matters central to the running of the school. Cotmore, commenting on the primary school council he studied, notes '[t]hat the school council had not disturbed the school as an organisation, despite its potential to do so, suggests that the school has successfully accommodated it within its existing decision making structures' (Cotmore, 2004: 64). However, he also notes that the children on the council still had an impact on the school and were not simply co-opted, rather their agency was contained by the boundaries the teachers put in place to limit the areas in which the school council could make a difference. Similar findings have emerged from research on other school councils (Thornberg & Elvstrand, 2012). For this process of limitation not to be the case, the adults (teachers) would need to reposition children as partners in the organisation and share power with them to enable that type of participatory position to be realised. This would require mutual trust across the generational order since joint decision-making would involve risks that the outcome of shared decision-making may not be in favour of one of the parties' interests. In reality, however, the challenge children's participation poses to intergenerational power relations is managed through systems which obviate the need for trust via procedures which govern both the agenda that can be addressed by these participatory bodies and the actions of those who are members of the council. The outcome of this is both positive and negative. On the one hand, the school council is invested with specific powers and can bring about change, and on the other hand the arenas in which change can be wrought are limited and the teachers retain ultimate power over how the school is organised and run, and also retain the power to veto those areas which are within the school council's remit (Thornberg & Elvstrand, 2012). System confidence works to facilitate participation but the lack of (adult) trust works to limit its effectiveness and range.

Our final arena in which to look at the characteristics of adult trust in children is that of voting age. Here we can see that the absence of trust and the presence of a negative confidence lead to the denial of a participatory right which would be attached to children solely on the basis of their being members of society independent of their status as children. In effect, the full rights of being a citizen.

Voting and suffrage

In most European countries now, the age at which a citizen has a vote is 18.[7] Grover positions voting as 'a prime manifestation of the basic human rights of free association and free expression' (Grover, 2010: 3). However, when it comes to youth voting rights, she argues, there has been a lack of interest by adults and nation-states at best and a delegimitisation and trivialisation at worst. Periodic arguments to lower the age of voting from 18 years to 16 years are mostly met with negative responses based on arguments that children are lacking in political competency (Chan & Clayton, 2006; Grover, 2010; Wagner et al., 2012). Entitlements to vote are presented within discourses of the need for the voter to possess or display maturity, social awareness and responsibility, all defined as being able to think through the implications of decisions and choices at a societal level as well as an individual one (see for example the report from the Electoral Commission, 2004: 24–5). Given some groups of adults, and some individuals, arguably also lack the particular competences presumed to be important for forming political views (Lau, 2012) the unconditional exclusion of all those under 18 years of age from the power of the ballot box and the unconditional inclusion of all those over the age of 18 years without age or other limitation on the right to vote,[8] suggests that the issue is an intergenerational one rather than a straightforward competency question. Whilst the reservation of the power of the ballot box for adults only is warranted in contemporary times on the basis that, in relation to children, adults are best placed as representatives of the 'common good' of the society, a consideration of the history of the civil right to vote reveals that this type of justification has been previously advanced to legitimate the withholding of power from others such as women, the poor, the working class, and particular religious groups.

The history of the civil right to vote and to be elected as a representative of the people, a form of democratic enlargement, has been a slow and at times painful process. Up until the middle of the twentieth century in many European countries voting rights were restricted to wealthy tax-paying or property-owning males (Przeworski, 2009).[9] Later extensions of suffrage rights to all males was ultimately conceded by those in power for self-serving political reasons such as a defensive response to fear of revolution (Przeworski, 2009: 313), a means of countering waning support for a party in power, or as a means of generating national loyalties amongst the masses (Kocka, 1990a, 1990b). Similarly, the eventual granting of women's voting rights[10] owed much to the desire of the governing party to be re-elected in the face of declining (male) support (Przeworski, 2009: 313–19). However, whilst these were the forces at work which brought about changes in who had the civil right to vote, the denial of the right was justified via discourses of incompetence and dependence. As Przeworski notes 'The assumption that women are not capable of exercising political rights was so self-evident to founders of representative institutions that Kant referred to it as 'natural'' (p. 313). This natural incapacity was bolstered by the argument that giving the right to vote to women would effectively double the male vote since women, like children, were not independent, had no (political) will of their own, and so would merely follow the views of their husbands/ fathers. Furthermore, it was argued that women's interests were already represented by the males in their households and through a tutelary, rather than an electoral, connection (Przeworski, 2009).

The same arguments of incompetence and dependence are now advanced in contemporary debates about lowering the age of voting to enfranchise young people. Chan and Clayton (2006) for example claim that:[11]

> The worry about extending the franchise is not that sixteen and seventeen-year-olds would not use their vote, but that too many of

them would vote and do so incompetently, in a way that would be detrimental to our democracy.

(Chan & Clayton, 2006: 538)

They conclude, on the basis of their research, that 'young people [between 16 and 18 years old] are, to a significant degree, politically less mature than older people, and that the voting age should not be lowered to sixteen' (Chan & Clayton, 2006: 533).

The validity of this argument as a justification for denying civil voting rights to those under 18 is of course undermined by the universal enfranchisement of all those over the age of 18 years, regardless of individual levels of political maturity. Given that the same arguments have been applied to other groups at different historical junctures and subsequently overturned by political expediencies, it is not unreasonable to conclude that the discourse of incompetence serves the maintenance of particular power relations, in this case intergenerational ones. The mobilisation of the risk (expressed as 'worry' by Chan and Clayton) that democracy would be degraded by children having the vote implies the role of adult trust in this question. We suggest that the risk here from the (enfranchised) adult perspective is that children's voting decisions will compromise adult interests as well as possibly what adults conceive to be children's own interests. However trust is only relevant to the question of granting civil voting rights since, *de facto*, a person who has voting rights has the right to express their view, however it is formed and on whatever it is based. In effect, the conferment of the *right* to vote renders trust irrelevant. If voting rights were granted to younger children there could be no discounting of their contribution on any grounds, unlike the situation where participation is mediated via voice groups and institutions established with a remit for children as the constituency such as school councils and children's parliaments.

Discussion

Current ideologies of children as dependent, vulnerable, and incompetent are used to legitimate adult authority over children in terms of making decisions on their behalf in particular (and many) circumstances and contexts (Archard, 1993) even if children's rights to participate in the decision-making process have been established in principle. This leads us to the conclusion that effective democratic participation for children is not possible whilst adults can mobilise discourses of trust and/or distrust in children's capacities to perform in the role of participative partners. On this basis it would appear that children make more progress as participative actors when participation is embedded in systems which eliminate the deployment of adult trust or render it irrelevant and are instead built on processes which secure relations between people in a regulatory or contractual way and eliminate or minimise unpredictably and risk (Smith, 2001: 291). However, such systems can also serve to curtail the effectiveness and range of participatory action and performance as we have shown, so adult trust in children remains important for participatory relationships, particularly those forms which, as Wall (2012) argues, constitute enlarged and alternative democratic spaces. As Khodyakov notes:

> The freedom provided by trust is the freedom to think for oneself and speak up with one's ideas. It includes as its consequence (not its cost) the freedom to be questioned and criticized – and the right to be recognized [...].
>
> (Solomon & Flores, 2001 cited in Khodyakov, 2007: 117)

Current theories of trust appear to provide an insufficient account of the role of trust in intergenerational relations.[12] In some ways, the mobilisation of trust by adults seems to be closer to what Javala (2003) argues characterises the Parsonian formulation of trust which Luhmann (1995) subsequently developed. The Parsonian concept of trust encompasses a 'competence gap' between (in his work) professionals and lay persons and so trust is only possible if both parties have shared norms, values and goals. This formulates trust as arising out of an initial sense, based on a feeling of familiarity about the person or the role the person occupies, of who can, or cannot, be trusted (Javala, 2003: 177–8). Children as a class are positioned by adults as known entities, known through the disciplinary gaze of developmental psychology and socialisation (Luke, 1989), and it is in this sense that Parsonian trust is relevant, although it's relevance comes through inversion and tautology, in that children as a class are familiar to adults as incompetent beings, and so are not trustworthy since they lack the competence needed to be so. However, the politics of participation, underpinned by various international rights conventions, national laws, and a politics of users and consumers, as well as the new sociology of childhood (Moran-Ellis, 2010) has made it untenable for children to be universally excluded from such processes in their relations with the state. This contemporary imperative for participation means that children must be engaged with by adults in ways which pose risks of unfavourable outcomes and this reintroduces the relevance of the Luh-mannian concept of trust. This sets up a tension between the familiar, in the form of the Parsonian competence gap, and the unfamiliar in the form of the risks that sharing power brings. In the case of children as participants in decision-making processes the tension is resolved via what Luhmann argues is system trust or confidence (Javala, 2003: 184; Smith, 2004) shored up by socialisation to engender shared norms and the ultimate retention of power by the professional (adult) to intervene as they see fit. This is evident in the ways in which voice groups and school councils are mediated by mechanisms of participatory conventions which embody adult norms and values, and how the risk posed by children's agency is circumscribed by the establishment of boundaries to that agency coupled with the retention by adults of powers of veto. The one mechanism which cannot be controlled in this way and so presents high levels of risk to adults – civil voting rights – is not granted to children.

Conclusion

The question of democratic participation is a serious one and the role of trust in it in the case of children needs close examination. As Bourdieu points out, for a fully democratic society, all individuals must have '[...] the feeling, be it socially scorned or supported, of being entitled to concern oneself with politics [...]' (1984: 639). Adorno's argument that as long as people do not yet 'own' their political subjectivity '[d]emocracy is perceived as one system among others [...] [and] is not identified with the people themselves as the expression of their political maturity' (Adorno, 1998: 93) can be understood in the same vein. The restriction of opportunities for children to feel entitled to engage politically and to experience democracy as part of a journey to the political maturity that is at the heart of democratic citizenship is not warranted by the rehearsal of arguments of incompetence or dependence. In addition, given the foundations of political subjectivity and citizenship are reflex-ivity, social judgement, and competence of political action, institutional or structural conditions which render certain forms of knowing as legitimate or illegitimate are intrinsic to mechanisms which enhance or restricts the opportunities of individuals to participate. As Bowles and Gintis (1987: 204) argue, strong democratic capacities flourish when institutions 'promote rather than impede the development of a democratic culture'. However, as Fischer warns, the rise in the political popularity of participation and public involvement does not guarantee that policy-makers will do more than 'go through the motions' of participation, nor that participation will not emerge as a means of managing citizens via mechanisms of bureaucracy (Fischer, 2009: 48). To counter these two dangers, he urges us to think of democracy as an ongoing convention of relations between all citizens, by which we in particular include children of all ages and in all circumstances (Moran-Ellis & Sünker, 2008; Sünker, 2009). The claim that children are the 'future' of society[13] obscures the social figuration of childhood as a subjecthood in the present. The main character in capitalism, the independent citizen, sits in opposition to the emphasis on dependency which characterises the lives of children. What is more, children as a social group are caught in the same web of limited self-realisation and commodification that Marx links to what he called 'the first form of society' in the evolution of society towards free individuality. Essentially, children are located in pre-modern conditions which structure and support the distribution of power between children and adults, and adult's contingent mobilisations of trust and distrust maintain that power relation. In *Grundrisse* Marx points to societalisation as the means of mediation between structure(s) and modes of relationships. Such mediation has important consequences for the promotion of human potential:

> Relations of personal dependence (entirely spontaneous at the outset) are the first social forms, in which human productive capacity develops only to a slight extent and at isolated points. Personal independence founded on *objective* (*sachlicher*) dependence is the second great form, in which a system of general social metabolism, of universal relations, of all-round needs and universal capacities is formed for the first time. Free individuality, based on the universal development of individuals and on their subordination of their communal, social productivity as their social wealth, is the third stage. The second stage creates the conditions for the third.
>
> (Marx, 1973: 158)

The utilisation of narratives of dependence and lack of independence to justify the withholding of trust from any group serves to reinforce the exclusion of distrusted groups from participation in society. At the same time, they are subject to processes of societalisation in anticipation of future entry into citizenship. We argue that these narratives of dependence and mediation are intrinsic to the social positioning of children in late capitalism, and indeed arise out of the workings of capitalist societies, the structures of which are inextricably woven through with relations of dependence, (apparent) independence, and inter-dependencies. Children are positioned in essentialised dependency relationships, however the potential for opening up spaces in which they can engage in a form of personal independence mediated via system confidence and adult trust is great, as is the scope for developing relations of mutual trust once the actualities of adult-child interdependencies have been fully acknowledged.

Notes

1 For the sake of brevity we use the term children, rather than children and young people.

2 See for example provision in *The Children Act 1989* in England & Wales (Department of Health, 1989), and *Kinder- und Jugendhilfegesetz, 1990* (Bundesministerium für Familia und Jugend) in Germany. Nicklett and Perron (2010), however, show that legal implementation of participation rights outside of industrialised countries is uneven.

3 For example: Young Minds (http://www.youngminds.org.uk/about/our_campaigns/consultations), date accessed 18 April 2012.

4 See http://www.un.org/documents/ga/res/44/a44r025.htm, date accessed 1 April 2012.

5 Surrey CAMHS Youth Advisors (http://www.surrey-camhs.org.uk/en/content/cms/cya/), date accessed 1 April 2012.

6 See http://nationaladvisorycouncilcmh.independent.gov.uk/ourwork.htm, although the Council has now been disbanded, date accessed 1 April 2012.

7 In some countries, the right to vote has been lowered to 16, but one might observe that these countries are often ones in which the governing power pays less attention to the electoral process: for example East Timor, North Korea. Austria is an exception and there are some German Länder which have a voting age of 16 for local elections.

8 In some countries, those who are involuntarily detained by the state in prison or other secure accommodation are not eligible to vote.

9 In Prussia additional restrictions were in operation in relation to social class wherein '[...] voters were distributed into separate electoral classes, according to their tax assessment' and those paying a higher level of tax had the right to elect a higher number of representatives (Steinmetz, 1993: 153–4).

10 Granted in 1918 in the UK for women over the age of 30 who were property-owners, and for all women over the age of 21 in 1928, and in Germany for women over the age of 18 in 1919.

11 See Hart and Atkins 2011 and Lau 2012 for opposite findings and conclusions. In addition, those who support voting at 16 often advance the argument that a lower voting age will help reverse the decline in voting as well as raise the general level of democratic engagement in the population – arguments that led to the change in franchise for women and other adults in the past (see Hart & Atkins, 2011; Wagner et al., 2012).

12 Endress argues for an examination of the role of what he calls 'functioning trust' which works at an un-reflexive or pre-reflexive level in daily interactions and actions as well as a notion of a meta-reflexive trust contextually operant at a conscious level but this still does not account for how trust plays in intergenerational contexts (Endress, 2002: 68–70).

13 In *Enlightenment* Kant argued from a teleological perspective against both the particular interests of ruling powers interested in the production of 'proper subjects' and the particular interests of parents, in which the instrumentalisation of children is inherent, who desire only that their own children 'get ahead' and are concerned with the production of the subjectivity that guarantees this. He insists that '[c]hildren should not be brought up according to the current state of the human race, rather to the future, possibly better one. That is to say: according to the idea of humanity and its entire definition' (Kant, 1968: 704).

Bibliography

Adorno, T. W. (1998) 'The meaning of working through the past', *Critical Models: Interventions and Catchwords*, New York: Columbia University Press, pp. 89–104.

Alderson, P. (2008) *Young Children's Rights: Exploring Beliefs, Principles and Practice*, 2nd edition, London: Jessica Kingsley.

Archard, D. (1993) *Children Rights and Childhood*, London: Routledge.

Badham, B. (2004) 'Participation – for a change: Disabled young people lead the way', *Children and Society*, 18: 143–54.

Barnes, M. & P. Cotterell (2012) *Critical Perspectives on User Involvement*, Bristol: Policy Press.

Beresford, P. & S. Croft (1993) *Citizen Involvement: A Practical Guide for Change*, Basingstoke: Macmillan.

Beresford, P. (2000) 'Service users' knowledges and social work theory: Conflict or collaboration?', *British Journal of Social Work*, 30: 489–503.

Bourdieu, P. (1984) *Die feinen Untershiede: kritik der gesellschaftlichen Urteilskraft*, Frankfurt: Suhrkamp.

Bowles, S. & H. Gintis (1987) *Democracy and Capitalism: Property, Community and the Contradictions of Modern Social Thought*, New York: Basic Books.

Brown, K. (2006) 'Participation and young people involved in prostitution', *Child Abuse Review*, 15: 294–312.

Bühler-Niederberger, D. & H. Sünker (2008) 'Theorie und Geschichte der Kindheit und des Kinderlebens' in H. Suenker and T. Swiderek (eds) *Lebensalter und Soziale Arbeit: Kindheit: Baltmannsweiler: Schneider Hohengehren*, pp. 5–46.

Bühler-Niederberger, D. & H. Sünker (2009) 'Interests in and responsibility for children and their life-worlds' in J. Qvortrup, W. Corsaro & M. Honig (eds) *The Palgrave Handbook of Childhood Studies*, Houndmills: Palgrave Macmillan, pp. 394–407.

Bundesministerium für Familia und Jugend (1990) *Kinder- und Jugendhilfegesetz, 1990*.

Burke, T. (2010) *Anyone Listening? Evidence of Children and Young People's Participation in England*, London: Children's Rights Alliance for England and National Children's Bureau.

Burman, E. & J. Stacey (2010) 'The child and childhood in feminist theory', *Feminist Theory*, 11: 227–40.

Burman, E. (1996) 'Local, global or globalized? Child development and international child rights legislation', *Childhood*, 3: 45–66.

Cashmore, J. (2002) 'Promoting the participation of children and young people in care', *Child Abuse and Neglect*, 26: 837–47.

Chan, T. W. & M. Clayton (2006) 'Should the voting age be lowered to sixteen? Normative and empirical considerations', *Political Studies*, 54: 533–58.

Coley, M. (2007) 'Children's voices in access and custody decisions: The need to reconceptualise rights and effect transformative change', *Appeal: Review of Current Law and Law Reform*, 12: 48–72.

Cotmore, R. (2004) 'Organisational competence: The study of a school council in action', *Children and Society*, 18: 53–65.

de Montigny, G. (1998) 'In the company of strangers: Being a child in care' in I. Hutchby & J. Moran-Ellis (eds) *Children and Social Competence: Arenas of Action*, London: Falmer.

Department of Health (1989) *Children Act, 1989*, London: HMSO.

di Luzio, G. (2006) 'A sociological concept of client trust', *Current Sociology*, 54(4): 549–64.

Electoral Commission (2004) *Age of Electoral Majority: Report and Recommendations*, London: Electoral Commission.

Elsely, (2004) 'Children's experiences of public space', *Children and Society*, 18: 155–64.

Endress, M. (2002) *Vertrauen*, Bielefeld: Transcript.

Eriksson, M. (2008) 'Participation in family law proceedings for children whose father is violent to their mother', *Childhood*, 15(2): 259–75.

Eriksson, M. (2011) 'Contact, shared parenting, and violence: Children as witnesses of domestic violence in Sweden', *International Journal of Law, Policy and the Family*, 25(2): 165–83.

Fischer, F. (2009) *Democracy and Expertise: Reorienting Policy Inquiry*, Oxford: Oxford University Press.

Gambetta, D. (2000) 'Can we trust trust?' in D. Gambetta (ed) *Trust: Making and Breaking Cooperative Relations*, Electronic edition, Department of Sociology, University of Oxford, pp. 213–37, www.sociology.ox.ac.uk/papers/gambetta213-237.pdf, date accessed 10 August 2011.

Grover, S. C. (2010) *Young People's Human Rights and the Politics of Voting Age*, London: Springer.

Hart, D. & R. Atkins (2011) 'American sixteen- and seventeen-year-olds are ready to vote', *ANNALS, AAPPS*, 633: 201–22.

Hill, M., J. Davis, A. Prout & K. Tisdall (2004) 'Moving the participation agenda forward', *Children and Society*, 18: 77–96.

Holland, S. (2001) 'Representing children in child protection assessments', *Childhood*, 8(3): 322–39.

Hutchby, I. & J. Moran-Ellis (1998a) (eds) *Children and Social Competence: Arenas of Action*, London: Falmer.

Hutchby, I. & J. Moran-Ellis (1998b) 'Situating children's social competence' in I. Hutchby & J. Moran-Ellis (eds) *Children and Social Competence: Arenas of Action*, London: Falmer, pp. 8–28.

Irwin, A. (1995) *Citizen Science: A Study of People, Expertise and Sustainable Development*, London: Routledge.

James, A. & A. James (1999) 'Pump up the volume: Listening to children in separation and divorce', *Childhood*, 6: 189–206.

James, A. & A. Prout (1990) *Constructing and Reconstructing Childhood: Contemporary Issues in the Sociological Study of Childhood*, London: Taylor Francis.

James, A., C. Jenks & A. Prout (1998) *Theorizing Childhood*, Cambridge: Polity Press.

Javala, J. (2003) 'From norms to trust: The Luhmannian connections between trust and social system', *European Journal of Social Theory*, 6: 173–90.

Kant, I. (1968) 'Über Pädagogik', *Werke Band 10*, Darmstadt: WBG, pp. 693–761.

Kerr, M., H. Stattin & K. Trost (1999) 'To know you is to trust you: Parents' trust rooted in child disclosure of information', *Journal of Adolescence*, 22: 737–52.

Khodyakov, D. (2007) 'Trust as a process: A three-dimensional approach', *Sociology*, 4(1): 115–32.

Kocka, J. (1990a) *Weder Stand noch Klasse: Unterschichten um 1800*, Bonn: Dietz.

Kocka, J. (1990b) *Arbeitsverhältnisse und Arbeiterexistenzen, Grundlagen der Klassenbildung im 19 Jahrhundert*, Bonn: Dietz.

Lansdown, G (1995) 'Children's rights to participation and protection: A critique' in C. Cloke and M. Davies (eds) *Participation and Empowerment in Child Protection*, Chichester, England: Wiley, pp. 19–38.

Lau, J. C. (2012) 'Two arguments for child enfranchisement', *Political Studies*, DOI: 10.1111/j.1467-9248.2011.00940.x, date accessed 27 March 2012.

Lee, N (1999) 'The challenge of childhood: Distributions of childhood's ambiguity in adult institutions', *Childhood*, 6: 455–74.

Luhmann, N. (1995) *Social Systems*, Standford, CA: Stanford University Press.

Luhmann, N. (2000) 'Familiarity, confidence, trust: Problems and alternatives' in D. Gambetta (ed.) *Trust: Making and Breaking Cooperative Relations*, Electronic edition, Department of Sociology, University of Oxford, pp. 94–107, www.sociology.ox.ac.uk/papers/luhmann94-107.pdf, date accessed 10 August 2011.

Luke, C. (1989) *Pedagogy, Printing and Protestantism: The Discourse on Childhood*, New York: State University of New York Press.

Marx, K. (1973) *Grundrisse: Foundations of the Critique of Political Economy (Rough Draft)*, London: Penguin Books.

Mayall, B. (1994) 'Children in action in home and school' in B. Mayall (ed.) *Children's Childhoods Observed and Experienced*, London: Falmer Press, pp. 114–27.

Moran-Ellis, J. (2010) 'Reflections on the sociology of childhood in the UK', *Current Sociology*, 58(2): 186–205.

Moran-Ellis, J. & H. Sünker (2008) 'Giving children a voice: Childhood, power and culture' in J. Houtsonen & A. Antikainen (ed.) *Symbolic Power in Cultural Contexts: Uncovering Social Reality*, Rotterdam: Sense, pp. 67–83.

Nicklett, E. J. & B. E. Perron (2010) 'Laws and policies to support the wellbeing of children: An international comparative analysis', *International Journal of Social Welfare*, 19: 3–7.

Przeworski, A. (2009) 'Conquered or granted?: A history of suffrage extensions', *British Journal of Political Science*, 39: 291–321.

Smith, C. (2001) 'Trust and confidence: Possibilities for social work in "high modernity"', *British Journal of Social Work*, 31: 287–305.

Smith, C. (2004) 'Trust and confidence: Making the moral case for social work', *Social Work and Social Science Review*, 11(3): 5–15.

Steinmetz, G. (1993) *Regulating the Social: The Welfare State and Local Politics in Imperial Germany*, Princeton: Princeton University Press.

Such, E. & R. Walker (2004) 'Being responsible and responsible beings: Children's understandings of responsibility', *Children and Society*, 18: 231–42.

Sünker, H. (2009) 'Democratic education – Educating for democracy' in E. Ropo and T. Autio (eds) *International Conversations on Curriculum Studies: Subject, Society and Curriculum*, Rotterdam: Sense, pp. 89–108.

Svanberg, J. & C. Street (2003) 'Where next? New directions in in-patient mental health services for young people', *Report 2: Issues Emerging: Views from Young People, Parents And Staff*, London: Young Minds.

Swiderek, T. (1999) 'The relevance of a children's policy and participation of young people in decision making in Germany – Municipal and local forms and models of co-determination', *Social Work in Europe*, 6(3): 14–22.

Thomas, N. & C. O'Kane (1998) 'When children's wishes and feeling clash with their "best interests"', *The International Journal of Children's Rights*, 6: 137–54.

Thomas, N. & C. O'Kane (1999a) 'Children's participation in reviews and planning meetings when they are looked after in middle childhood', *Child and Family Social Work*, 4: 221–30.

Thomas, N. & C. O'Kane (1999b) 'Experiences of decision-making in middle childhood: The example of children "looked after" by local authorities', *Childhood*, 6(3): 369–87.

Thornberg, R. & H. Elvstrand (2012) 'Children's experiences of democracy, participation and trust in school', *International Journal of Educational Research*, DOI.

United Nations (1989) *Convention on the Rights of the Child* A/RES/44/25 http://www.un.org/documents/ga/res/44/a44r025.htm, date accessed 1 April 2012.

van Nijnatten, C. & E. Jongen (2011) 'Professional conversations in divorce-related child welfare inquiries', *Childhood*, 18: 540–55.

Vis, S. A., A. Holtan & N. Thomas (2012) 'Obstacles for child participation in care and protection cases – Why Norwegian social workers find it difficult', *Child Abuse Review*, 21: 7–23.

Vis, S. A., A. Strandbu, A. Holtan & N. Thomas (2011) 'Participation and health – Research review of child participation in planning and decision-making', *Child and Family Social Work*, 16: 325–35.

Wagner, M., D. Johann & S. Krtizinger (2012) 'Voting at 15: Turnout and the quality of vote choice', *Electoral Studies*, DOI 10.10.16/j.electstud.2012.01.007, date accessed 27 March 2012.

Wall, J. (2012) 'Can democracy represent children? Towards a politics of difference', *Childhood*, 19: 86–100.

Wattam, C., J. A. Hughes & H. Blagg (1989) *Child Sexual Abuse: Listening, Hearing and Validating the Experiences of Children*, London: Wiley.

Woodhead, M. (1990) 'Psychology and the cultural construction of children's needs' in A. James & A. Prout (1990) *Constructing and Reconstructing Childhood*, London: Falmer.

Worrall-Davies, A. (2008) 'Barriers and facilitators to children's and young people's views affecting CAMHS planning and delivery', *Child and Adolescent Mental Health*, 13(1): 16–18.

Wyness, M. (2003) 'Children's spaces and interests: Constructing an agenda for student voices', *Children's Geographies*, 1(2): 223–39.

Wyness, M. (2005) 'Regulating participation: The possibilities and limits of children and young people's councils', *Journal of Social Science*, 9: 7–18.

Wynne, B. (1992) 'Misunderstood misunderstanding: Social identities and public uptake of science', *Public Understanding of Science*, 1: 281–304.

3
Trust Building and Violation During Childhood Consequences for Children's Wellbeing and Dispositions for Trust in Later Life

Julia Grosse and Hanne Warming

This chapter examines trust dynamics in children's lives from a combined *being* and *becoming* perspective. In the early days of the new social studies of childhood, researchers advocated replacing the traditional developmental 'becoming perspective' on children's lives and life conditions with a 'being perspective' (see for example Qvortrup, 1994). However, more recent contributions suggest that children must be conceptualised both as becomings and beings (Lee, 2001; Halldén, 2005; Uprichard, 2008). In keeping with that idea, this chapter examines childhood experiences in terms of insecurity/security, trust building/violation, and the consequences of these experiences for children's wellbeing and self-esteem as well as for dispositions for trust in later life. Given all the societal (Welch et al., 2005; Putnam, 1993, 2000; Rothstein, 2009; Fukuyama, 1995; Uslaner, 2002) and individual (Ward & Meyer, 2009; Helliwell & Wang, 2011) benefits that trust is known to generate, we urgently need to expand our knowledge about how trust is formed within the ecological system that frames children's lives and development (Bronfenbrenner, 1979; see also introduction to this book). Thinking along these lines means acknowledging that 'society shapes the individual' (James et al., 1998: 23), recognising the impact of adults (parents, teachers and others), peers and the local environment (see for example Stolle & Nishikawa, 2011; Jantzer et al., 2006), and regarding children as actors who shape their own futures, which is consistent with a life course perspective (Elder, 1994; Elder et al., 2003; Giele & Elder, 1998).

The empirical data on which this chapter is based primarily resulted from a Swedish research project on trust viewed from a life course perspective (Grosse, 2012). That study is based on individual semi-structured life world interviews with 27 adults, strategically sampled for the purpose of sociodemographic variation,[1] and a survey of a representative sample of the Swedish population. In this chapter, we present findings from the qualitative part of that study. These findings are supplemented by data on children's experiences from a Danish research project on trust dynamics in social work with children at risk.[2] The empirical data consist of qualitative life world interviews and exploratory workshops with 17 Danish children aged 7 to 17. This combination of life course interview with adults and participatory research with children makes an excellent basis for examining trust dynamics from the double perspective of becoming and being. Combining cross-national data in this way requires awareness of the impact of national context. However Sweden and Denmark are very close culturally as well as with regard to welfare.

In everyday life, the concept of trust is rarely problematised, even though it is actually used to refer to a number of quite different phenomena both in everyday conversation and in theory. In accordance with a life world approach, this chapter firstly offers a hermeneutic phenomenological analysis of: a) these different everyday meanings of trust, and b) the ways in which our interviewees perceive processes of trust building and violation and the consequences of these processes for their wellbeing and trust attitudes later in life as a child and in adulthood (Kvale, 2007: 51). We start with a brief presentation of our findings concerning the different everyday meanings of trust, which we relate to theoretical conceptualisations of trust. Next, we offer a brief state of the art on research addressing the relationship between childhood experiences and trust attitudes. This is followed by the main section of the article, namely an analysis of how our interviewees perceive processes of trust building and violation during childhood, and how these experiences influence their wellbeing as well as development of disposition for trust later in life. We frame this analysis using Luhmann's concepts of trust in trust, social trust, system trust and his distinction between trust and confidence. The analysis is structured around the phenomenologically identified meanings that our interviewees attribute to trust.

Meanings of trust

One definition of trust, which emerged from our interviews, has to do with inner security and a feeling of safety. Inner security is very close to the concept of basic trust (Erikson, 1950; Bowlby, 1971) and the concept of trust in trust (Luhmann, 2005; see also Warming, Chapter 1 in this book). Feelings of safety are closely related to fear of crime (Hale, 1996), or rather the absence of fear of crime in public space, and can be seen as a more specific form of trust in trust – or as confidence in the Luhmannian sense if related to a specific place or type of space.

Another way of understanding trust, which can be identified, is as an attitude based on an intuitive or reflexive evaluation of familiar people, strangers and institutions as trustworthy. This definition includes what Luhmann (1988) conceptualises as familiarity, confidence and trust, although the interviewees do not systematically make the difference between these. Further, it includes his concepts of social trust, that is trust in persons, and system trust, that is trust in institutions (see also Warming, Chapter 1). In value research that is based on large-scale surveys, it is very common to distinguish between particularised and generalised trust, signifying a more intimate and a more abstract type of trust respectively (Uslaner, 2002; Freitag & Traunmüller, 2009). While the former include what Luhmann conceptualises as social and system trust as well as confidence and familiarity, the latter addresses his concept of trust in trust.

A third way of defining trust in our interviews is as a maxim or moral imperative to be trustful, that is as a mirror of one's more general view of society. From this perspective, trust can be seen as a kind of value, similar to what Uslaner (2002) conceptualises as moral trust.

Research on the significance of childhood experiences for trust in later life

Research on the consequences of childhood experiences for trust dispositions in later life is rare and has primarily been carried out in the field of pure developmental psychology. In this research – as in the general field of trust research (see Introduction of this book) – many different definitions and uses of the concept of trust exist. In the following review, we adhere to the definitions in the reviewed literature, whereas we in the analysis of the interviews primarily use Luhmann's concepts, as they are more precise and nuanced. We start out by reviewing research focusing on the significance of early attachment for later social behaviour with regard to trust, self-esteem and self-confidence, features which are all proven to correlate with generalised trust later in life (Rothstein, 2009).

Psychological research stresses the importance of the quality of early attachments for later attachment patterns, social behaviour in general and self-esteem both throughout childhood and as an adult (Bowlby,

1971; Ainsworth et al., 1978; Lund, 2001). This assumption is based on Erikson's life stages model of children's development, where attaining basic trust is the first and most important stage that determines the following stages (Erikson, 1950, 1968; Erikson & Erikson, 1997; see Warming, Chapter 1, for a critique of this model). Empirical studies support the idea that early attachment patterns influence children's later self-esteem, self-confidence and ability to create trustful social bonds, and there is an impressive degree of cross-generational similarity and influence in the findings from this research (Ainsworth & Eichberg, 1993: 161; Hesse, 1999; Main, 1991; Fonagy et al., 1991, 1995). A recent example is Kopp-Smith's study which demonstrates how people, who have lost a parent early in life, are more afraid of intimacy, more anxious and withdrawn and have lower levels of trust and confidence which negatively affect their later romantic relationships (Kopp-Smith, 2010).

Despite a proven correlation between early attachment patterns and trust in later life, it is still quite unclear to what extent such patterns matter for inner security and interpersonal trust in adulthood (Bridges, 2003; Christiansen, 2001). Among other things, this is because it is difficult to distinguish between attachment patterns in childhood and other experiences, such as parental divorce, that might lead to other types of insecurity in the child's social situation (Lewis et al., 2000), and because of the complex interplay between risk and protective factors (Rutter, 1997; Schaffer, 1992). Thus, while the literature convincingly shows that early attachment patterns are significant for different dimensions of trust, it is also clear that these do not single-handedly predetermine the personality and attitudes of adults (Clarke & Clarke, 1998; Kryger, 2004).

Longitudinal studies show generalised trust to be quite stable throughout life (see for example Stolle & Hooghe, 2004), suggesting that generalised trust in later childhood and adulthood is mainly determined by primary socialisation, irrespective of later experiences. However, this argument is often made indirectly, following the idea that if trust is not shaped by experiences in adult life it must have been created in early childhood (Sturgis et al., 2007; Uslaner, 2002). It remains quite unclear how this generalised trust is created during childhood: for instance, what is the significance of parents' generalised trust? Whereas Katz and Rotter (1969) and Campbell (1979) found a direct correlation between parents' and children's generalised trust and political confidence, a more recent study by Stolle and Nishikawa (2011) showed much higher levels of parental social trust compared to their children's.

The role of parents is dealt with in different ways. Of these, we have already addressed attachment patterns. Here, for instance, An and Cooney (2006) and King (2002) find that a trustful relationship with parents is correlated with the ability to trust in intimate relationships in adulthood.

Another parental role that has been identified in relation to trust is parents' function as 'moral teachers', as role models and their role in shaping the child's attribution styles (Uslaner, 2002; Seligman, 1991). Uslaner further indicates that an anti-authoritative parenting style, which gives children the opportunity to make their own decisions, contributes to high levels of generalised trust (Uslaner, 2002). Conversely, children who have been warned to be careful and not trust strangers have been found to have lower levels of generalised trust (Uslaner, 2002; Stolle & Nishikawa, 2011). In line with such findings, Stolle and Nishikawa (2011) explain children's comparatively low levels of generalised trust in an American context in terms of parental warnings, which according to the parents were motivated by the heavy reporting of crimes towards children in recent years.

Finally, other researchers have explored the significance of certain events in childhood for trust in later life, particularly events that are thought to erode trust. The impact of parental divorce on children's ability to build up and maintain intimate relationships is often stressed, but a closer look reveals a more complicated picture. Some studies have found a negative relationship between divorce in the parental home, generalised trust and trust in intimate relationships (van Schaick & Stolberg, 2001; Duran-Aydintug, 1997; Franklin et al., 1990). However this correlation might also be attributable to the effects of parents' conflicts or their bad relationship, rather than to the divorce *per se* (King, 2002; Franklin et al., 1990).

Another critical event that matters in terms of trust creation is bullying, which has proven to have serious negative effects on children's social trust, wellbeing and self-esteem (Craig et al., 2009; Due et al., 2011). Jantzer et al. (2006) further demonstrates that bullying in childhood diminishes trust among young adults, particularly among college peers, but does not affect later romantic relationships. Shyness levels are also higher, and life satisfaction lower, compared with individuals who have not suffered from bullying. Salmi et al. (2007) investigated the impact of different types of crimes on teenagers and found that having been bullied has the strongest correlation with low social trust of all types of victimisation, including theft or physical violence.

Altogether, the literature provides evidence of a correlation between trust and children's wellbeing, including self-esteem, and between childhood experiences and trust attitudes in later life. How exactly these correlations work is not yet clear, but it serves to provide us with some theoretical and empirical working ideas about the dynamics that might be at play, notably an awareness of the complexity of this field. Trust research is dominated by a quite traditional developmental psychology approach, which tends to position children as objects of adult actions rather than as agents (James et al., 1998). Yet children – just like adults – are both objects of policies, other people's agency and interpretive agents in their own lives (Redmond, 2010). Thus, there is a need for research that acknowledges children's agency as part of the complex set of processes that shape their experiences and which investigates the consequences of these experiences for trust in later life. In the following analysis, we make a first attempt to fill this gap.

Experiences of trust dynamics

Feeling (in)secure

Most of the adult interviewees remember their childhood as being characterised by feelings of security and confidence in their parents. They consider this secure childhood to be the main foundation of their later ability to trust and feel self-esteem. On a general level, this finding can either be interpreted as empirical support for theories that stress the importance of security and early attachment patterns (e.g. Erikson, 1950; Bowlby, 1971; Ainsworth & Eichberg, 1993), and of children as objects of parents' agency, or as a mirroring (and being a product of) the discursive power of these theories. In the following, we dig a bit deeper by analysing negative experiences of insecurity and lost confidence and looking at how children respond to these.

Those of our adult interviewees, who recall their childhood as generally insecure, mainly relate this to lack of confidence towards their parents, rather than towards other relationships and/or systems. Interestingly however, although Denmark, like Sweden, is characterised by low crime rates and high standards of healthcare and welfare, the findings from the Danish interviews and workshops with children at risk reveal these factors as relevant. In fact, the Danish children relate their feelings of insecurity to threats of crime, illness, poverty and also adult professionals such as teachers to a much higher degree than the Swedish adults recalling their childhood – although their parents also play a central role in the Danish children's narratives. One explanation of this difference between the results from the two projects might be the 'at risk' status of the Danish participating children. Another would be the role of dominant discourses on the adults' narrative remembering process (Fentress & Wickham, 1992; Rosenthal, 1993).

The participants' feelings of insecurity towards their parents are expressed in many different ways in the interviews. One is a feeling of being constantly assessed or judged, which can be interpreted as parents communicating that they distrust their child. Another is a general feeling of abandonment, that is that their parents were not really there for them. A third is related to experiences of domestic violence and parents' alcohol abuse. The latter two experiences can be regarded as a form of violence towards children's confidence in their parents. Less obvious experiences, such as being played off by one parent against the other, parental envy, not being encouraged, or living in a very restrictive milieu with a lot of do's and don't's and unrealistically high expectations of performance are also linked to feelings of insecurity in our interviews. In some cases, interviewees talk about insecurity as a constant impression of not having been welcome as a child, as in the following quotation:

> I: I would say that her [her mother's] first four children were ok, but then ... Then she should have stopped having more children.
> J: So she was more interested in them?
> I: Yes, and they had a different father. With me, it was my father who wanted to have children. And then she had a strange desire for power, which made her have another child [the interviewee] even though she didn't really want to have it. So I might have felt better if I had grown up with my dad.

During the interview, it transpires that childhood experiences of being unwanted has contributed significantly to long-term negative self-esteem, which in turn produced difficulties with social trust, especially when it comes to romantic relationships and friendships. These findings are in line with Baker (2005).

Compensating mechanisms

Conversely, other interviewees who also report insecure childhoods do not have difficulties showing confidence and trust towards other people in later life neither as a child nor in adulthood. In some cases, this may be attributed to compensating mechanisms such as a close confidant or a supportive and caring person, for example a preschool or other teacher or a grandparent. In the Danish data, social workers are also often mentioned. Some of these children report that they had heard from other children that they could be allocated a 'contact person' (a social worker who spends time with the child, compensating for parents' inadequate care) and that they have actively taken steps to be assigned to such a person. Likewise, they report how they use this person to re-establish security in insecure situations. An eight-year-old girl whose mother is in treatment for alcoholism explains: 'I just call her [the social worker], and then she advises me about what to do, and afterwards she talks to my mother. It really makes me feel much more secure'. The children emphasise how important such a person can be: 'He makes me smile, even when I'm totally down', or 'she makes me feel safe and calm, makes me believe in life and go on "fighting" again'. In line with this, a middle-aged man narrates how his grandmother was an oasis of safety and calmness:

> Trust has a lot to do with self-esteem and expectations, of course. What kind of expectations did I have of my parents? Of my mother? None at all, only that she wouldn't break her neck when she was drunk. And my whole life, I hoped my dad would contact me, which he never did. [...] But at Christmas, grandmother, fabulous, calm, she was just there. Wonderful.

Other children, such as friends and siblings, can also have compensating functions. Our interviewees especially emphasise loyalty as important in such relationships, that is having a person who 'vouches for' you and demonstrates unconditional love and support both on a symbolic and practical level.

Security through support

The youngest group among our Swedish interviewees report how expectations and experiences of support from their parents contributed to their feelings of security. Conversely, the middle-aged interviewees tend to report that they lacked this kind of parental support, both when they were children, and later as (young) adults, which is in accordance with Ule's findings from Slovenia (Chapter 9).

A young woman describes a turning point in her life related to an unintentional pregnancy and abortion, when her confidence in receiving support from her family was undermined:

> I: I was pregnant and had an abortion, and my family and relations, they just tried to hush it up. 'Don't talk to anyone. We don't talk about things like that. It's not happening'. So everyone I had trusted until then just vanished. They weren't there for me.
> J: Vanished completely, or just when it came to talking about it?

I: No, for me it was a big let down. So then I lost all trust in them.

J: Completely?

I: Yes, completely. At that time, my basic trust disappeared.

Here, her expectation that her relatives would support her more than anybody else means that she experienced very intense disappointment when they let her down. She talks about the long-term effect of this in terms of her generally negative expectations of other people, that is lack of trust in trust:

There was no one who just told me: 'No matter what, we will always be there for you when you feel down' – this type of security. So I started to feel that this world wants to hurt me.

So, what she first describes as the disappearance of confidence in her family is reinterpreted as a starting point for mistrusting everyone, that is erosion of trust in trust. Thus, several dimensions of trust are affected by this incident: the confidence she had in her family and relatives, and trust in trust which has consequences for her inner security and dispositions towards social and system trust.

Scare stories

Some interviewees recall their lack of security as caused by stories told by their parents. One middle-aged woman provides an example of such a story:

I have always been – until ten years ago – incredibly afraid of the dark. What can I say? Scared of ghosts, supernatural things. Not as an insecurity, but as fear that someone might want to hurt me. And then, one day, my mum and dad told me how to handle my own children: 'You should do what we did with you. Remember how you could never sleep as a child. So your dad and I decided to tell you about the Knack.' And this [the Knack] was a dark, horrible guy, who came at night if you weren't sleeping. So I got the picture of this little frightened child who pulled the blanket up to her nose thinking: 'I have to sleep, I have to sleep, I have to sleep. Otherwise the Knack will come and get me.' And then I realised this story was at the root of everything.

The story told by her parents undermined her feelings of security in situations of darkness both as a child and as an adult. In this case, the child had confidence in her parents. However, her parents used this confidence to instil fear in her for sleep discipline reasons. This raises the question, whether she would have been better off – and felt more secure – if she had questioned her parents' story, and on a more general level whether a critical attitude in some cases is more protective than confidence and trust.

Parents' intentional educational actions: Warnings

Parents' impact on their children's attitude development occurs partly through intentional educational actions by parents, such as encouraging children to act in a certain way or warning them against certain kinds of people, situations or behaviours; and partly, indirectly, through role model functions (Stolle & Nishikawa, 2011: 286).

Many of our interviewees recall being warned explicitly against risk. However this mostly has to do with things they perceive as obvious sources of danger: 'common things'. Interestingly, some of our middle-aged interviewees tend to follow this up with an explanation for why such warnings were so rare, for example that the world was less dangerous then, or that people in general, and their parents in particular, were not aware of potential risk. This indicates that they do not share their parents' attitude of confidence, and will probably give their own children more warnings than they were given. This may be because they question whether their parents' attitude was appropriate, or because they perceive life to be more risky today than when they were children. Thus, world views and related attitudes of confidence, trust and mistrust are not uncritically passed on from the older generation to the younger, but are influenced by other kinds of information. This is reflected in the following exchange:

J: When you're travelling, do you ask people to help you with your luggage?
I: No, I don't do that. That kind of trust, I just don't have it. Not these days.
J: Not these days? Terror threats, drugs?
I: Yes, exactly. Before, I guess you could do that. But now it's different from the 70's. Then it wasn't a problem.

According to the literature, trust in trust and social trust is positively correlated both to not having received many warnings as a child and to anti-authoritative parenting styles (Uslaner, 2002: 102). However, as we shall see, our analysis both supports these ideas but also nuances them.

Parents' intentional educational actions: Encouragement to try new challenges

Several interviewees report that they have received sound advice from their parents and even been encouraged to try new challenges. They have not been brought up to think that society and life were dangerous. The Danish children claim that this helps them learn to take action in their own lives, and – if these actions prove successful – improve their trust in trust. For instance, one boy was encouraged to travel alone between his parents' home and the residential home where he lives. By facing this challenge, he realised that he could actually manage on his own and that he could ask strangers for support. This increased his trust in trust and his independence.

Refraining from giving too many warnings, and not being too restrictive towards children, can be regarded as an expression not only of confidence in society or trust in trust, but also more specifically of parents' trust in their children to act competently and manage possible risk. Children explain how such expressions of trust encourage them 'to prove that I am worthy of her trust', which increases their self-esteem. Conversely, warnings and restrictions can be experienced as distrust, with negative consequences for their ability to engage with others, their self-esteem and their trust in adults.

Parents' influence on children through role models

The narrative accounts by our Swedish interviewees comprise a rich body of material on the impact of parents as role models for children's development of a trusting attitude, that is, how parents transfer their attitudes and values about trust and others' trustworthiness to their children through their own behaviour patterns (see for example Uslaner, 2002: 77; Seligman, 1991). A young woman recounts:

> I: Let's say we have workmen at home. I always put away my jewellery case. I don't leave it where it usually is, in the bedroom. I hide it in the wardrobe behind some clothes. I still do this. We've always done that at home whenever we left the house.
> J: Not because anything ever happened, but because your parents did that?
> I: Yes, you put away things like this when you leave the house. That's just the way you do things.

This story is an example of transferral: the uncritical copying of a mistrustful attitude towards strangers. However there are also examples of the opposite. Thus, some interviewees, who characterise their parents as very suspicious towards most people, particularly strangers, actively distance themselves from their parents' attitude, as in the case of this middle-aged woman:

> She [her mother] had a quite pessimistic attitude towards people she met. And this made me become the total opposite. I was always wondering 'why?' When she saw someone in the street, she was like: 'Why are they acting like that?' Whereas I would say: 'But there might be a good reason.' […] And I had a childcarer who was the complete opposite. She was rather positive. So I saw the difference. So I wanted to become more like her than like my mum.

The quote illustrates both her dissociation from her mother's attitude, and the possible significance of other adults as role models for children's trust attitudes. The existence of more than one role model, and differences in their attitudes, makes it possible for a child to make a reflexive choice.

Parental separations

The literature review showed that parental divorce has been found to influence trust in later life, both negatively and positively. Our interviewees' narratives support this, but also contribute new understandings. We found that divorce *per se* may not be the crucial factor; rather, maintaining a good relationship with both parents may be more significant in line with Franklin et al. (1990) and King (2002). Several of our interviewees report experiencing the divorce as a relief, particularly if there were lots of conflicts between the parents while they were still living together:

> I remember really well when I thought for the first time – I still lived at home at that time, I can't have been more than 14 or 15 years old – when I thought for the first time that I wished they would break up, that I really wished they would separate. Before that, everything was extremely tense and anxious. I didn't want that [the divorce] to happen, but I could see they ought to do it … The best thing would have been if they could have lived together, because I wanted to be with both my mom and my dad. But I still remember when the idea came into my head for the first time. What if they could live their lives happily instead of destroying and undermining each other?

A survey among Danish school children (Nyby, 2011), as well as qualitative interviews with children experiencing their parents' divorce

(Warming, 2002), echoes this ambivalent experience of, on the one hand, a heartfelt wish to live with both parents, and on the other the burden of living with parents who are continually arguing and who are not very emphatic and attentive to them, all of which make them feel insecure.

Several interviewees report practically losing contact with their father as a consequence of their parents' divorce. They describe their self-image as having been partly formed by their father's absence, and they describe this experience as predominantly negative. One middle-aged interviewee kept bringing up her father's absence as the main cause of her feelings of insecurity in relationships in general (both romantic relationships and friendships), that is for her lack of trust in trust in adult life. Significantly, all the interviewees who had lost contact with their fathers due to parental divorce early in life were single, even though they longed for a romantic relationship. This picture fits well with the results of Franklin et al.'s (1990) findings that parental divorce rarely has significance for children's trust in general, but does affect their ability to trust love partners and their chances of enjoying lasting love relationships.

However, having had divorced parents does not necessarily undermine one's ability to have confidence in a partner later in life. One example of the opposite is a middle-aged woman, whose parents had divorced, and who experienced feelings of insecurity and of not being loved unconditionally by her parents during her childhood. She tells that a trustful partnership was very natural to her and made her feel secure in her adult life:

> But he [her husband] has been a very important person in my life, since he has always been there. He has always told me that he will be there: 'I will be there, even if you change, as long as I can accept the change.' He is my security. So he was the first 'root' I put down somewhere I felt I wanted to stay. I was quite restless before that.

Finally, we should point out that not all the participants with separated parents associate divorce with conflicts, nor do they see their parents' broken and conflictive relationship as undermining their own chances of enjoying positive love relationships. Several individuals describe their experience of the divorce as quite undramatic, simply as 'that's life'. This suggests that divorce can be unproblematic for children's trust, at least in Sweden, Denmark and other parts of the Western world, since nowadays it is very common there. Being aware of that, and having peers with similar experiences, appears to lead to a form of externalisation where the child views the separation as something normal in society, rather than as a catastrophic failure on the part of his or her parents. Divorce thus becomes less critical for trust.

Bullying

One institution that almost every child experiences is school. Though school experiences were not included as a separate theme in our semi-structured interviews, bullying in school came up in several interviews. These interviewees present themselves as rather suspicious or wary in one or more respects, that is low level of trust in trust. It appears that bullying critically influences the interviewees' disposition for trust. One woman talked about the long-term consequences:

> It [being bullied] didn't make me negative towards people I meet, but it made me think: 'Wow, she's spending time with me. Why is she doing that? Does she like me? And if she likes me, what is it that she likes? In that case, I'd better keep doing what I'm doing so she keeps liking me'.

Although she starts out by saying that she does not have a negative attitude towards others, her story shows that she has negative expectations of how other people will perceive and relate to her (low level of trust in trust). Whether the reason for this is bad self-esteem, bad experiences or both, the end result is an attitude of mistrust. Elsewhere in the interview, she describes several situations where she acts extremely carefully towards others, in particular strangers.

Based on the interviews and workshops with Danish children, the negative effects of bullying appear to be exacerbated if people in whom the child has trust or confidence, for example a friend or a teacher, know about the bullying, but do nothing to prevent it. This is experienced as a kind of betrayal, which has consequences for future confidence and trust in that person and sometimes in people in the same role or at the same kind of institution (the school). In both the Swedish and the Danish research projects, several bullying victims report that their schools turned a blind eye to the bullying. The following quote is from the Swedish interviews:

> J: Did the school do anything to stop the bullying in any way?
> I: No, it was more like... there's no bullying at our school.
> J: No one saw it?

I: Nobody cared. They might have seen it, but they didn't care.

J: What do you think about that?

I: Well … it happens all the time in Swedish schools. I doubt that there's a single school without a bully. I don't believe that for a second.

The adults who realise what is going on, but refrain from taking appropriate action, may be teachers, parents or other adults. This situation can be regarded as a kind of double exposure: to the act of bullying itself and to neglect by the social environment. Some interviewees, who were bullied as children but received no adult support, express a distinctly low level of trust in institutions, that is low level of system trust both during childhood and as adults.

The relationship between trust and bullying is not only one-way, however. The interviews provide example of how individuals who possess trust in trust as children sometimes take action to break the negative spiral of bullying and bad self-esteem in their lives. Sometimes they do this by boosting their self-confidence in arenas outside school, which then stops the bullying and/or limits its negative long-term effects (see Jantzer et al., 2006). In other cases, they seek outside help, as the following quote shows:

> There was a girl who left our class, who had been a friend of mine, and we continued to write letters to each other. And there were two girls in my class who I sometimes said hello to. I mean I talked to them, but we didn't really spend time with each other. Anyway, we talked to each other. And they saw one of the letters. I don't really know why. Well, I gave them one of the letters. And in that letter I also mentioned the problems in the class. And that was the reason we started seeing each other. Then the others realised 'Ok, she's not on her own any more', and then they lost interest in teasing me.

This shows how a child may take action to reinstate him or herself in the social milieu of the classroom. In this case, the girl took the risk of sharing her letter with her peers and thereby showing them trust which turned out to be well founded, and which resulted in a shift in her social position in the class towards inclusion and less bullying.

Conclusion

Our analysis demonstrates the significant role of family and school in shaping different dimensions of trust in childhood, with serious consequences for the child's life quality as well as for dispositions for trust in later life. However, it also shows that children are not passive puppets who are determined by neither adults' actions nor institutional structures. Furthermore, other persons and institutions can play a compensating and modifying role which opens up space for children's reflexive choices and agency.

The significance of childhood, and especially early childhood as structured by family bonds, is related to the fact that early attachment patterns and identity formation form the basis for later identity work (Ainsworth & Eichberg, 1993; Nsamenang, 2008). Negative identity formation with regard to trust can have different causes, though a common feature is a loss of confidence in the parents' or significant others' expected support. A secure childhood requires confidence in the primary care persons, typically the parents. Our examples show that if this confidence is breached, a direct shift from confidence to distrust can occur. However, our data also show cases of more gradual learning processes where children revise their perception of their parents and reshape their own attitudes in a less radical fashion. In such cases, a child's wellbeing and identity development with regard to trust in trust depends on his or her access to supportive and caring others, be these adults or peers.

Conflicts between significant others, typically parents, erode the child's confidence in the home as a secure space, with an ensuing risk of negative consequences for his or her self-esteem and sense of security. Yet, several interviewees do not remember their parents' divorce in itself as catastrophic and most of them do not experience long-term damage to their trust in trust, not even with regard to love relationships. This resonates with Hamilton's (2000) and Duran-Aydintug's (1997) findings. Loss of contact or strained relations with a parent might be more critical for trust in love relationships.

Another critical factor for a child's wellbeing and trust development is bullying and social exclusion by peers, which matters both in terms of trust in themselves, social trust and wellbeing. Here, we identified a double exposure consisting of the bullying itself on the one hand and on the other failure to take action to stop bullying on the part of the people whom the child expected to support him or her, for example teachers, peers and parents.

Our analysis shows that the different types of events mentioned above matter more or less for trust – both towards people or institutions and in terms of identity formation regarding trust in trust – depending on the significance that people ascribe to them. Two factors appear to be particularly important: the first is the extent to which the individual interprets the event as an attack on his or her inner security, which is often correlated to his or her emotional bond to the trust object in question. The second is the type of role expectations a person has with regard to relationships that are included in the experiences which she or he relates to trust. Such expectations derive partly from former real experiences with, and perceived promises by, the trust object; and partly, as pointed to by Weber and Carter (2003) and Baier (1986), from characteristics that are socially constructed as naturally related to certain positions or occupations, such as teachers or parents. If one assumes that certain individuals can be 'counted on' because they hold certain positions or because of an emotionally close relationship, violations of those expectations are experienced as particularly distressful.

In addition to feelings of security and attachment patterns, socialisation in the form of active teaching and role modelling plays a role in children's identity development regarding trust in trust. That said, our interviews show that some interviewees are less trustful than their parents were and taught them to be, and some are more so. Some individuals actively distance themselves from their parents' attitudes when they become adults, while others do so already as children. Thus, we found that children can – especially if other role models are available – reflexively shape their own attitudes so that they differ from those of their parents and from their own upbringing.

Once we acknowledge that trust is significant to children's wellbeing and that childhood experiences are significant for identity formation and trust development during childhood and in later life, several important implications arise. First, there is clearly a need for greater commitment to supporting children wherever possible, for example through preventive and active social work such as family therapy, coaching for insecure parents and ensuring that attentive adults are present in schools and daycare institutions. Second, those involved should acknowledge children's own perspectives and attempts to take action, with a view to providing concrete support and avoiding signalling distrust in the child. Third, children's ability to make reflexive choices and take action in their own lives should be strengthened by increasing the number of significant and confident others in their lives, for example contact persons or staff in schools and daycare institutions. These people should have the time, competences and commitment to support the child, thus offering an alternative, more trustful but not naïve, role model. In this way, children will be empowered to build up and maintain confidence, trust and timely critical caution both as children and later as adults.

Notes

1 Twelve interviewees were young adults. Six of them were met twice within a two-year period. Fifteen interviewees were middle-aged. Strategic sampling was applied for the purpose of sociodemographic variation. The interviews were taped, transcribed and coded in the Nvivo software for qualitative data analysis.

2 The project about trust in social work with children is funded by the Danish National Research council. Further information can be found at http://www. tillid.ruc.dk.

Bibliography

Ainsworth, M., M. Blehar, E. Waters & S. Wall (1978) *Patterns of Attachment*, Hillsdale, NJ: Erlbaum.

Ainsworth, M. D. S. & C. Eichberg (1993) 'Effects on infant-mother attachment of mother's unresolved loss of an attachment figure, or other traumatic experience' in C. M. Parkes, J. Stevenson-Hinde & P. Marris (eds) *Attachment Across the Life Cycle*, London and New York: Routledge, pp. 160–86.

An, J. S. & T. M. Cooney (2006) 'Psychological well-being in mid to late life: The role of generativity development and parent-child relationships across the lifespan', *International Journal of Behavioral Development*, 30(5): 410–21.

Baier, A. (1986) 'Trust and antitrust', *Ethics*, 96(2): 231–60.

Baker, A. J. L. (2005) 'The long-term effects of parental alienation on adult children: A qualitative research study', *The American Journal of Family Therapy*, 33(4): 289–302.

Bowlby, J. (1971) *Attachment and Loss*, Harmondsworth: Penguin.

Bridges, L. J. (2003) 'Trust, attachment, and relatedness' in M. H. Bornstein, L. Davidson, C. L. M. Keyes & K. A. Moore (eds) *Well-being: Positive Development Across the Life Course. Crosscurrents in Contemporary Psychology*, Mahwah, N.J.: L. Erlbaum Associates, pp. 177–89.

Bronfenbrenner, U. (1979) *The Ecology of Human Development*, Cambridge, MA: Harvard University Press.

Campbell, B. A. (1979) 'Theory building in political socialization. Explorations of political trust and social learning theory', *American Politics Quarterly*, 7(4): 453.

Duran-Aydintug, C. (1997) 'Adult children of divorce revisited: When they speak up', *Journal of Divorce and Remarriage*, 27: 1–2.

Christiansen, R. (2001) 'Overlevelsens hylster: forholdet mellem tillid og risiko i moderniteten', *Psykologisk Pædagogisk Rådgivning*, 38(4): 285–99.

Clarke, A. & A. Clarke (1998) 'Early experience and the life path', *The Psychologist*, 11(9): 433–5.

Craig, W., Y. Harel-Fisch, H. Fogel-Grinvald, S. Dostaler, J. Hetland, B. Simons-Morton, M. Molcho, M. G. de Mato, M. Overpeck, P. Due & W. Pickett (2009) 'A cross-national profile of bullying and victimization among adolescents in 40 countries', *International Journal of Public Health*, 54(2): 216–24.

Due, P., C. S. Brixval & B. E. Holstein (2011) 'Mobning' in M. Rasmussen & P. Due (eds) *Skolebørnsundersøgelsen 2010*, pp. 81–3, http://www.hbsc.dk/downcount/HBSC-Rapport-2010.pdf.

Elder, G. H. (1994) 'Time, human agency, and social change: Perspectives on the life course', *Social Psychology Quarterly*, 57(1): 4–15.

Elder, G. H., M. Kirkpatrick Johnson & R. Crosnoe (2003) 'The emergence and development of life course theory' in J. T. Mortimer & M. J. Shanahan (eds) *Handbook of the Life Course*, New York: Kluwer Academic/Plenum Publishers, pp. 3–19.

Erikson, E. H. (1950) *Childhood and Society*, New York: W. W. Norton.

Erikson, E. H. (1968) *Identity, Youth and Crisis*, New York: W. W. Norton.

Erikson, E. H. & J. M. Erikson (1997) *The Life Cycle Completed*, New York: W. W. Norton.

Fentress, J. & C. Wickham (1992) *Social Memory*, Oxford & Cambridge: Basil Blackwell Publisher.

Fonagy, P., M. Steele, H. Steele & G. S. Moran (1991) 'The capacity for understanding mental states: The reflective self in parent and child and its significance for security of attachment', *Infant Mental Health Journal*, 12(3): 201–18.

Fonagy, P., M. Steele, H. Steele, T. Leigh, R. Kennedy, G. Mattoon & M. Target (1995) 'Attachment, the reflective self, and borderline states: The predictive specificity of the Adult Attachment Interview and pathological emotional development' in S. Goldberg, R. Muir & J. Kerr (eds) *Attachment Theory: Social, Developmental and Clinical Perspectives*, Hillsdale: NJ: Analytic Press, pp. 233–78.

Franklin, K. M., R. Janoff-Bulman & J. E. Roberts (1990) 'Long-term impact of parental divorce on optimism and trust: Changes in general assumptions or narrow beliefs?', *Journal of Personality & Social Psychology*, 59: 743–55.

Freitag, M. & R. Traunmüller (2009) 'Spheres of trust: An empirical analysis of the foundations of particularised and generalised trust', *European Journal of Political Research*, 48(6): 782–803.

Fukuyama, F. (1995) *Trust: The Social Virtues and the Creation of Prosperity*, New York: Free Press.

Giele, J. Z. & G. H. J. Elder (1998) 'Life course research: Development of a field' in J. Z. Giele & G. H. J. Elder (eds) *Methods of Life Course Research: Qualitative and Quantitative Approaches*, Thousand Oaks, CA: Sage, pp. 5–27.

Grosse, J. (2012) Kommer tid kommer tillit?: Unga vuxnas och medelålders erfarenheter. [Trust from a life course perspective: Young and middle-aged Swedes' experiences]. Dissertation, Stockholm: Stockholm University, Department of Social Work.

Hale, C. (1996) 'Fear of crime: A review of the literature', *International Review of Victimology*, 4(2): 79–150.

Halldén, G. (2005) *The Metaphors of Childhood in a Preschool Context*, paper presented at AARE conference, Sydney, 27 November–1 December, http://www.aare.edu.au/05pap/hal05001.pdf.

Hamilton, C. E. (2000) 'Continuity and discontinuity of attachment from infancy through adolescence', *Child Development*, 71(3): 690.

Helliwell, J. F. & S. Wang (2011) 'Trust and wellbeing', *International Journal of Wellbeing*, 1(1): 42–78.

Hesse, E. (1999) 'The adult attachment interview. Historical and current perspectives' in J. Cassidy & P. R. Shaver (eds) *Handbook of Attachment. Theory, Research, and Clinical Applications*, New York, London: The Guilford Press, pp. 395–433.

James, A., C. Jenks & A. Prout (1998) *Theorizing Childhood*, Cambridge: Polity Press.

Jantzer, A. M., J. H. Hoover & R. Narloch (2006) 'The relationship between school-aged bullying and trust, shyness and quality of friendships in young adulthood: A preliminary research note', *School Psychology International*, 27(2): 146–56.

Katz, H. A. & J. B. Rotter (1969) 'Interpersonal trust scores of college students and their parents', *Child Development*, 40(2): 657–61.

King, V. (2002) 'Parental divorce and interpersonal trust in adult offspring', *Journal of Marriage & Family*, 64: 642–56.

Kopp-Smith, A. K. (2010): *Parental Bereavement and the Romantic Relationships of Adults*, PhD dissertation. Adelphi University, The Institute of Advanced Psychological Studies.

Kryger, L. (2004) 'Tilknytning til andre mennesker', *Psykolog Nyt*, 18: 32–43.

Kvale, S. (2007) *Doing Interview*, The Sage Qualitative Research Kit, London: Thousand Oaks; New Delhi, Singapore: Sage.

Lee, N. (2001) *Childhood and Society. Growing Up in an Age of Uncertainty*, Maidenhed: Open University Press.

Lewis, M., C. Feiring & S. Rosenthal (2000) 'Attachment over time', *Child Development*, 71(3): 707–20.

Luhmann, N. (1988) 'Familiarity, confidence, trust: Problems and perspectives' in D. Gambetta (ed.) *Trust: Making and Breaking Cooperative Relations*, Oxford: Basil Blackwell, pp. 94–107.

Luhmann, N. (2005): *Tillid – en mekanisme til reduktion af social kompleksitet*, København: Hans Reitzels Forlag.

Lund, M. (2001) 'Tillit och mänsklig utveckling' in G. Aronsson & J. C. Karlsson (eds) *Tillitens ansikten*, Lund: Studentlitteratur, pp. 29–47.

Main, M. (1991) 'Metacognitive knowledge, metacognitive monitoring, and singular (coherent) vs. multiple (incoherent) models of attachment – Findings and directions for future research' in C. M. Parkes, J. Stevenson-Hinde & P. Marris (eds) *Attachment Across the Life Cycle*, London: Routledge, pp. 127–59.

Nsamenang, B. (2008) 'Constructing cultural identity within families' in L. Brooker & M. Woodhead (eds) *Developing Positive Identities. Early Childhood in Focus 3*, Margate: Thanet Press Ltd, p. 16.

Nyby, T. K. (2011): *Familieformer og skilsmisse*, København: Børnerådet.

Putnam, R. D. (1993) *Making Democracy Work: Civic Traditions in Modern Italy*, Princeton, N.J.: Princeton University Press.

Putnam, R. D. (2000) *Bowling Alone: The Collapse and Revival of American Community*, New York: Simon & Schuster.

Qvortrup, J. (1994) 'Introduction' in J. Qvortrup, M. Bardy, G. Sgritta & H. Wintersberger (eds) *Childhood Matters: Social Theory, Practice and Politics*, Aldershot: Avebury, pp. 1–23.

Redmond, G. (2010) 'Children's agency and the welfare state: Policy priorities and contradictions in Australia and the UK', *Childhood*, 17(4): 170–84.

Rosenthal, G. (1993) 'Reconstruction of life stories' in R. Johnson & A. Lieblich (eds) *The Narrative Study of Lives*, Vol. 1, London: Thousand Oaks; New Delhi: Sage, pp. 59–91.

Rothstein, B. (2009): *Tillitens mekanismer*, Svensk Höst, the SOM Institute, report no. 46.

Rutter, M. (1997) *Den livslange udvikling*, Hans Reitzels Forlag.

Salmi, V., M. Smolej & J. Kivivuori (2007) 'Crime victimization, exposure to crime news and social trust among adolescents', *Young*, 15(3): 255–72.

van Schaick, K. & A. L. Stolberg (2001) 'The impact of parental involvement and parental divorce on young adults' intimate relationships', *Journal of Divorce and Remarriage*, 36(12): 99–121.

Seligman, M. E. P. (1991) *Learned Optimism*, New York: Knopf.

Schaffer, H. R. (1992) 'Early experience and the parent–child relationship: Genetic and environmental interactions as developmental determinants' in B. Tizard & V. Varma (eds) *Vulnerability and Resilience in Human Development*, London: Jessica Kingsley, pp. 39–65.

Stolle, D. & M. Hooghe (2004) 'The roots of social capital: Attitudinal and network mechanisms in the relation between youth and adult indicators of social capital', *Acta Politica*, 39(4): 422–41.

Stolle, D. & L. Nishikawa (2011) 'Trusting others – How parents shape the generalized trust of their children', *Comparative Sociology*, 10: 281–314.

Sturgis, P., R. Patulny & N. Allum (2007) *What Makes Trusters Trust?*, paper presented at the 'Reciprocity: Theories and Facts' Conference, University of Milan-Bicocca, Milan.

Uprichard, E. (2008) 'Children as "beings and becomings": Children, childhood and temporality', *Children and Society*, 22(4): 303–13.

Uslaner, E. M. (2002) *The Moral Foundations of Trust*, New York: Cambridge University Press.

Weber, L. R. & A. Carter (2003) *The Social Construction of Trust*, New York: Kluwer Academic/Plenum Publishers.

Welch, M. R., R. E. N. Rivera, B. P. Conway, J. Yonkoski, P. M. Lupton & R. Giancola (2005) 'Determinants and consequences of social trust', *Sociological Inquiry*, 75(4): 453–73.

Ward, P. & S. Meyer (2009) 'Trust, social quality and wellbeing: A sociological exegesis', *Development and Society*, 38(2): 339–63.

Warming, H. (2002) *Det er lidt svært – men jeg må jo sige min mening*, København: Frydenlund.

4
Betrayal of Trust: Victims of Maternal Incest

Jackie Turton

As the chapters in this book indicate, the concept of trust is complex as it is used to inform numerous and diverse discourses (Bessant et al., 2005). The virtual notions of trust and trustworthiness are even more problematic when considering the relationships and responses of children and young people to the adult world. The intention of this chapter is to identify some of the particular problems experienced by victims of maternal incest. Here we explore the interplay between the individual dimensions of trust, concerning the child's intimate and emotional relationship with an important other, alongside the broader social dimensions that should enable the sexually abused child to disclose.

Children have few strategies for coping with sexual abuse. The very act of being given the identity of 'child' publically exposes a lack of legal and social status leading to inadequate personal and practical resources for protection (Bessant et al., 2005). Furthermore, sexual abuse is such a betrayal of trust that it can affect all future relationships for the victim, particularly if the perpetrator is a familial figure (Welldon, 1988; Gittens, 1998; Peter, 2006). The difficulties are exacerbated for a child when the offender is female, even more so in cases of maternal incest (Elliott, 1993; Rosencrans, 1997; Mitchell & Morse, 1998; Denov, 2004; Turton, 2008). The controlling and gendered construction of the family has generated a series of hurdles for victims to negotiate. We will discuss some of the social contexts that disable the child and highlight ways in which their inability to trust or find someone trustworthy blocks access to protection and social participation.

There are two key social elements which work towards preventing disclosure. The first concerns the wider social constructs that create an atmosphere of disbelief that women can sexually abuse their children and the second element highlights the interpersonal problems for children concerning disclosure and who to trust. While these two extreme concepts of trust may seem rather disparate, according to Sztompka there are strong links between 'the various types of trust [...] that operate according to the same logic [...] behind all of them there looms the primordial form of trust – in people and their actions' (1999: 45).

Methods

The data for this chapter is drawn from a wider qualitative research project concerning the sexual abuse of children by women, using a sociological rather than a psychological framework. There are only a few studies (Denov, 2004) relating to female abusers that consider the social context of the events and their stories. Since access to these offenders is limited, the original work included a number of perspectives in an attempt to contextualise the female perpetrator. A series of in-depth interviews were undertaken with child protection professionals (including police and probation officers, social and health workers and counsellors), three female offenders and eight survivors.

All of the interviews were thematic in approach offering the respondents an opportunity to tell their stories and the themes were taken from the child sexual abuse literature, the limited research on women as abusers and the researcher's 'subjective adequacy' (Bruyn, 1966). But more generally the information gathering took a grounded theory approach (Glaser & Strauss, 1967) to ensure that as new information and ideas were accumulated they were fed into the research.

It is worth saying more about the process in terms of ethical considerations since this relates to issues of trust and what stories are told (London et al., 2005). This is a very sensitive area of research. At each stage it was important to develop bonds of trust with gatekeepers in order to gain access to respondents and then develop trusting relationships with the interviewees to enable them to 'tell their stories'. Plummer (1995) has noted elsewhere that sexual stories require a willing audience. For instance, he suggests that the stories from paedophiles still remain so unacceptable they cannot be heard in public. To compensate for this exclusion, perpetrators tend to use a variety of rationales and justifications (Lyman & Scott, 1970; Taylor, 1972; Turton, 2008) in attempts to make their experiences more socially acceptable. The victims in the original study (Turton, 2008) were abused by their mother or mother-figure. This chapter uses the data to consider the problems of trust when children are abused by their maternal figure and how these difficulties are intertwined with our inability to recognise and accept that some mothers sexually abuse their children.

Trust and the social constraints

There are tensions between knowledge and action in nearly all cases of familial sexual abuse. Richardson identified the paradox that exists as 'a constant tension between the willingness to know, and the desire not to know (which) condemns awareness of child sexual abuse to a fluctuating and conflicting state' (Richardson, 2001: 198). Cases concerning female sexual abusers are no different and there are a number of particular issues that are worth exploring in more depth since they relate to the availability of trustworthy adults and the consequential credibility awarded to the disclosure stories of child victims.

Do women sexually abuse children?

In the first instance, perhaps one of the primary concepts to accept is that women, including mothers, do sexually abuse children. The concerns about child sexual abuse have been high on the public agenda for at least the last three decades, fuelling public anxiety, media uproar and political debate (Jenkins, 1998; Kitzinger, 2004). In the main this has been depicted as a gendered problem with discussion concentrated around male offenders and female victims. There is no doubt the statistical evidence would indicate that men are much more likely to be sexual abusers of children than women. In England and Wales females made up just 2.9 per cent of all arrests for sexual offences in the year 2009–10 (Povey et al., 2011). This figure includes all sex offences, not just child sexual abuse, but it does offer us a gendered picture. It is important to note when viewing these figures that for evidential reasons very few child sex abusers – whether male or female – reach the criminal courts in the UK. So for these two reasons the statistical evidence forms a very loose guide to the prevalence of female abusers.

Other estimates of prevalence rates of female perpetrators are variable. Early research by Russell and Finkelhor (1984) suggested that female perpetrators were involved with the sexual assault of 20 per cent of all abused boys and 5 per cent of all abused girls. Turner and Turner's (1994) review of the literature showed that between 6–14 per cent of all cases of sexually abused children in the USA involved a female offender. A more recent review by Kite and Tyson (2004) indicates that the offending rate for female sexual abusers varies from 4–24 per cent with retrospective victim reports offering rates in the higher ranges. Generally, researchers in the field (Bunting, 2005) have accepted that about 5 per cent of all cases of child sexual abuse involve a female perpetrator. While all of these may be helpful indicators, perhaps a more relevant statistic in the UK comes from ChildLine[1] whose 2008–09 figures show that of the 12,268 children who called during that year to talk about sexual abuse, 54 per cent said the perpetrators were men and 17 per cent cited women as their abusers. Within this latter group mothers were disclosed as the perpetrators by 4 per cent of the abused girls and 20 per cent of the abused boys (NSPCC, 2009). So while the recorded and estimated figures for women who sexually abuse children are lower than that for male perpetrators they demonstrate that females form a significant minority.

What harm can they do?

The second concept to consider is the question of harm, which has been raised on a number of occasions and remains part of the mythical illusion about female sexual abuse even amongst some professionals (Denov, 2004). It was Mathis who first voiced the question of women and sexual harm: 'that she might seduce a child into sex play is unthinkable and even if she did so what harm could she do without a penis?' (Mathis, 1972: 54). But as we know sexual abuse involves more than just penetration by a penis. It is important to recognise that abuse by a female can range along a continuum from the more ambiguous voyeuristic behaviour to overt sexual violence such as sodomising and penetrating with objects, burning, pinching, biting breasts and genitals (Mathews et al., 1989; Lawson, 1993; Faller, 1995; Ramsey-Klawsnik, 1990; Saradjian, 1996; Nathan & Ward, 2002). However, often it is not the physical but the emotional trauma of abuse, especially by a mother, that can have a lasting effect, as voiced by two adult survivors. 'I was an object by which she got relief from her sexual frustrations' (May[2]). 'She used to tell me I was a nobody [...] it's all this feeling and all this pain [...] you don't know what to do with all this pain' (Petra[3]).

It is worth just adding here another concern about harm. Some male victims may deny, or choose not to recognise that sexual relationships with their mothers are abusive (Elliott, 1993; Mellor & Deering, 2010). Roth discovered with her client group that this was not uncommon amongst all victims of maternal incest. 'Up to the moment of acceptance, clients who were sexually abused by their mothers are *absolutely* sure they were *not* abused by their mothers' (Roth, 1993: 122, italics in the original). Particularly for male victims, such a stance could be linked to social notions of masculinity and femininity – what has been called the masculinisation of aggression and the feminisation of victimisation (Sepler, 1990; Mendel, 1995). Adopting this perspective presents a range of problems concerning disclosure, trust and protecting children more generally since any notions of harm and risk can be easily ignored under the premise that female sexual abuse is just harmless titillation or, in some cases where the victims are male, perhaps a 'rite of passage' (Mellor & Deering, 2010; Denov, 2004). However, some research has found that a high percentage of rapists and sexual offenders claim to have experienced sexual abuse by an adult female (Groth, 1979; Petrovich & Templar, 1984; Briere & Smiljanich, 1993), indicating that their sexual aggression may be as a consequence of unresolved childhood trauma.

Accepting that women, including mothers, can, and do, sexually abuse children and that the abuse can be harmful is important, as 'not being believed' is one of the key concerns for victims prior to disclosure (Roth, 1993; Paine & Hansen, 2002). If we also include reports from victims who find female sexual abuse, particularly by a close relative, more shameful and emotionally damaging than that committed by male offenders (Rosencrans, 1997; Mendel, 1995; Sgroi & Sargent, 1993), then perhaps we can begin to identify just some of the difficulties that victims have in finding someone to trust with their story.

Media responses

The media reporting of child sexual abuse has concentrated on the high profile cases raising concerns about the male-stranger paedophile and conveniently skirting around the fact that sexual abuse is most commonly a familial crime (Wykes & Welsh, 2009). Apart from the 'ordinariness' of familial sexual abuse, any reporting on any cases heard through the family courts is heavy restricted in the UK. Yet, the media is one of the main providers of public information and knowledge about child abuse (Kitzinger, 2004) so it is easy to understand the popular misconception that the male-stranger is the primary predictor and therefore against whom children require protection (Kitzinger, 2004), since these are the cases that most commonly reach the press. When incidents of female perpetrators do become public, readers tend to be 'alternately horrified and titillated by the accounts' (Lawson, 2008: 331). Recent reports have shown[4] maltreatment of a child by a woman especially a mother is very newsworthy (Coward, 1997). These cases often construct the female perpetrator as some monstrous 'other' – not feminine – not normal – not 'like us'. Therefore she can be discounted as real women do not behave this way; a notion that is sometimes adopted by child protection workers. 'She had long hair but with all due respect there was nothing feminine about her [...] always wore trousers [...] very dowdy looking [...] a bit smelly [...] there was nothing feminine about her at all' (social worker).

Thus the case of the maternal incest offender becomes simplistically conflated with the essentialist, expected traits of femininity and nurturing; 'good enough' mothers are low risk offenders (Turton, 2010). Sexual abuse that occurs in the home tends to be either absent from media reporting or in extreme cases 'spectacularised' in such a way as to make it seem an aberration.

There are two key points here. In the first instance, because paedophiles tend to be publicly identified as male strangers, the home and family structure remains a sanctuary and the place of containment and control that most western societies rely on even though we know 'the family is one of the most dangerous places for children to live' (Jenks, 1996: 91). Secondly, any female perpetrators may be disproportionately vilified and discounted as 'other', either unfeminine or crazy (Peter, 2006), since normal mothers protect, not abuse, their children. Given this situation, those children who are abused by female family members face particular issues concerning who to trust and who will believe their disclosures. But it is not only disbelief that silences child victims; there are other influences especially in terms of the family and the social expectations of the mothering role.

Trust and social participation

Of course for many children the home is a sanctuary, but concentrating on the stranger paedophile 'masks the fact that most child sexual abuse is perpetrated within families or by those known to (victims)' (Green, 2001: 161). 'Stranger-danger' reinforces the notion that the ideal type of family offers a safe private haven against a public world of crime and disorder (Saraga, 2001); it works towards protecting idealised images of the maternal role; it offers a rationale for condoning the controlling elements of the family that limits the child's opportunity to seek trustworthy adults outside of the household.

The family

As outsiders we often have fixed concepts of family that easily blur the reality of what lies just beneath the surface (Gittens, 1993) and may create an aura of disbelief amongst some professionals when abusive incidents are identified (Denov, 2004; Turton, 2008). This blurring between the fixed notions of the ideal family and the reality that Gittens (1993) refers to in her work, encourages public displays that reinforce the ideal type. For example, Mitchell and Morse (1998) discuss how easy it is for female abusers to act out the perfect mother role in public, 'a saintly attitude' and 'very sweet to people' then change moods dramatically in private. And victims have voiced the ambiguities that this mirage of home life presents.

> [...] the family were seen by outsiders as loving and affectionate [...] the outer side was very upper middle class and yet all the horrible stuff was going on underneath (Penny[5]).

> You had to go home [...] in the evening you had to go home. It was like having a big stone in your stomach everyday of your life [...] (Petra).

> [...] things would have looked OK. We had a car; we had a TV; we went on holiday [...] on Sunday we would have Sunday lunch and tea would be on a trolley [...] we did a lot of entertaining (Louise[6]).

The family remains an important socialising structure within western societies where adults have state sanctioned control over children. In abusive households this presents a child with conflicting emotions that are intensified in cases of maternal incest leading to a consideration of the interplay between societal expectations, the maternal abuser and the child. All these dimensions leave little room and few options for the child victim to disclose the abuse being suffered. Research (Goodman-Brown et al., 2003; London et al., 2005) suggests that disclosing any familial abuse can be very difficult for children for a variety of reasons, including concerns about complicity, embarrassment, guilt, shame and fears of abandonment. Furthermore, the closer the relationship with the victim the less likely the child is to disclose (Wyatt & Newcomb, 1990; DiPietro et al., 1997; Smith et al., 2000) and Sas (1993) reported that over 80 per cent of victims in his sample delayed or never disclosed the abuse. On occasions when the opportunity to talk with a trusted adult does arise, it is the close bond that actually works to inhibit disclosure as the child attempts to protect their one precious relationship.

> [...] they (aunt and grandmother) were very important to me as a child [...] I never [...] I don't think [...] ever felt like telling [...] I just felt I could behave like a child with them and be safe and secure in that [...] (May).

> But you see I never did tell her (grandmother) about the abuse. She asked me; she asked me lots of times [...] but I never did tell her [...]

I don't know why but I guess it's [...] I was afraid of losing her (Petra).

Both May and Petra had very close links with their grandmothers, formed trusting bonds and loving relationships that they were determined as children not to taint with stories of abuse. In these particular cases the interpersonal trust formed between the child victims and their grandmothers did not appear 'safe' enough to lead to disclosure. Although rationalised by May and Petra as a way of protecting their important others, the risk of not being believed, of letting them down, of losing their relationship, and with this the risk of disappointment is high. Penny, another child victim of maternal incest, found this out the only time she tried to disclose as a child, '[...] but she's your mother dear, of course she wants a cuddle' (Penny). Trust and risk are closely related – trust is required to combat the risky situation (Sztompka, 1999; Luhmann, 1988) but not being able to trust reduces the options for alternative actions (Sztompka, 1999). In the case of these victims the fear of trusting outweighed the value of disclosure and the promise of protection, refraining from action means the risk is negated (Luhmann, 1988). They are not able to trust and thereby unable to access the route to protection.

For most children the family is a space that should offer a safe haven enabling them to grow emotionally and develop a sense of understanding and trust. But for abused children this becomes eschewed. May and Petra, quoted above, found their only safe relationships were too important to risk losing, which perhaps suggests that at least in some cases of maternal incest, finding someone to trust and accessing a trustworthy adult may not be the complete solution.

The mother role

In turning to consider the role of mothering, I would like to highlight the problems created by the idealisation of motherhood and the assumption that all mothers will love their children. The two issues are closely connected to the underlying problems for the victims of maternal incest since they can lead to a sense of distrust[7] (disbelief) between protection workers, as well as society more broadly.

The ideology of femininity assumes all women share a universal nurturing role (Forna, 1998); as Glenn has suggested 'woman is conflated with mother, and together appears as an undifferentiated and unchanging monolith' (Glenn, 1994: 13). In western society women are expected to be nurturing and protective (Roth, 1993), often judging themselves and other women in terms of their ability to care (Cockburn, 2005). Alongside the caring image we expect children and their mothers to have a special relationship – the close loving bond between mother and child that offers the mother a licence to be intimate.

> She must be completely devoted not just to her children, but to her role. She must be the mother who understands her children, who is all-loving and [...] all giving. She must be capable of enormous sacrifice [...] she must embody all the qualities traditionally associated with femininity such as nurturing, intimacy and softness. That's how we want her to be. That's how we intend to make her.
>
> (Forna, 1998: 3)

We already know from our discussion above that child sexual abuse by women is very unusual, so it is the rarity of the event alongside the social expectations of maternity that can offer mothers who sexually abuse the opportunity to disguise or rationalise their behaviour as childcare. Thus, the social expectations of the maternal role cause problems for some women as it disallows ambivalent feelings to be revealed and ignores female perversity (Welldon, 1988). Research has indicated that there seems to be 'a reluctance or unwillingness on the part of professionals to acknowledge or identify sexual offending by females, as it seems shocking, unnatural and to contravene our understanding of the dynamics of sexual abuse' (NSPCC, 2009: 22).

In cases of maternal abuse, mothers who experience problems are unlikely to seek advice and they are more likely to put on the show of 'happy families' to the world. Such fantasies of an essential harmony between mothers and children can hamper decisions made by professionals (Featherstone, 1997) or even lead to unintentional collusion with the abuser (Denov, 2004; Turton, 2008). As one probation officer identified, '[the] social image of motherhood and femininity often masks abusive behaviour [...] professionals may collude with these mothers by assuming they are the protectors [...]' (Veronica).

So we can begin to build a picture indicating the social constraints on victims of maternal incest in terms of social denial of the event, denial of harm and the over-riding assumption that all mothers love their children or can be made to do so (Featherstone, 1997). Women in the household, especially mothers, are perceived as low risk offenders by the adults that children come into contact with – such as teachers and other professionals, in other words the adults children might choose to trust with any concerns. The low risk assessment encourages a sceptical approach to disclosures allowing for minimisation or even denial by child protection professionals of suspected abusive behaviour (Denov, 2004; Turton, 2008). Even in cases where there are indicators of abuse the risk may be downgraded as there is 'no socially acknowledged place to put this behaviour, because maternal sexual abuse completely defies our logic concerning femininity and motherhood' (Peter, 2006: 284). As a result, stories from these children may be referred to as 'over enthusiastic childcare' or misinterpretation by the child (Turton, 2008). Finding an adult to trust when your story is considered 'untrustworthy' is problematic and as a consequence these children may be left unable to voice their concerns.

Trust and finding a voice

While broader social structures have significant impact on protecting children, for the victim the problem lies in finding the pathway to access the right to a voice. This process is not a simple one since the emotional ties of intimate relationships can create serious barriers. Sometimes the action of the very system designed to protect children becomes a hindrance.

Liberation or protection?

The current welfarist approach to protecting children is problematic. Of course the young child does need some protection but there are hidden dangers within the system itself since encouraging the maintenance of innocence feeds into the opportunity for grooming by perpetrators, including incest abusers (Kitzinger, 1988; Warner, 2001). In other words, keeping children dependent may not protect them against abuse (Scott et al., 1998). In fact, there may be ulterior motives to protecting children linked with the ways in which we have created childhood as separate and children as 'specialisms' (Weeks, 1989).

Gittens takes this further by suggesting that the innocent child is 'largely created, maintained and defined by adults for their own reasons' (Gittens, 1998: 151). The very process of protecting children inside the family environment can deny them their rights to participation and their own voice about sex and sexuality (Kitzinger, 1988; Jenkins, 1998), as highlighted by Liz: 'A child's right to her body, autonomy and privacy is still a radical concept which would require the transformation of family power relations' (Liz, 1982: 21).

We are therefore left in a rather ambiguous situation since the very system designed to ensure children's safety could disempower them and leave them less able to seek protection, increasing their 'isolation and confinement with the family' (Kitzinger, 1988: 81). It is the isolation and disempowerment that presents key problems; these children need recognition as subjects of rights not just subjects of protection to avoid them becoming even more vulnerable. In their case this is not easy to resolve, partly linked to the family structure as suggested by Liz, but some child victims may have already adopted a powerless sense of self in order to accommodate[8] their abusive situation.

> [...] it is precisely the children who are the most vulnerable, eager to please and easily-led who obstinately reject any idea that they have 'rights' and refuse to develop a 'sense' of their own power. Such unexpected conviction from the most vulnerable children is understandable if we accept the 'sense' of powerlessness may in fact reflect their internal reality. Children are sometimes hopeless because there is no hope, helpless because there is no help and compliant because there is no alternative.
>
> (Kitzinger, 1997: 181)

It is not just powerlessness within the family that controls and silences victims. Despite the work that has been achieved to secure children's rights,[9] questions about accessibility remain: how do children get to know about their rights and get to exercise them? Not much has changed since Kitzinger's comment in one of her early discussions,

> Young people are politically disenfranchised, economically restricted and denied the legal rights and responsibilities that are considered part of full citizenship [...]. If we are to tackle the roots of child sexual abuse we have to think about the position of children in society.
>
> (Kitzinger, 1988: 83)

The sense of powerlessness that engulfs incest victims is difficult enough for all children who have been abused but it is exacerbated for the very young child, a common maternal incest victim (Faller, 1987; Finkelhor et al., 1988; Rudin et al., 1995; Saradjian, 1996; Rosencrans, 1997; Bunting, 2005). Furthermore, the philosophy of children's rights sits rather awkwardly alongside maternal incest. After all, as suggested above, the mother is generally supposed to be the child's most faithful champion. It is difficult to know how we can challenge this situation for children especially within the UK since our recently reformed Children Act, 2004, continues to recognise the parent's right to 'reasonable chastisement' and thereby highlights the tension that exists 'between [the] preservation of family forms and the protection of children' (Saraga, 2001: 232).

What this means is that for incest victims finding a voice and someone to trust outside of the family is made more complex by the legal process designed to protect their welfare. As a result we cannot problematise child sexual abuse without problematising childhood 'as a structured position in society' (Kitzinger, 1997: 184). If this is the case then understanding child sexual abuse is itself constrained by the social institution of childhood; they are inextricably linked embodying notions of loss, risk, trust and trustworthiness.

Attachment and loss

The other issue I want to raise here concerns the strong emotional ties that bind the child to their important other – the concept of maternal attachment and loss. Psychologists (Bowlby, 1998; Salter-Ainsworth, 1991) have explained attachment theory as an internal response of a child to the primary adult figure. Rather than get into any lengthy debates about nature/nurture, it does seems appropriate to suggest two aspects to understanding the special relationship that a child has for a parent – usually the mother in the first instance – as it is a combination between the psychological and the social environment. So in the case of maternal incest, 'we have the internal psychological desire for a close intimate relationship with our maternal figure and [...] we are socialised into accepting the mythical mothering role' (Turton, 2008: 78). This is pivotal to understanding the relationship between the abusive mother and child, as the failure of the 'ideal' maternal model presents problems for victims as well as professionals. Victims can find it difficult to deal with the sense of maternal loss and they may not feel able, or may not want, to express that loss to the outside world. Rosencrans highlights this very point by suggesting that '[...] more than any other person, mother can convince the world that we are worthwhile human beings. Mothers can convince us of that [...] abused children want it' (Rosencrans, 1997: 33). The difficulty of confronting abusive mothers is further expressed by a survivor in Elliott's work on female sexual abusers.

> There's something about a mother [she] gives you love and care. So when she abuses you, it leads to an even greater sense of despair than when your father does it. In my dreams I castrate my father

and suffocate him. But I can't attack my mother. I am torn between love and hate.

(Survivor cited in Elliott, 1993: 10)

The above quote does appear to confirm the psychologists' suggestion that loss of the primary attachment figure can represent a loss of everything to the child (Bacon, 2001) and that, like most children, abused children experience their primary attachment figure as necessary for survival. Consequently victims are left with huge dilemmas.

> The child abused by a primary attachment figure suffers in multiple and complex ways. There is the pain, confusion and fear of the abuse itself; there is the extreme contradiction inherent in the source of danger and the source of protection residing in one person. Perhaps most terrifying of all there is the fear of loss of attachment relationship, which children often believe will happen if they try to protect themselves from being abused by a parent.
>
> (Bacon, 2001: 49)

In terms of maternal incest the iconic status of the mother role plays a part in the conflict between fear of abuse and fear of loss. Since mothers are so socially important in families, victims, like Louise, find themselves unable to tell and unable to give up on their mother. 'I can remember at Christmas crying that I wanted me mum. I cried loads of times wanting me mum, but not the mum I got' (Louise).

The risk of permanent loss of the maternal can be another factor in the failure to 'trust' and in some cases the desire to retain the mother figure appears to be so deeply embedded that abused children may both fantasise their attachment and defend 'their inappropriate mothers' (Roth, 1993: 122). The following quotes suggest the subsequent inertia victims experience.

> I know that some people who have not been sexually abused by their mothers have deep emotional relationships with them, but I feel that the emotional bond I have with my mother is unnaturally intense. At time I feel we are almost the same person ... from a very early age it felt like my body was just an extension of hers (Alice[10]).
>
> [...] if you have been sexually abused by your mother you can't discard her entirely. Apart from anything else she carried you in her womb and delivered you [...] so you are inextricably linked

together, whether you like it or not. Trying to deal with this ... is very difficult (May).

Survivors on the one hand want to be loved by their mothers even if on the other they hate them for the abuse they have inflicted. While these two victims appeared to feel a maternal link, there was a tension between this bond and their fear, shame and inability to escape the situation. By disclosing the abuse 'child victims of maternal incest have to disillusion the social world by shaking motherhood from its pedestal and at the same time risk permanent loss of the primary maternal attachment' (Turton, 2008: 34). Furthermore, since mothers are assumed to be champions of their children, they are assumed to be trustworthy. The loss of the bond is not just a loss of the maternal attachment for the child but perhaps a more socially 'iconic' notion of trust.

So while many of the academic discussions focus around insecure or inadequate attachments (Frederick & Goddard, 2008), victims sometimes find a problem for disclosure, and the ability to trust other adults, is linked to the inability to disengage – or detach – from the maternal. If not a psychological loss, then at the very least the cultural implications of severing the link with the primary attachment figure may prove too strong for child victims, creating a state of inertia due to the inability to trust or inability to take the risk of disclosing the abuse.

Conclusion

What this discussion reveals is a series of hurdles for both victims and professionals when encountering maternal incest. It is important to recognise that barriers exist for both victims and child protection workers since children need to be ready to tell and professionals need to be ready to hear. The trust dynamic is a two-way process. The problematic is also two dimensional. On the one hand, the skewed and abusive relationship within the close intimate family unit creates an environment of emotion and distrust, silencing the victim. On the other, we are confronted with gendered social structures that obscure women who sexually abuse and idolise, both psychologically and socially, the maternal figure. This clouds any stories of female sexual abuse with disbelief. While challenging this situation is not easy, we do need to refocus our approach.

For instance, professionals require an understanding of female sexual perpetrators to avoid falling into the trap of denial or minimisation of the behaviour. This is not an easy process since calling into question the relationship, especially the sexual status, of a mother with her child has to contend with numerous social taboos. But perhaps a more in-depth consideration of the diversity of motherhood could, as Featherstone (1997) suggests, move us away from a romanticised version of the mother-child relationship that influences decisions and judgements in child protection (Kelly, 2002). For the sake of the child victim the final outcome has to be acceptance and recognition of maternal incest by protection workers and society more generally. These victims need somebody to trust and someone who will believe their story.

However, having access to a trustworthy adult is just one side of the problem. The disconnection between the experiences of maternal sexual abuse and the social expectations of mothering can leave victims 'feeling ostracised and alone' (Peter, 2006: 298) and unable to make sense of their abuse and unable to tell their stories to the outside world. Mendel's (1995) research considers male victims of female perpetrators, many of whom are maternal incest victims. He identified that all child victims feel a sense of betrayal of trust; the closer the familial relationship the greater the sense of betrayal resulting in '[...] extreme dependency or impaired ability to trust others, difficulty judging the trustworthiness of others, anger, hostility, grief and depression' (Mendel, 1995: 75). This sense of betrayal suggests that even given the access to trustworthy adults, children may be unable to disclose. The quotes from May and Petra above discussing their relationships with grandparents indicate that this is the case and that it can continue to affect relationships into adulthood for some victims. Penny simply says '[...] your capacity to know who to trust, who to love has been warped'. But Louise is much stronger in her response.

> [...] but how has it affected me? It has affected me in having relationships. It has affected me in that I don't trust ... umm ... actually I would say it's more about women than men ... I have more trust in men than women ... I still haven't got confidence ... All those people see this external thing that Louise can do this, that and the other and suggests this, that and the other but inside I'm not ... (Louise).

All maternal incest victims find it difficult to talk about their abuse and while we can make some headway by considering the response of professionals, or challenging vulnerability by the enactment of children's rights or even questioning the Madonna versions of mother-hood, improving the opportunities for some children may be limited. Sgroi and Sargent (1993) indicated why the problems for these victims are not readily resolved.

> It simply may generate too much cognitive dissonance for [survivors] to acknowledge to self or to others that he or she was sexually abused by her or his mother. In other words, to view oneself as so powerful a sexual object that 'my own mother succumbed to the temptation to have sexual contact with me,' may be a belief that is too threatening and overwhelming for the child to integrate and absorb.
>
> (Sgroi & Sargent, 1993: 24)

It is the abusive intimate relationships within the lives of some of these victims that corrupt the process of trust. But it is the broader social structures that compound any distrust that results in disclosure being a risk too far.

Notes

1   ChildLine is a free confidential 24-hour helpline for children and young people. It was set up as a registered UK charity in 1986 and is now part of the National Society for the Prevention of Cruelty to Children (NSPCC).
2   May was sexually abused by her mother from infancy until she was five years old. Then she was sexually abused by her brother, his friend and his friend's father.
3   Petra was sexually abused by her mother and father from the age of three.
4   The recent arrest in the UK of Vanessa George (2009), mother and nursery worker caused public outrage and widespread media condemnation.
5   Penny suffered emotional and sexual abuse at the hands of her mother from about the age of two.
6   Louise was sexually and physically abused by her mother from an 'early age'.
7   Distrust here is used as the negative mirror image of trust suggested by Sztompka (1999).
8   For more discussion see Summit (1983) who identified the *child sexual abuse accommodation syndrome* that outlines why children are reluctant to disclose familial abuse.
9   The United Nations Convention on the Rights of the Child was ratified by the UK in 1999 and is reflected within the Children Act 2004. Alongside the legislation changes within the court system – with the additional remit of an appointed guardian for children and new policy documents for child protection workers have included elements to include the child victims in discussions and decision-making.
10 Alice was sexually abused by her mother from an 'early age'.

Bibliography

Bacon, H. (2001) 'Attachment, trauma and child sexual abuse: An exploration' in S. Richardson & H. Bacon (ed.) *Creative Responses to Child Sexual Abuse*, London: Jessica Kingsley, pp. 44–59.

Bessant, J., R. Hil & R. Watts (2005) 'Introduction' in J. Bessant, R. Hil & R. Watts (eds) *Violations of Trust: How Social and Welfare Institutions Fail Children and Young People*, Aldershot, UK: Ashgate, pp. xx–xxvi.

Bowlby, J. (1998) *A Secure Base: Clinical Applications of Attachment Theory*, London: Routledge.

Briere, J. & K. Smiljanich (August, 1993) *Childhood Sexual Abuse and Subsequent Sexual Aggression Against Adult Women*, paper presented at the 101st annual convention of the American Psychological Association, Toronto Canada.

Bruyn, S. (1966) *The Human Perspective in Sociology*, New Jersey: Prentice Hall.

Bunting, L. (2005) *Females Who Sexually Offend Against Children: Responses of the Child Protection and Criminal Justice System*, London: NSPCC.

Cockburn, T. (2005) 'Children and the feminist ethic of childcare', *Childhood*, 21(1): 71–89.

Coward, R. (1997) 'The heaven and hell of mothering' in W. Hollway & B. Featherstone (eds) *Mothering and Ambivalence*, London: Routledge, pp. 122–9.

Denov, M. (2004) 'The long-term effects of child sexual abuse by female perpetrators: A qualitative study of male and female victims', *The Journal of Sex Research*, 40(3): 303–14.

DiPietro, E. K., D. K. Runyan & D. D. Fredrickson (1997) 'Predictors of disclosure during medical evaluation for suspected sexual abuse', *Journal of Sexual Abuse*, 6: 133–42.

Elliott, M. (1993) *Female Sexual Abuse of Children: The Ultimate Taboo*, Harlow: Longman.

Faller, K. C. (1987) 'Women who sexually abuse children', *Violence and Victims*, 2(4): 263–76.

Faller, K. C. (1995) 'A clinical sample of women who have sexually abused children', *Journal of Child Sexual Abuse*, 4(3): 13–30.

Featherstone, B. (1997) 'I wouldn't do your job! Women, social work and child care' in W. Hollway & B. Featherstone (eds) *Mothering and Ambivalence*, London: Routledge, pp. 178–203.

Finkelhor, D., L. Williams & N. Burns (1988) *Nursery Crimes: Sexual Abuse in Day Care*, Newbury Park, CA: Sage.

Forna, A. (1998) *Mother of All Myths: How Society Moulds and Constrains Mothers*, London: HarperCollins.

Frederick, J. & C. Goddard (2008) 'Living on an island: Consequences of childhood abuse, attachment disruption and adversity in later life', *Child and Family Social Work*, 13: 300–10.

Gittens, D. (1993) *The Family in Question*, London: Macmillan.

Gittens, D. (1998) *The Child in Question*, London: Macmillan.

Glaser, B. G. & A. L. Strauss (1967) *The Discovery of Grounded Theory: Strategies for Qualitative Research*, Chicago: Aldine.

Glenn, E. (1994) 'Social constructions of mothering' in E. Glenn, G. Chang & L. Forcey (eds) *Mothering: Ideology, Experience and Agency*, London: Routledge, pp. 1–29.

Goodman-Brown, T., R. Edelstein, G. Goodman, D. Jones & D. Gordon (2003) 'Why children tell: A model of children's disclosure of sexual abuse', *Child Abuse and Neglect*, 27(3): 525–40.

Green, L. (2001) 'Children, sexual abuse and the child protection system' in P. Foley, J. Roche & S. Tucker (eds) *Children in Society: Contemporary Theory, Policy and Practice*, Basingstoke, UK: Palgrave with Open University Press, pp. 160–9.

Groth, N. (1979) *Men Who Rape*, New York: Plenum.

Jenkins, P. (1998) *Moral Panic: Changing Concept of the Child Molester in Modern America*, New Haven, CT: Yale University Press.

Jenks, C. (1996) *Childhood*, London: Routledge.

Kelly, N. (2002) 'Using document analysis to reveal narratives of mothering' in C. Horrocks, K. Milnes, B. Roberts & D. Robinson (eds) *Narrative, Memory and Life Transitions*, University of Huddersfield, pp. 189–97.

Kite, D. & G. A. Tyson (2004) 'The impact of perpetrator gender on male and female police officers' perceptions of child sexual abuse', *Psychiatry, Psychology and Law*, 11(2): 308–18.

Kitzinger, J. (1988) 'Defending innocence: Ideologies of childhood', *Feminist Review*, 28(Spring): 77–87.

Kitzinger, J. (1997) 'Who are you kidding? Child, power and the struggle against sexual abuse' in A. James & A. Prout (eds) *Constructing and Re-constructing Childhood*, London: Routledge Falmer, pp. 165–89.

Kitzinger, J. (2004) *Framing Abuse. Media Influence and Public Understanding of Sexual Violence Against Children*, London: Pluto Press.

Lawson, C. (1993) 'Mother-son sexual abuse: Rare or under-reported? A critique of the research', *Child Abuse and Neglect*, 17(2): 261–9.

Lawson, L. (2008) 'Female sex offenders' relationship experiences', *Violence and Victims*, 23(3): 331–43.

Liz (1982) 'Too afraid to speak', *The Leveller*, 2–15 April: 18–21.

London, K., M. Bruck, S. Ceci & D. Shuman (2005) 'Disclosure of child sexual abuse: What does the research tell us about the ways that children tell?', *Psychology, Public Policy and Law*, 11(1): 194–226.

Luhmann, N. (1988) 'Familiarity, confidence and trust: Problems and alternatives' in D. Gametta (ed.) *Trust: Making and Breaking Cooperative Relations*, Oxford: Basil Blackburn, pp. 74–108.

Lyman, S. & M. Scott (1970) *A Sociology of the Absurd*, California: Goodyear.

Mathews, R., J. K. Matthews & K. Spletz (1989) *Female Sexual Offenders: An Exploratory Study*, Orwell, VT: Safer Society Press.

Mathis, J. (1972) *Clear Thinking About Sexual Deviations*, Chicago: Nelson-Hall.

Mellor, D. & R. Deering (2010) 'Professional response and attitudes toward female-perpetrated child sexual abuse: A study of psychologists, psychiatrists, probationary psychologists and child protection workers', *Psychology, Crime & Law*, 16(5): 415–38.

Mendel, M. (1995) *The Male Survivor: The Impact of Sexual Abuse*, Beverley Hills, CA: Sage Focus.

Mitchell, J. & J. Morse (1998) *From Victims to Survivors: Reclaimed Voices of Women Sexually Abused in Childhood by Females*, Washington, DC: Taylor and Francis.

Nathan, P. & T. Ward (2002) 'Female sexual offenders: Clinical and demographic features', *Journal of Sexual Aggression*, 8(1): 5–21.

NSPCC (2009) *Children Talking to ChildLine about Sexual Abuse*, London: NSPCC, http://www.nspcc.org.uk/Inform/publications/casenotes/children_talking_to_childline_about_sexual_abuse_wda69414.html, date accessed 23 March 2010.

Paine, M. L. & D. J. Hansen (2002) 'Factors influencing children to self-disclose sexual abuse', *Clinical Psychological Review*, 22(2): 133–43.

Peter, T. (2006) 'Mad, bad or victim? Making sense of mother-daughter sexual abuse', *Feminist Criminology*, 1(4): 283–302.

Petrovich, M. & D. Templar (1984) 'Heterosexual molestation of children who later become rapist', *Psychological Report*, 54: 810.

Plummer, K. (1995) *Telling Sexual Stories*, London: Routledge.

Povey, D., R. Mulchandani, T. Hand & P. Lakhvinder Kaur (2011) *Police Powers and Procedures in England and Wales 2009/10*, second edition, Home Office Statistical Bulletin, London: Home Office.

Ramsey-Klawsnik, H. (April 1990) *Sexual Abuse by Female Perpetrators: Impact on Children*, paper presented at the National Symposium on Child Victimisation, Atlanta, GA.

Richardson, S. (2001) 'Maintaining awareness of unspeakable truths: Responses to child abuse in the longer term' in S. Richardson & H. Bacon (eds) *Creative Responses to Child Sexual Abuse*, London: Jessica Kingsley, pp. 197–220.

Rosencrans, B. (1997) *The Last Secret: Daughters Sexually Abused by Mothers*, Brandon, VT: Safer Society Press.

Roth, N. (1993) *Integrating the Shattered Self*, New Jersey, USA: Jason Aronson Inc.

Rudin, M., C. Zalewski & J. Bodmer-Turner (1995) 'Characteristics of child sexual abuse victims according to perpetrator gender', *Child Abuse and Neglect*, 19(8): 963–73.

Russell, D. & D. Finkelhor (1984) 'Women as perpetrators' in D. Finkelhor (ed.) *Child Sexual Abuse, New Theory and Practice*, New York: The Free Press, pp. 171–87.

Salter-Ainsworth, M. (1991) 'Attachments and other affectional bonds across the life cycle' in C. Murray-Parkes, J. Stevenson-Hinde & P. Marris (eds) *Attachments Across the Life Cycle*, London: Routledge.

Saradjian, J. (1996) *Women Who Sexually Abuse Children*, Chichester: Wiley.

Saraga, E. (2001) 'Dangerous places: The family as a site of crime' in J. Muncie & E. McLaughlin (eds) *The Problem of Crime*, London: Sage, pp. 191–238.

Sas, L. (1993) *Three Years After the Verdict*, London, Ont. Canada: London Family Court Clinic Inc.

Scott, S., S. Jackson & K. Bartlett-Milburn (1998) 'Swings and roundabouts: Risk, anxiety and the everyday worlds of children', *Sociology*, 32(4): 689–705.

Sepler, F. (1990) 'Victim advocacy and young male victims of sexual abuse: An evolutionary model' in M. Hunter (ed.) *The Sexually Abused Male: Prevalence, Impact and Treatment*, Vol. 1, Lexington, MA: Lexington.

Sgroi, S. & S. Sargent (1993) 'Impact and treatment issues for victims of childhood sexual abuse by female perpetrators' in M. Elliott (ed.) *The Last Taboo*, London: Longman, pp. 15–38.

Smith, D. W., E. J. Letiourneau, B. E. Saunders, D. G. Kilpatrick, H. S. Resnick & C. L. Best (2000) 'Delay in disclosure of childhood rape: Results from a national survey', *Child Abuse and Neglect*, 2: 273–87.

Summit, R. (1983) 'The child sexual abuse accommodation syndrome', *Child Abuse and Neglect*, 24: 689–700.

Sztompka, P. (1999) *Trust, a Sociological Theory*, Cambridge, UK: Cambridge University Press.

Taylor, L. (1972) 'The significance and interpretation of replies to motivational questions: The case of the sex offender', *Sociology*, 6: 23–39.

Turner, M. & T. Turner (1994) *Female Adolescent Sexual Abusers: An Exploratory Study of Mother-Daughter Dynamics With Implications for Treatment*, Vermont, USA: Safer Society Press.

Turton, J. (2008) *Child Abuse, Gender and Society*, Abingdon, UK: Routledge.

Turton, J. (2010) 'Female sexual abusers: Assessing the risk', *International Journal of Law, Crime and Justice*, 38(4): 279–93.

Warner, S. (2001) 'Disrupting narratives of blame: Domestic violence, child sexual abuse and the regulation of experience and identity', *Psychology of Women Section Review*, 4(1): 3–17.

Weeks, J. (1989) *Sex Politics and Society: The Regulation of Sexuality Since 1800*, second edition, London: Longman.

Welldon, E. (1988) *Madonna, Mother, Whore*, New York: Guilford.

Wyatt, G. E. & M. D. Newcomb (1990) 'Internal and external mediators of women's sexual abuse in childhood', *Journal of Consulting and Clinical Psychology*, 58: 758–67.

Wykes, M. & K. Welsh (2009) *Violence, Gender and Justice*, London: Sage.

5

Trust Relationships Between Children, Social Welfare Professionals and the Organisations of Welfare

Sharon Pinkney

This chapter explores the dynamics of trust between children and social welfare professionals. I argue that this is an important aspect of child welfare as trust is closely related to participation and child protection and is therefore one of the most significant areas of child welfare. This important area of trust has been under-theorised in relation to child welfare and protection. The chapter assesses some of the constraints in the process of development of trust by using examples of empirical data from social policy texts, interviews with welfare professionals and from consultation documents written up after participation events with groups of children who are Looked After[1] in residential or foster care in the UK. Extracts from interviews and policy texts are used to illustrate some of the complexities and issues involved in building trust relations between children, young people and welfare professionals.

The first part of this chapter examines these individual relationships between children and welfare professionals, such as social workers or children's rights workers and advocates. The conditions of labour within managerialised welfare contexts where resource constraints lead to staffing difficulties are considered in relation to the difficulties they can create for building trust between children and welfare professionals. Listening to children is developed as one illustration of the potential complexities involved in participation practice and building trust between the child and welfare professional. The chapter then shifts to exploring aspects relating to institutional trust and mistrust before considering wider issues of trust within the broader context of societal attitudes towards children and young people. This third level of analysis takes us into the arena of children's rights and social justice. These three levels of analysis and the interrelationship between them are explored to help us unravel some of the complexities involved in the dynamic relations of trust between children, young people, welfare professionals and the organisations of welfare.

Theorising trust in relations between children and welfare professionals

From the early 1950s Erikson (1963) discussed the idea of trust as one of a number of important developmental psychological stages in infancy and childhood. Erikson argued that resolving the crisis of developing basic trust in others takes place during infancy. The proposition was that the infant needed to establish faith in the environment and those who care for them and would show heightened vulnerability in infancy, potentially leading to mistrust if this developmental stage was unsuccessful. Erikson's approach became known as a lifespan developmental approach with trust as one of the basic stages of psychological development within childhood.

Erikson's work was influential and was broadly adopted and developed by others who used more sociological approaches, such as Giddens (1994), who argued that the child learns to trust itself, others and systems within early childhood. This developmental stage is viewed as important in developing resilience and the ability to adapt to change and threats which create insecurity. This early theorising can be viewed as representing a traditional and functionalist analysis of trust where the child passes through developmental stages successfully and learns to trust.

Goffman (1961) identified that trust is an unintended outcome of social interaction. In this perspective trust was regarded as an essential element in social interaction and created a sense of predictability and normality. While acknowledging that Goffman's work was important, I argue that it was most helpful in understanding how confidence is developed, which is slightly different than trust (more on this later).

I will use the approach developed by Warming (Chapter 1) who argues that these earlier theories of trust run counter to the theorising within the sociology of childhood. The emphasis in the literature within the sociology of childhood has been on the child as an active rather than passive recipient of relationships and trust is therefore viewed as relational.

For Misztal (2001), trust plays an important part in the socially learned and confirmed expectations individuals have of one another, as well as of the organisations and institutions in which they are involved. In this perspective, trust therefore becomes an essential part of citizen engagement and democratic participation. This is helpful in developing an analysis of trust at the societal level and one that includes participative democracy and social justice. Following Misztal, I argue that trust in the organisations and institutions of welfare forms an essential part of the public's relationship to welfare agencies and organisations.

Bauman argued that scepticism and fear developed towards the idea of experts in child welfare and protection (Bauman, 1990). For Bauman the 'big society' involved community networks based on trust, reciprocity and social capital which is rooted in informal social networks. We can see how the concept of trust has an important relationship within Bauman's theory of social capital. Putnam also argued that trust enables and promotes social capital and as such is empowering (see Warming, Introduction).

For Luhmann (1988) trust is regarded as part of the way we manage risk and uncertainty. It is a component part of making choices and taking action; if we take no actions then we run no risk. This changing pattern of risk and uncertainty is part of the wider context within which social work with children and families operates. Luhmann makes an important distinction between trust and confidence with trust emerging as a more essential concept for active citizenship. For Luhmann, confidence can enhance participation but trust becomes a way of managing uncertainty, complexity and lack of confidence within modern globalised societies. Beck (1992) argued more widely that a number of features were associated with increased uncertainty including the production of a 'risk society' and that attention would inevitably turn towards damage limitation and ways to make safe, regulate and identify 'dangerousness'.

Baraldi and Farini (Chapter 7) argue that confidence is a prerequisite for the reproduction of social systems in society, such as the economy, politics and education, whereas trust assures the reproduction of the specific social relationships included in these systems. In this chapter it is the field of communication processes and the relational dynamic between the social worker, for example, and child or young person that is the main focus. I therefore argue that the public may have confidence (or mistrust) in the institutions of welfare but the child needs to be able to develop trust with the social worker.

Earlier in this book, Warming (Chapter 1) helpfully suggested combining Bourdieu and Luhmann, to enable a critical analysis of trust dynamics that is attentive to power relations. In this chapter I also aim to capture the dynamics of power within relations of trust between welfare professionals and children.

Trust in welfare professionals

In this part of the chapter the focus is on the process of trust building with individual welfare professionals within social welfare settings. Development of trust between a child and a social worker, for example, involves time, continued and ongoing relationships and a commitment to listen to and take seriously the child's views and opinions. This sounds simple enough but further examination reveals that it can be problematic in relation to children who are Looked After in residential or foster care or deemed at risk of child abuse.

Participation and children's rights literature tell us that trust takes time to develop between a child and professional (Thomas & O'Kane, 1998). The importance of the development of trust is evident in all kinds of professional, family and other relationships but with children who are involved with welfare services it takes on an elevated level of significance. These children often have reasons to be particularly cautious about trusting adults because of their lived experiences of abuse and violations of trust. For children in public care building trust can be a long, time consuming and complex process, often involving counselling, therapeutic intervention and support. In this context where the child is likely to be fragile, feeling hurt, anger and pain the task for the social worker is a complex one demanding high levels of experience, creativity, skills and sensitivity. Child protection is complex territory for social work professionals who must attempt to build trust with both the parent(s) and child, while also being honest about their concerns. In this situation the child often has a different perspective on the problem and their situation and the social worker has to hear their views. Communication skills for professionals are of prime importance and require professional sensitivity when talking with children and young people, ascertaining their views, asking difficult questions and avoiding the child feeling pressurised. The Office of the Children's Commissioner report (Cossar et al., 2011) argues that continued professional development and training should focus on these important professional skills. 'You've got to trust [the social worker] and she's got to trust you. Otherwise there's no point' (Cossar et al., 2011).

The second aspect for the child in building trust with a social worker is the importance of continuity in the relationship. Children, like adults, do not wish to tell their story to several different professionals. Given the telling is likely to cause anxiety and distress, it is important that when they disclose, the experiences are heard and listened to, and that the adult or professional does not go away. The child may experience the latter as hurtful or rejecting and may feel unworthy if the social worker is not able to continue working with them. If this happens several times it is likely that the child may withdraw and decide not to tell again. In terms of therapeutic support for a child who has experienced abuse this disruption in professional relationships is at the least unhelpful and at worst potentially damaging to their future wellbeing. This fragmentation and lack of continuity in the relationship between a child and a professional is a source of distress for children and also a contributor to poor outcomes. *Care Matters* (Department of Children, Schools and Families, 2008) reports that children in care wish to choose who they relate to and be able to build trust with that professional and rely on them communicating on their behalf. Importantly they do not wish to have to build strong relationships with a range of professionals within their care network.

The Office of the Children's Commissioner (Cossar et al., 2011) reports in relation to child protection that if children trust a social worker they are more likely to tell when tensions are increasing in the family. The report also argued that professionals should consider who is a trusted adult for the child and include them in protecting the child. The importance of this relationship between the children and their social worker was emphasised and the children who had a trusting relationship felt they were part of making positive changes in their lives. The children interviewed as part of this research again confirmed their wish that their social worker should not change so often.

Therefore, one of the key tenets of child protection is that of listening to and communicating with children and young people. This is an important aspect of building trust between the child and professional social worker. The legislation, guidance and Inquiry reports have all emphasised the importance of listening to children. The Children Act 1989 (Department of Health, 1989), The Utting Report (Department of Health, 1991), Every Child Matters (HMSO, 2003) and Working Together (Department for Children, Schools and Families, 2010) all emphasise the importance of listening to and hearing what children say as well as that children may need time and more than one opportunity in order to develop sufficient trust to communicate any concerns they may have. In all these reports there was increasing recognition that principles, rules and guidance were not sufficient. Enhancing participation of children and young people in decision-making processes has been one of the key outcomes of pressure from children's rights organisations as well as professional support for social justice claims by children and young people.

Ascertaining the child's wishes and feelings through his or her participation within welfare decision-making processes was firmly embedded as a central part of any assessment of the child's welfare. Listening to children has been seen as a skill requiring sensitivity and skills. Alongside this was the need to balance the child's own expressions of distress or hurt with the perspectives of parents and other professionals. Schofield and Thoburn (1996) argued that a betrayal of trust within a family is likely to prejudice the children's capacity to make sense of their experiences. They were careful to point out that this is not an argument for not listening to children but more an argument for professionals developing skills and experience, as well as having the time, to listen and help children think through their situation. They argued about the importance of a relationship with a trusted adult in maximising children's participation.

The psychosocial lens helps us view the ways that individual professionals and the organisations of welfare sometimes avoid listening to and hearing children. This is part of a complex process of minimising the emotional impact of participation work with children. Not hearing can also mean being absolved of having to do anything to change the situation (Pinkney, 2011a). The relationship between the emotional dimensions of participation work and building trust with children is important to understand. If children feel they are not listened to and heard it will impact on their future participation. If they do not participate in decision-making the outcomes are likely to be less positive for them.

In my earlier research I argued that contested meanings do not seem to be adequately captured within the Guidance and Legislation where it is assumed that 'listening' to children is important but also that it is simple (Pinkney, 2005). In her study of Looked After children and their social workers, McLeod found that professionals and children have very different understandings of what is involved in listening. Interestingly the young people in her research had an active view of listening involving action, practical support and self-determination. The children felt strongly that their personal feelings should remain private. The social workers by contrast generally saw listening as a more receptive and passive activity involving having a respectful attitude, offering emotional support and encouraging self-expression. Her research revealed a situation where social workers felt that they were listening to young people while those same young people said they wanted to be heard but the social workers were not listening (McLeod, 2000).

For McLeod the paradox that seemed to be built into the relationship between a social worker and a young person could only be explained by concluding that they have different understandings of the meaning of 'listening'. McLeod's findings concur with a growing body of evidence that suggests that young people are not convinced that their social workers listen to their views (Sinclair, 1998; O'Quigley, 2000; Morris & Wheatley, 1994). Jones and Myers (1997) showed how listening to children in care is easier to say than it is to do.

In another study of children experiencing their parents' separation, Smart and Neale (2000) considered that children's views were increasingly listened to and sought, although they noted that there was some filtering of information. As a result they warned against professionals being deaf to what they might consider unpalatable views. They favoured a principle of asymmetrical reciprocity where children's views are respected but where adults take responsibility for difficult decisions. An important arena of debate is that around the extent to which we can expect children to be autonomous, responsible and independent when age and development often presuppose dependence, inequality, trust, care and intimacy.

In my research one Authority asked children in its care why they should be listened to. The following were the reasons the children gave:

- Because we're our own people and should have some privacy and make our own decisions
- Because without children Social Services would not exist
- Because what we say is important
- We think Social Services should listen to us because it's our lives and we know what we want
- By listening, Social Services will enable us to achieve what we want
- Because they have to listen!
- Because we know what we want and how we feel
- Because Social Services is here for young people not the other way round
- There is no reason why not
- Because I want you to

(Department F)

The children make a range of comments about the reasons they feel they should be listened to and similar comments were made across many different Authorities in various participation and consultation events. These comments range from assertive statements to more cautious ones about why their views and opinions should be valued. They are all clear that professionals should listen to children. This juxtaposition of the consistent messages from consultation events with children and the sense that welfare organisations are not always able or willing to listen to these comments creates a tension between the advocates of children's rights and the institutions of social welfare, which was evidenced throughout my research.

For this constituency of children trust is multidimensional, dynamic and complex. For children either in care or who have been abused, the idea of having trust in adults, being cared for and intimate with care-givers become potentially problematic. The underlying assumption is the presence of a benevolent adult who can be trusted and depended upon. It is worth considering here whether developing trust is always positive for a child. For some children who have experienced abuse, and particularly sexual abuse, part of the therapeutic process of work with the children may be to help them to reduce their level of disclosure about the abuse. Talking about abuse can cause problems for a child, in school for example or with their peers. An important element of the child protection and support work with the child may be to get him or her to be less trusting of adults or peers. It is salutary to reflect upon this less positive dimension within the relational dynamic of trust. If we reify trust we potentially overlook examples where it may have less positive and often unintended consequences and outcomes for children and young people. Including this more complex and sensitive aspect into any theorising, policy or practice on the dynamics of trust relationships between children and welfare professionals is essential.

Children of sufficient age and understanding often have a clear perception of what needs to be done to ensure their safety and wellbeing. Listening to children and hearing their messages requires willingness, training and special skills, including the ability to win their trust and promote a sense of safety. Most children feel loyalty towards those who care for them, and have difficulty saying anything against them.

The social worker, on the other hand, is also likely to feel emotional attachment to a child who has talked openly to them and disclosed experiences of abuse or neglect. The professional is likely to have a high investment in future protection and safeguarding of the child. Part of their job satisfaction involves the development of relationships of trust with children and their families. Feeling that they are able to offer good quality support for children is important to the social worker's professional identity and is often cited as one of the key motivations for entering the welfare profession.

One of the practical difficulties encountered by welfare professionals is that constraints on social work time and pressure of heavy caseloads often means the relationship with the child is fragmented or the time spent with the child is curtailed and squeezed with the demands of other competing priorities. The high numbers of children who do not have an allocated key-worker or social worker is testimony to this pressure on welfare services. The material conditions of labour where there are shortages of social workers, high reliance on agency and temporary contracted social work staff in field and residential care means that many distressed and hurt children will not have access to a professional who they can build a trusting relationship with.

By way of illustration, the following extract is taken from an interview with a Children's Rights Officer debating the difficulties around resourcing social welfare:

CRO: ... if your social workers are on their knees ... a lot of the areas of Local Authorities I work in are 50 per cent down in social workers in each team. That means each team is 50 per cent short.

SP: And are they using agency social workers to fill those gaps?

CRO: No they can't. They are just 50 per cent down and can't recruit.

SP: So in that environment 'good practice' even if it's in your head is not achievable?

CRO: It can't be, it absolutely can't be. So you commission a children's Rights Service and employ two part-time workers across a vast rural Authority.

(CRO 3, Department A8)

In the next extract another interviewee, who is employed as a Participation Officer, discusses similar problems:

PO: ... And there are ... sort of ... problems unique to Social Services, like the turnover of social workers, which is a big problem in London. So it takes a while for the young people to build up a relationship and then they keep changing, ... I don't think participation will deal with this but that is a key problem for young people because they lose out.

(PO, Department Y)

In this next extract from an interview in another Authority with a Child Care Consultant (CCC) the consequences of constant staffing crises are explored further:

CCC: ... So with a lot of young people who are Looked After the case isn't even allocated to a social worker. And that is a worry. Last year I think we had about 20 per cent of Looked After cases not allocated and the Social Services Inspectorate was threatening us with 'special measures' if we didn't do something about it. And we employed a whole lot of unqualified people just to allocate these kids to ... and then recently there's been a cash crisis, so we've had to make them all redundant, so we've got the kids unallocated again. It's just a disaster.

... We've also had a shortage of Team Managers in parts of the County ... so in (area) for example there's been nobody to supervise social workers if they've had the social workers. In (another area) there's been managers but no social workers. So it is really difficult. And it is quite difficult to carry on working and being positive in that environment.

(CCC, Department D)

The limits of participation within scarce resource context are explored within these interview texts although this was not a research topic I was intending to gather data on. During the interviews it became clear that the material conditions of staffing and resourcing social welfare was having a direct impact on the quality of participation and social work with children and young people. The sense of vulnerability and exposure for the young people in this situation as well as for the staff was an unexpected feature of these research interviews. The idea of 'special measures' relates to the climate of failure within social welfare within the UK. One interpretation is to view this as an illustration of how placing an authority in special measures can result in short-term solutions but not longer-term improvement in continuity of support for vulnerable children.

These research participants were all deeply committed to working with children in a positive and dynamic way. The weariness and strain of the experience of continuously trying to work in this environment became evident during the interviews. All welfare and children's rights professionals I interviewed located participation work with children in the wider contexts of resource shortfalls and low staff morale. The comments generally reflect the situation across most Local Authority Children's Services where 'good practice' is compromised by material shortfalls (Rapoport, 1960; Satyamurti, 1981; Pithouse, 1996). All the interviewees insisted that this resource and staffing crisis places incredible pressures on practitioners, professionals and Authorities. The comment was made that it is surprising that anything at all happens in this environment. Analysing these interview texts lead me to view participation as a socially constructed process accomplished by professionals and practitioners within the wider context and constraints of organisational and individual imperatives.

The evidence from my research interviews is that professionals feel they are too pressurised to be able to really involve, listen to and, importantly in this context, build trust with children. These interviews were conducted with staff with a vested interest in and high level of commitment to participation and children's rights. The interview texts illustrate an alternative view of a particular sort of 'reality', which is, what happens in practice and what happens to social work and children's rights and professionalism within the conditions of managerialism. Part of these narratives can therefore be viewed as the stories the profession tells itself about how difficult it is to deliver services in this environment and under these conditions. We can see here that the professional social workers sometimes lose confidence in their own organisations of welfare.

Another interpretation of these interview texts is to view this as the discourse of liberal professionalism under pressure. Professional discourse may be displaced, subordinated and appropriated but material, ethical and emotional strain or discomforts are still voiced. The interviewees are talking about the emotional 'strains' of being professionals in public welfare services. Children's Rights Officers and similarly positioned staff are possibly uniquely situated as both radicalised and uncomfortably marginalised professionals within social and welfare work with children in the UK. The interview texts in my research demonstrate the tension between professionalism and managerialism within child welfare services.

Managerialism legitimises and extends the right to manage and involves competing discourses of how to manage (Clarke & Newman, 1997; Clarke et al., 2000). The rise of new public management within public sector and welfare organisations since the late 1980s has been well documented (Clarke et al., 2007; Newman, 1998; Pinkney, 1998; Froggett, 2002). Managerialism was developed under Conservative regimes during the 1980s and continued to develop with New Labour administrations since 1997 as well as within the current UK coalition government since 2010. It seems almost certain that there will be further continuity of the managerialist agenda because it is firmly embedded in Labour, Conservative and Liberal Democrat policies. In my research I was interested in the extent to which the discourse of managerialism had permeated social care contexts.

The reason this is relevant here is that the conditions of increased managerialism and administration in social welfare mean that time is a scarce commodity for welfare professionals charged with advocating, representing and assessing 'the best interests' of children and young people. Within my research, participation is being viewed as a socially constructed and performative process accomplished by professionals and practitioners within the wider context and constraints within their organisations. As I argued earlier, professionals often feel they are too pressurised to be able to really involve, listen to, take seriously and importantly in this context, build trust with children. The process of participation and building trust takes time, which as we have seen is an increasingly scarce commodity in social welfare settings. The interviews illustrate what happens to children's participation and trust within the conditions of managerialism. As I argued earlier, these narratives can be viewed as the stories the profession tells about the difficulty of delivering services in this pressurised environment:

> Overall morale is very low, staffing is very short, everybody is under terrible pressure, workload is excessive and inevitably standards of practice drop because people just do the absolute minimum. And the important bits which are about the direct one to one relationship with the individual child are the bits that get lost when you've got too many cases.
>
> (Interview with a Consultation Policy Officer, Children's Services, Department D)

Managerialism carries within it the promise that better management will improve services. This magic of management can be viewed in part as a response to the discourse of failure that developed after three decades of inquiries into child abuse where welfare services and professionals were viewed as failing to protect children. In the research interviews there was evidence of the discourses of displaced, subordinated and appropriated professionalism. Professionals are able to sometimes resist subject positions created by powerful discourses, such as managerialism. This resistance usefully highlights attempts to disrupt power relations and the undermining of colonising discourses (Marston, 2004). I argued elsewhere that the formal social policy texts in my research show an increased focus on management, efficiency, customers, best value, accountability and performance and how managerialism forces the procedural and customer version of rights. The question remains whether this particular version of rights within the customer discourse enhances children's rights and participation (Pinkney, 2011b).

Social workers often talk about the increased burden of administration and complex recording systems that prevent them from spending time with children. As I argue above, time is an essential component in the trust building process between child and welfare professional. While it is clear that good administration and recording is an essential element of child protection, spending time with a child has to be the most important aspect of the social worker's task. Freeing social worker time to develop continuity and relationships of trust with children must be given higher priority if these children are to be protected in future.

Up to now the focus of this chapter has been on the importance of relationships of trust between children, young people and individual welfare professionals. Within the next section the focus is shifted to trust in the institutions and organisations of child welfare.

Trust in the institutions of welfare

Beck (1992) argues that the plausibility of experts was only superficially undermined by child deaths and 'accidents' between 1914–70 but that this period was characterised by institutional repression of 'troublesome information' which served to bolster public confidence and trust in child welfare services. After the 1970s the effect of inquiry reports into child deaths led to ambivalence about child welfare services (Pinkney, 1998). The problem of identifying and managing 'risk' led to the proliferation of risk assessment and risk management within social welfare contexts. The role of professionals within welfare organisations therefore became to identify and manage risk and dangerousness. Part of the difficulty with this is that welfare agencies and professionals are supposed to manage risk and dangerousness within an environment where hardly anyone has faith or trust in them being able to do this.

Howe (1992) argued that as audit and inspection became a routine feature of welfare organisations and new systems of regulation were continuously introduced and implemented, the focus became that of making 'defensible decisions' rather than the 'right decisions'. Douglas (1992) argued that refined blaming systems were part of the 'risk society' where nothing goes wrong without it being attributed to someone and him or her being held to account. The Inquiry Reports into child abuse during the 1970s and 1980s are testimony to the need to apportion blame to an individual, institution or organisation. Tunstill argued that consequently the discourse of risk dominated the development of childcare policies during the 1980s and 1990s (Tunstill, 1999). From the 1990s UK welfare organisations saw a flourishing of complaints procedures, disciplinary mechanisms and litigation, which were all consequences of the attempt to minimise risk.

The Cleveland child sexual abuse crisis in the UK in 1987 is an example where there was a breach of trust in the institutions of welfare in relation to child sexual abuse (HMSO, 1988). Parents voiced fears at bringing their children to hospital or doctors for routine medical checks. Ferguson (2004) argues that this illustrates well how trust, or lack of it, in child welfare systems can be influenced and shaped by experiences at the access points to welfare services. For Ferguson one of the outcomes from Cleveland was a structural transformation in trust relations which overturned earlier accommodation and suppression of child sexual abuse to a situation where child sexual abuse could be acknowledged.

Giddens (1994) argued that the development of active trust in child welfare services is one of the biggest challenges for the institutions of welfare. He went on to argue that this building of active trust is essential if the public, neighbours and families are to disclose concerns about abused children.

We can therefore see that there is an essential problem of lack of confidence between children, families and the public with child welfare institutions. Child protection relies on public and community confidence in reporting cases of suspected child abuse or neglect. Negative imagery of the institutions of welfare and of the legal system, for example, can mitigate against the development of confidence. On the other hand, stories of victims finding support and acknowledgement of abuse can positively influence others to disclose and enhance confidence.

Social recognition and identity is closely related to the process of building trust. Not being regarded as trustworthy can generate insecurity in an individual's social relationships but also in relationships with organisations and in this context with welfare professionals and the institutions of welfare. Being viewed with mistrust is a common complaint of young people in the UK when the media has often been accused of having an unbalanced focus on negative aspects of youth culture. Looked After young people in residential or foster care have experienced particular problems with being trusted:

> Some people go to foster care and they get bullied – like for having hearing aids. The thing I don't get is the independence – I asked my

foster carer once if I could go for a walk but she shouted at me and was really nasty 'No you can stay here where I can see you'.

(Foster child, Department A8)

I don't like to be classed as a special person. I want to go to 'normal' playscheme activity.

(Foster child, Department G)

These comments were made during consultation events with children who position themselves as 'disabled'. They relate to general concerns about bullying but add another specific dimension in relation to the specific vulnerability and difficulties with trust for children with disabilities. The second comment relates both to the difficulty of constructing normalised narratives of self as well as to the dilemma about the difficulty in referring to children with specific needs whilst avoiding pathologising those children. Both extracts involve children's perceptions that they are not trusted. The examples provide illustrations of the ways that Looked After children have difficulty maintaining a normalised narrative of self as they are constantly reminded of their subject position and identity as Looked After children.

CRO: Yes I mean that came across from the young people I interviewed. One of them said something like ... she was in a children's home in a rather posh residential area ... and there was a lot of hostility to it ... and she said 'people round here look at us as if we've got televisions on our heads or something, what do they think we are, we're just a bunch of kids who haven't got anywhere else to live? And they think you must be a murderer or a rapist or something if you're in care. When you say you're in care people say "well what did you get done for?"'

(Children's Rights Officer 1, Department D)

In this extract the Children's Rights Officer is talking about young people challenging the dominant representations of Looked After children. The underlying assumption is that being in care means wrongdoing on the part of the child rather than that they are more likely to be in care as a result of having wrong done to them or through family breakdown. The strong sense of not being trusted in the neighbourhood where they reside comes through.

The following extract is about problems of trust in the process of participation and institutions of child welfare and protection. The CRO is talking about comments from children and young people about their formal and informal participation in decision-making processes:

> SP: ... so where do those informal comments to you go?
>
> CRO: well at the moment it goes from us to our management but it doesn't go into a strategic plan. There is no system in place that feeds those day-to-day comments into a strategic plan.
>
> SP: that's really interesting in relation to the process of policy making and how the informal processes feed into the formal policy documents and plans. Do the comments you receive from young people feed into any formal processes and policy?
>
> CRO: Not really no. My experience ... I'm not trying to be really negative here ... but my experience is that young people can be helped on an individual basis sometimes depending on the issues they raise. But there is nowhere that is gathering this information and correlating it and asking has this arisen before? Is it something we can integrate into our policy and practice? And that is not just comments to me. I'm also thinking of the complaints procedure and reviews. Where does information from reviews go? It goes in a box and doesn't get looked at and evaluated. It's the same with complaints and recommendations, transitions reviews for disabled children ... where do they go to?
>
> SP: ... so nobody is taking the strategic overview and evaluating the information which is there? It isn't making a difference to what happens?
>
> CRO: No it's not. The only time it makes a difference is if there's an inspection where they pick up things and ask organizations like ourselves or ask young people directly.
>
> (Children's Rights Officer 3, Department A8)

This extract illustrates some of the difficulties and tensions about trust within the processes of participation and consultation from the perspective of children's rights professionals. We feel the Children's Rights Officer's sense of dismay and frustration of not being able to make any difference after hearing what young people say at participation and consultations events. This provides a comment about children's rights work being a difficult arena to work in because of the slow pace of change and limited evidence of the impact and outcomes of children's participation beyond individual children who may benefit from their participation. It has been argued that this may be a common experience of consultation and service user participation in different policy and service delivery contexts (Danso et al., 2003; Carr, 2004).

Societal mistrust of children

Kelly (2005) argues that institutional mistrust of youth is a common feature of developed societies. He cites the example of CCTV cameras being installed in school toilets to deal with problems of drug abuse and bullying in Australian schools. Following the work of Foucault (1977, 1983) and in particular his work on surveillance, disciplinary power and governmentality, Kelly explores issues of institutionalised mistrust, surveillance and regulation of contemporary populations of young people. Adult and professional anxieties about young people and risk are not new but they have translated into policies and practices relating to young people. Youth has historically occupied the 'wild zones' and been viewed as 'ungovernable', 'dangerous' and lacking in self-regulation. These views of youth have fundamentally been shaped by race, class and gender and situated in relation to normative ideas about youth (Bessant & Watts, 1998). This means the consequences of this mistrust of youth is experienced differentially by different groups of young people. We can argue therefore that this more generalised sense of mistrust in young people is evident in a range of adult and professional interventions in their lives on the basis of professional and expert concerns about their welfare. Constructing young people as (un)governable subjects, Rose (1999) illustrates the tendency towards illiberal and authoritarian governmentalities that continue to dominate discourses of youth in Western societies.

Trust then informs many of the discourses associated with children and young people generally but in particular in the context here of those who live away from home with foster carers or in residential care. Being 'in care' brings with it certain expectations of being supported, cared for, nurtured and having positive relationships with those who do the caring. Sometimes this relationship is formalised within a contract or agreement between parents, children and young people and relevant professionals. The institutions of welfare take seriously this aspect of trust between families, children, professionals and their organisations. The trust that is placed within welfare professionals and institutions is subjected to great scrutiny and when things go wrong it results in critical inquiry reports and negative media attention being directed at the services and professionals that care for children and young people. Examining the rationales and normative justifications carried within institutional policies and practices is an important part of critical social policy projects.

Bessant et al. (2005) argue that the cultural, historical and socio-economic conditions that shape the day-to-day work with children needs to be understood and that it is at the point of routine institutional governance that the grim realities of the policies and practices of trust and mistrust are played out. For Bessant et al., too much focus has been directed at the individuals and institutions themselves and not enough at the prevailing attitudes, discursive practices, modalities of power and government that underpin these institutions. This is a powerful argument about the way institutional harm and abuse of trust has to be understood within the wider context of societal attitudes towards children and young people.

Conclusion

This chapter has considered the relations of trust between children and young people, welfare professionals and the institutions of welfare. In doing this it has considered the individual relationships as well as the resource context they operate within the UK. The organisations and institutions of welfare were examined in relation to structural aspects of the possibilities for trusting relations between children and welfare professionals. Lastly, consideration was given to wider societal attitudes towards children and youth and the way this frames and shapes these relations of trust. I introduced extracts from my earlier research as well as other research findings to illustrate the narrative of trust within welfare organisations and professionals. The example of listening to children seems a basic presumption of building trusting relations but was shown to be fraught with difficulties and complexity within both a practice and policy environment.

I argue that the dynamic interaction between the process of participation of individual children and young people in everyday governance as well as within institutions of welfare and broader societal attitudes to children is critical. The focus on active 'voice' for children and young people and processes of participation and consultation within social welfare is welcome. Violations of trust when they occur often go beyond the failure of individual professionals to follow policy and practice guidance to the wider social, cultural and economic status of child and youth. The challenge is for individual professionals as well as the institutions of child welfare to recognise the significance of the process and relations of trust within this often fraught and contested arena of social welfare work with children. The wider implications of societal attitudes towards children and youth bring us into the broader arena of human rights and social justice.

Note

1   Within the UK the term Looked After has been used to describe children and young people who are living either in foster or residential care.

Bibliography

Bauman, Z. (1990) *Modernity and Ambivalence*, Cambridge: Polity Press.
Beck, U. (1992) *Risk Society: Towards a New Modernity*, London: Sage.
Bessant, J. & R. Watts (1998) 'History, myth making and young people in a time of change', *Family Matters*, 49: 5–10.
Bessant, J., R. Hil & R. Watts (eds) (2005) *Violations of Trust: How Social and Welfare Institutions Fail Children and Young People*, Aldershot, UK: Ashgate.
Carr, S. (2004) *Has Service User Participation Made a Difference to Social Care Services?*, London: Social Care Institute for Excellence.
Clarke, J., S. Gewirtz & E. McLaughlin (2000) 'Reinventing the welfare state' in J. Clarke, S. Gewirtz & E. McLaughlin (eds) *New Managerialism New Welfare?*, London: Sage, pp. 1–26.
Clarke, J. & J. Newman (1997) *The Managerial State: Power, Politics and Ideology in the Remaking of Social Welfare*, London: Sage.
Clarke, J., J. Newman, N. Smith, E. Vidler & L. Westmarland (2007) *Creating Citizen-Consumers: Changing Publics and changing Public-Services*, London: Sage; New Delhi: Thousand Oaks.
Cossar, J., M. Brandon & P. Jordan (2011) *'Don't Make Assumptions': Children and Young People's Views of the Child Protection System and Messages for Change*. Office of the Children's Commissioner, University of East Anglia, Norwich, UK.
Danso, C., H. Greaves, S. Howell, M. Ryan, R. Sinclair & J. Tunnard (2003) *The Involvement of Children and Young People in Promoting Change and Enhancing the Quality of Services*, London: Social Care Institute for Excellence.
Department of Children, Schools and Families (2008) *Care Matters; Time to Deliver for Children in Care: An Implementation Plan*. Nottingham: DCSF Publications.
Department for Children, Schools and Families (2010) *Working Together to Safeguard Children: A Guide to Inter-agency Working to Safeguard and Promote the Welfare of Children*, Nottingham: DCSF Publications.
Department of Health (1989) *An Introduction to The Children Act 1989*, London: HMSO.
Department of Health (1991) *Children in the Public Care: A Review of Residential Care Carried Out by Sir William Utting*, London: HMSO.
Douglas, M. (1992) *Risk and Blame: Essays in Cultural Theory*, London: Routledge.
Erikson, E. H. (1963) *Childhood and Society*, second edition, New York: Norton.
Ferguson, H. (2004) *Protecting Children in Time: Child Abuse, Child Protection and the Consequences of Modernity*, Basingstoke, United Kingdom: Palgrave Macmillan.
Froggett, L. (2002) *Love, Hate and Welfare: Psychosocial Approaches to Policy and Practice*, Bristol: Policy Press.
Foucault, M. (1977) *Discipline and Punish*, London: Penguin Press.

Foucault, M. (1983) 'The subject and power' in H. L. Dreyfus & P. Rabinow (eds) *Michel Foucault: Beyond Structuralism and Hermeneutics*, Chicago: University of Chicago Press, pp. 208–26.

Giddens, A. (1994) 'Living in a post traditional society' in U. Beck, A. Giddens & S. Lash (eds) *Reflexive Modernization*, Cambridge: Polity.

Goffman, E. (1961) *Asylums: Essays on the Social Situation of Mental Patients and Other Inmates*, Harmondsworth: Penguin.

HMSO (1988) *Report of the Inquiry into Child Abuse in Cleveland 1987: Presented to the Secretary of State for Social Services by the Right Honourable Lord Justice Butler-Sloss*, London: DBE.

HMSO (2003) *The Green Paper: Every Child Matters*, Norwich: The Stationary Office.

Howe, D. (1992) 'Child abuse and the bureaucratisation of social work', *Sociological Review*, 40(3): 491–508.

Jones, J. & J. Myers (1997) 'The future detection and prevention of institutional abuse: Giving children a chance to participate in research', *Early Childhood Development and Care*, 113: 85–92.

Kelly, P. (2005) 'Dangerousness, surveillance and the institutionalised mistrust of youth' in J. Bessant, R. Hil & R. Watts (eds) *Violations of Trust: How Social and Welfare Institutions Fail Children and Young People*, Aldershot, UK: Ashgate.

Luhmann, N. (1988) 'Familiarity, confidence, trust: Problems and alternatives' in D. Gambetta (ed.) *Trust: Making and Breaking Cooperative Relations*, Oxford: Department of Sociology, University of Oxford, pp. 94–107.

Marston, G. (2004) *Social Policy and Discourse Analysis: Policy Change in Public Housing*, Aldershot, Hampshire: Ashgate.

McLeod, A. J. (2000) *Listening But Not Hearing: Barriers to Effective Communication Between Young People in Public Care and Their Social Workers*, PhD thesis, Lancaster: University of Lancaster.

Misztal, B. A. (2001) 'Normality and trust in Goffman's theory of interaction order', *Sociological Theory*, 19(3): 312–24.

Morris, S. & H. Wheatley (1994) *Time to Listen: The Experiences of Young People in Foster and Residential Care*, London: ChildLine.

Newman, J. (1998) 'Managerialism and social welfare' in G. Hughes & G. Lewis (eds) *Unsettling Welfare: The Reconstruction of Social Policy*, London and New York: Routledge.

O'Quigley, A. (2000) *Listening to Children's Views: The Findings and Recommendations of Recent Research*, York: Joseph Rowntree Foundation.

Pinkney, S. (1998) 'The reshaping of social work and social care' in G. Hughes & G. Lewis (eds) *Unsettling Welfare: The Reconstruction of Social Policy*, London and New York: Routledge.

Pinkney, S. (2005) *Competing Constructions of Children's Participation in Social Care: Analysing Text and Talk*, unpublished PhD thesis, Milton Keynes: Open University.

Pinkney, S. (2011a) 'Participation and emotions: Troubling encounters between children and social welfare professionals', *Children & Society*, 25(1): 37–46.

Pinkney, S. (2011b) 'Discourses of children's participation: Professionals, policies and practices', *Social Policy and Society*, 10(3): 271–83.

Pithouse, A. (1996) 'Managing emotion: Dilemmas in the social work relationship' in K. Carter & S. Delamont (eds) *Qualitative Research: The Emotional Dimension*, Aldershot, Brookfield USA: Avebury, pp. 87–104.

Rapoport, L. (1960) 'In defence of social work: An examination of stress in the profession', *Social Science Review*, 34(1): 62–74.

Rose, N. (1999) *Powers of Freedom: Reframing Political Thought*, Cambridge: Cambridge University Press.

Satyamurti, C. (1981) *Occupational Survival: The Case of the Local Authority Social Worker*, Oxford: Blackwell.

Schofield, G. & J. Thoburn (1996) *Child Protection: The Voice of the Child in Decision Making*, London: Institute for Public Policy Research.

Sinclair, R. (1998) 'Involving children in planning their care', *Child and Family Social Work*, 3(2): 137–42.

Smart, C. & B. Neale (2000) '"It's my life too" – Children's perspectives on post-divorce parenting', *Family Law*, 30: 163–9.

Thomas, N. & C. O'Kane (1998) 'The ethics of participatory research with children', *Children and Society*, 12(5): 336–48.

Tunstill, J. (1999) 'Social services provision for children and young people: Answer or problem?' in J. Tunstill (ed.) *Children and the State: Whose Problem?*, London and New York: Cassell, pp. 118–39.

6

Trust, Social Work and Care Ethics An Exploration of the Luhmannian Concept of Trust and Social Work with Children at Risk: Relating Luhmann's Concept of Trust to the Ethics of Care

Michael Christensen

This chapter proposes that the Luhmannian concept of trust can serve as a powerful way to understand the situated positions in which social workers carry out their work with children in positions at risk. It also addresses the social worker both as a representative of the social system and a person 'in between' the social system and the specific child. Luhmann's concept of trust is explored in the light of the growing recognition of children as valid actors with meaningful opinions and an increased focus on children's inclusion and involvement in decisions about their personal cases. Thus, the chapter explores the Luhmannian concept of trust, how it enables an analytical framework that allows for a focus on the social worker's position within a specific system logic, but at the same time allows for a focus on the relation between social worker and the specific child. Luhmann's concepts of trust, distrust and confidence are related here to considerations about the ethics of care/ethics of rights, thereby introducing a distinction between concrete situations and abstract, generalised practices and between relationships/morality contra universal rights and rules. The chapter seeks to nuance the immense volume of research that addresses the relationship between social workers and children at risk and suggests that we understand this relationship in terms of trust.

The following four quotations come from fieldwork carried out as part of the research project 'Trust in social work with children in positions at risk. How does the institutional set-up hinder or facilitate trustful relations between social worker and child?'.[1] The quotations raise important issues relating to the ethics of care/ethics of rights and the role that trust can play in social work with children and young people and they provide the foundation for the main ideas put forward in the chapter. The quotations will be analysed with a view that demonstrates the strengths of the Luhmannian concept of trust.

> Those who have something to do with foster children should be better at listening to the children, because they often have experiences from life that enable them to take a great deal of responsibility for their own lives.
>
> (Adda, 19 years old) Quotation 1

> Well, [the work is organized] in a strange way [...] but we have this municipality that looks at figures and times for the case process, and then there's us [the social workers]. We look at what is going on in real life. Every time I do something related to a case I have to write it in my journal, then I have to fill in a form to document how far I am with the case – so that someone higher up in the system can check up on me. And then I have to write it up in my own calendar, which can also be checked. But I do love my job, even though I'm constantly being checked up on, I still love it – I think I can make a difference.
>
> (Social worker in a Danish municipality X) Quotation 2

> If new social worker students knew how much time we spend on citizens [face-to-face relations] and documentation, writing, meetings etc. they would run away screaming – I know I would.
>
> (Social worker in a Danish municipality X) Quotation 3

> [Social Worker in a Danish municipality Y]: Now, tell me again, why did you want a meeting with me?
>
> [Dana, 14 years]: I called you because I don't know what's going on. Everybody tells me different stuff, so I don't know what to do and I want you to tell me.
>
> [Social Worker]: Let me make one thing clear: If anyone thinks they can decide for you, they're wrong. You make the decisions and if you're not sure what to do, you come to me. If others have a problem with that then they answer to me, not to you. I'm glad you called me so we can sort this misunderstanding out. (Quotation 4)

The new childhood paradigm has produced an increasing focus on children's rights and involvement in their own cases, especially children at risk. However, recent work suggests that efforts to ensure inclusion, listening to and recognition of children at risk are struggling to survive under institutional conditions which do not facilitate such approaches (Smith, 2001) and that children at risk experience a lack of inclusion which leads to unsatisfactory case histories (Smith, 2001; Knudsen, 2001; Dalrymple, 2003; Grover, 2004; Warming, 2005; Leeson, 2007; Gaskell, 2010). Parton (1998) argues that the 'new' focus on social work strategies in children's involvement in social work has emerged in tandem with various discourses focusing on 'objective' factors that constitute risk (those which can be measured and controlled) rather than on face-to-face relationships. Likewise, Meagher and Parton (2004) and Ruch (2005) point out that social work is increasingly subject to various control mechanisms, such as audits and documentation, which measure 'performance'. Because of this 'performance turn', social work, understood as an intersubjective meeting between people who are dependent on one another, is disregarded or at best overlooked. Along similar lines, Cockburn (among others) stresses the importance of not regarding children solely as *recipients* of care (Cockburn, 2005). According to Smith (1997), the relationship between social worker and child cannot be reduced to a normative fulfilment of children's objective rights. Rather, social work (with children) is also about assessment, judgement and dialogue (Smith, 1997). Thus, Smith sees trust as *the* fundamental characteristic for enabling 'social work to work' (Smith, 2001: 298). Smith's objection to today's brand of social work is that it is characterised by issues of confidence rather than of trust, since the social worker's role is, in many instances, reduced to that of a technical operator or 'manager' focusing on output according to various predefined indicators designed to ensure compliance with the specified 'package of care' (Smith, 2001: 289). While recognising national and theoretical differences regarding what constitutes a social worker, in this chapter the term is used to refer to a person employed within the official Danish municipality-based social system to carry out social work with children at risk – a so-called 'case manager'.

I further recognise that there in terms of 'childhood matters' (Qvortrup et al., 1994) is a stronger theoretical focus on children at risk in respect of their rights than of the involvement in their own cases (Satka & Eydal, 2004; James et al., 1998) and that there is increasing emphasis on cost effective measures, performance, documentation of practice in social work and so on (Mik-Meyer, 2001; Smith, 2001; Sehested, 2002). Against that background, it becomes pertinent to investigate the situated position from which social workers carry out social work, how they navigate between the different system demands, and based on that to understand the relationship between social workers and children, which requires that we invoke the concepts of trust/distrust and confidence. This allows us to shed light on the important role that trust plays in the enabling of children's participation and citizenship when dealing with children's encounters with social workers in municipality-based social work. The Luhmannian concept of trust can help to conceptualise the social worker not solely as a representative of the social system (authoritative trust) or as a co-player with the child (personal trust). Instead, we can begin to see the social worker as a reflexive hybrid situated and navigating in between these two positions.

Before unfolding Niklas Luhmann's concept of trust, the chapter briefly presents considerations about the ethics of rights and the ethics of care in order to set the scene for how the Luhmannian concepts of trust, distrust and confidence can offer a powerful perspective on the social worker's role within a specific social system.

The ethics of care and the ethics of rights

Besides providing insight into the individual social workers' understanding of their professional habitus, the quotations above suggest that involving children is difficult within institutional conditions that are not conducive to an inclusive participatory environment. This is because systemic demands impose a different way of understanding social work than that expressed in quotations 1–3. However, as the social worker in quotation 4 points out, child-initiated involvement, equivalent to the eighth rung in Hart's *Eight Rung Ladder of Participation* (Hart, 1992), *is* possible and can be implemented in practice in social work. As readers will recall, the eighth rung on Hart's Ladder is characterised by: 'Youth initiated shared decisions with adults' (Hart, 1992: 8). The obvious question which this raises is: Why are the quotations from social workers in municipality X and Y so different? The answer to this question, while at first glance seemingly straightforward, is actually extremely complex. We can shed some light on the issue by looking at it through the lens of Luhmann's concepts of trust, distrust and confidence, as well as from perspectives from the ethics of care and the ethics of rights.

Most of the abovementioned perspectives on social work are, in various ways, reflected in debates about the ethics of rights and care respectively (Lee, 1999; Carey, 2003; Dickens, 2006). Although Orme (2002) has demonstrated a logical connection between the ethics of rights and the ethics of care, the quotations in the opening lines suggest that there are debates in social work today about whether the focus should primarily be on rights or care. Feminist critiques have highlighted the problems of focusing exclusively on the ethics of rights in social work. These critiques are based on a carefully thought out perspective on social work that focuses on relationships instead of rights and rules, and on concrete, bounded situations rather than informal, abstract ones (Cockburn, 2005). Along similar lines, Meagher and Parton consider the ethics of care as a means to reflect upon the character of social work (political as well as institutional) with a view to conceptualising new relationship-based practices in the social sphere. This, in turn, makes it possible to discuss social work practice as a principle-based activity where institutional (or legal) practices are given primary status and where it is the competence of the individual social worker that constitutes the quality of the social work (Meagher & Parton, 2004). Despite substantial (and justified) critiques by ethics of rights advocates warning against solely focusing on feminist aspects of care, the feminist ethics of care nonetheless seems to offer powerful tools to rethink the relationship between social workers and users (the specific children at risk) and to understand institutional demands both from a theoretical and a practical perspective. While the critiques that solely focus on rights or on care illustrate the complexity of the social work, the two approaches are not theoretically equipped to adequately explain the individual social worker's situated perspective – especially not in terms of trust. Therefore, it is relevant to relate Luhmann's concepts of trust, distrust and confidence to the dynamics that play out between the social worker and the child at risk and thereby situating trust in the context of the ethics of care and ethics of rights discussion.

The Luhmannian concepts of trust, distrust and confidence

Although trust is far from a new concept, few sociologists have worked extensively with the concept (Lewis & Weigert, 1985; Luhmann, 1988; Misztal, 1996; Misztal, 2001). As Luhmann points out, trust relations must be empirically investigated and documented instead of remaining as theoretical abstractions (Luhmann, 2005). Related to this, one of the main challenges in conceptualising trust is how to differentiate it from confidence. Luhmann himself first fully conceptualised the difference in *Familiarity, Confidence, Trust: Problems and Alternatives* (1988); his earlier work from 1968 (2005) does not distinguish clearly between trust and confidence. The key differences of the two will be elaborated later in the chapter, but for now it will be sufficient to mention the differences in risk assessment, expectations towards other people and complexity as constitutive differences between trust and confidence.

Like Luhmann, Misztal (1996) finds that the key difference between trust and confidence should be understood in terms of expectations of another person's actions and, by extension, how complex the inter-personal relationship is considered to be by the person who is in a position to choose to trust or distrust. Where confidence relates to rela-tively certain expectations about another person's actions (for instance confidence that a plumber will repair your blocked drain), trust involves personal risk and is thereby a more '[...] difficult task of assessment of other people's capacities for the action' (Misztal, 1996: 16). This implies that trust enters into the equation when the other is unknowable; '[...] when behaviour cannot be imputed or predicted, because either a) there is no system within which sanctions can be imposed or b) there is no underlying sense of or terms of familiarity or sameness that would allow such prediction' (Seligman, 1998: 393). Without neglecting the social and systemic implications of trust, Seligman's notion b) has impor-tant implications for the social worker/child at risk relationship. These have to do with the child's initial contact with the social system, the nature of his or her involvement with the system and the way in which prior trust and distrustful relations shape the possibilities for future trustful relations with the system. In order to understand trust/distrust relations in social work with children at risk, and in seeking a concept-ualisation of trust that is sensitive to context and situation and thereby also attentive to the empirical matter under investigation, I take my point of departure in Luhmann's notion of trust as a means to reduce complexity:

> Trust, in the broadest sense of confidence in one's expectations, is a basic fact of social life. In many situations, of course, man can choose in certain respects whether or not to bestow trust. But a complete absence of trust would prevent him from getting up in the morning. He would be prey to a vague sense of dread, to paralysing fears. He would not even be capable of formulating definite distrust and making that a basis for precautionary measures, since this would presuppose trust in other directions. Anything and everything would be possible. Such abrupt confrontation with the complexity of the world at its most extreme is beyond human endurance.[2]
>
> (Luhmann, 1979: 4)

These are the opening lines of Luhmann's book on trust (2005). It is quite a strong statement that without trust you are not able to get out of bed in the morning – and in more general terms, to claim that human action is not possible without this existential 'leap' of trust.

First of all, Luhmann's point of departure is systems theory, inspired by Parsons, in which trust is viewed in terms of its function. This starting point is the reason why Luhmann can theorise about trust/distrust in a normatively neutral way.[3] Luhmann is not interested in whether trust is better than distrust. For Luhmann, trust and distrust are functionally equivalent tools in the struggle to reduce complexity, however, trust is more desirable than distrust in psychological terms as trust reduces complexity more cost efficiently than distrust (Luhmann, 2005).

Time and risk and how they relate to trust

For Luhmann, trust comprises both structure and process and he develops the concept against a systems theory background that focuses on system environment differentiation. This perspective forces one to look closer at two different ways of defining time. Time can be seen either as incident or as preservation. At first glance, this distinction may appear irrelevant to this article, but in fact it is crucial in understanding how people assess risk and hence how they decide whether to trust or distrust. The following discussion of the concept of time will be followed by a closer consideration of its implications for social work.

Luhmann argues that things can be understood either as incidents or preservations. An incident is fixed at a certain point in time and is independent of the way in which it is understood at that time. Incidents are conceptualised as things that slither forward on the timescale, continually turning particular points in the present time into the past. Incidents are therefore independent of whether one recognises them as past, present or future. However, these notions of time are needed in order to understand the nature of the specific incident and to make it 'real' in the present. Preservation, for its part, concerns something that lasts regardless of the passage of time, but which can only be grasped in the present (Luhmann, 2005). Neither conceptualisation is adequate in itself – they complement each other. This rather abstract definition of time is relevant to trust, as trust is closely connected to uncertainty about the future and is thereby connected to potential risk. The problem of trust is that the future holds a lot more potential than can be realised in the present. Not all potential futures can become present and, because of this complex uncertainty about the future, it is necessary to reduce complexity in order to be able to take action. This is not an easy task, since the spectrum of future possibilities surpasses the individual's capability of calculating 'everything'. Put another way: the present future is open, complex and intangible. You can imagine a range of possible futures, but you can never be sure what the outcome of the future will be. As the present moves forward into the future, it produces new presents through various selections, but at the same time it produces new possibilities for the future (Luhmann, 2005). Seen from this perspective, the notion of trust as a contingency guarantee is very appealing. It strengthens preservation at the expense of incidents and thereby increases the threshold for ambiguity. However, this does not tell us much about the nature of trust, its complexity or how it relates to risk assessment. In the following, I therefore also address the difference between confidence and trust, as expounded by Luhmann.

Trust – confidence and agency

First and foremost, Luhmann differentiates between personal trust and system trust. This chapter focuses primarily on a hybrid of the two – trust in representatives of a system and personal trust. This hybrid form may be found in intersubjective encounters that require face-to-face interaction in the sense that one subject is compelled to recognise another subject and thereby relate to a possibly different interpretation of a given situation. This approach does not favour the psychological dimension of trust over the social and systemic dimensions of trust. Rather, the three aspects are given equal importance. Confidentiality is the basis for trust and distrust in that it facilitates relatively certain expectations and thus to some extent absorbs potential risk, hence it offers a certain amount of order.[4] As Luhmann puts it, 'Confidence is the structure of existence, not the structure of action' (Luhmann, 2005: 53). Whereas confidence is related to the past – and to a certain degree to the present – trust is oriented towards the future. But trust is also related to confidence because one cannot exhibit trust without some sort of pre-experience of similar incidents (Jalava, 2003). The past consists of an already reduced complexity given that there is no longer an alternative. Hindsight is confidential; it does not change and is thereby 'over'. This is not to say that a certain incident is fixed in time and has one universal interpretation which cannot be changed. Confidence points towards possible contingencies – not guarantees, only possible outcomes. This does not mean that trust is a causal function of the past (consisting of potentially positive as well as negative trust experiences), but rather that confidence is the basis for trust or distrust. In the case of the child at risk, historical confidence in the system is not likely to be a factor, given that contact to the social services may be absent *or* prior contact may have been distrustful or troublesome. In this sense, confidence is about what can be taken for granted in a particular situation. The leap into trust is, according to Luhmann, related to actions in which critical alternatives exist (Luhmann, 2005). These actions are defined by the 'amount of damage' connected to a breach of trust. If the potential amount of damage created by a breach is greater than the *potential* advantage of showing trust; then trust is involved (Deutsch, 1958; Luhmann, 1988, 2005). I have added the term *potential* since – as I mentioned earlier – complete knowledge is not an option. Knowledge is more a blend of knowing and not knowing. By the same token, the distinction between confidence and trust depends on the individual's perception of the situation and the potential risk (Luhmann, 1988; Möllering, 2001).

It should now be clear that Luhmann's trust/distrust distinction is fundamental. In every social relationship, the issue of trust is present. It can be dominant or implicit, but it functions as a mediator between subjects and their expectations about each other's actions. Rather crudely, one might say that a person is trustworthy when he or she stands by the things (especially actions/gestures/reactions) she or he says and does, consciously or unconsciously. Trust is therefore also about self-representation in the sense that it is based both on an assessment of others' trustworthiness and the extent to which they display trustworthy actions (Luhmann, 2005). While important, my emphasis on trustworthy behaviour should not be interpreted to mean that trust is only a matter of the psychological system, indeed in my view the psychological aspects of trust should not be overemphasised. In Luhmannian terms, trustworthiness can be regarded as a problem of acting in a way that functionally favours the social system or, in strictly system-terms, communicating in a way that underpins the autopoiesis of the system. Seen from this perspective, trust and trustworthiness capture both structural/institutional as well as personal aspects of trust. The specific characteristics of these two types of trust must be examined more closely with a view to deploying them in analyses of the relationship between social workers and children at risk.

Personal trust and trust in system authorities

The operative notion in the above discussion is the term trustworthiness. This is clearly a very subjective notion.[5] Yet at the same time, interaction between two subjects is rife with symbolic actions, spontaneity and intentions. Luhmann talks about motivation structures (Luhmann, 2005), which consist of the intentions or motives in which one engages in relationships with other people. One can try to increase one's trustworthiness through various self-representation strategies. However, such self-representation should not be regarded as entirely synonymous with Erving Goffman's considerations about 'passing' and other strategies for not standing out as non-normal (Goffman, 1983), though many similarities can be found in both authors' concepts of self-representation. What primarily concerns Luhmann in Goffman's work is the latter's attention to individual, microsociological strategies. Although Luhmann is inspired by these strategies, he also emphasises the structural pressures that frame individual expectations of person-to-person relations (for instance media coverage of the social work system and the legitimacy of the system). The strategic element is essential to Luhmann's understanding of personal trust and it contains a notion of process. Luhmann is rather unclear about this: he refers to the so-called 'small steps principle', a type of learning process which eases the social conditions on which trust relations are founded. These small steps may take the form of 'probes' used to test the other's trustworthiness. In some cases, these tests, though seemingly risky, actually do not imply any risk for the person doing the testing.

One last characteristic of personal trust should be mentioned. Although trust requires an initiative from the person who displays trust, personal trust is essentially a mutual action. Trust cannot be forced, it must be bestowed based on prior gestures the person shown trust must act upon (Luhmann, 2005). For the person showing trust, these prior gestures constitute a form of vulnerability that initiates the trust relationship. However, this does not fully apply to the situation at hand; the relationship between social workers and children at risk. This relationship is not necessarily initiated voluntarily. It is somewhat more asymmetrical than personal trust (although this can also be asymmetrical). This is because the social worker is a representative of an abstract and complex system and the child at risk is potentially compelled to engage in the relationship on an involuntary basis. However, although the relationship might be initiated involuntarily, the decision to trust or distrust may be more voluntary. For instance, the child may be distrustful towards the social system in general, but still exhibit trust in the specific social worker in charge of his or her case.

The positioned social worker

So what is the trust relationship between social worker and child at risk really about? Complexity in the world is growing and an increasing amount of selection is required in order to make sense of it. Selection is facilitated through differentiated social systems (Luhmann, 2000). As chains of selection become increasingly complex, motivation structures and patterns also proliferate, widening the gap between the individual and the social system (Luhmann, 2005). In this increasing complexity, with ever-more differentiated selection systems which in turn produce their own rationalities, how can individuals trust the various social workers' communications, actions and ability to reduce complexity? In order to answer this question, we must first address the situated and positioned nature of the social worker's work. First, it seems reasonable to consider the social worker as an authority who represents complexity and a systematised body of knowledge which cannot be made completely explicit.

The social worker is an exponent for a complex, systematised body of knowledge which he or she has to follow, at least to some extent (the legal framework), although a certain amount of flexibility is possible, since the precise measures taken in each case must be adjusted to the individual child at risk. In investigating how the flexibility inherent in social work is intertwined with the more rigid institutional and legal guidelines for social work, we are dealing with what Luhmann calls 'internal system trust alertness' (Luhmann, 2005: 135–7). This makes the trust relationship more complex and transforms trust into a kind of tactic. As mentioned in the introduction, Smith (2001) emphasises trust as the key to making social work *work*. This depends on how one views social work. Social work is a mixture of two different ways of conceptualising system trust. In the first, the system yields trust; in the second, trust is required in order for the system to function. Thus, the dynamics between social worker and child at risk are asymmetrical in the sense that the social worker has the power to make decisions about the child's life. Therefore in order to be able to function properly, the social worker as a representative of the system must earn the right to be trusted. This renders the former view on system trust (system yields trust) inadequate, since it considers matters of self-representation irrelevant, whereas we know that in relationships between social workers and children at risk self-representation motives are highly relevant. In this perspective, system trust in the form of an authority blends together with personal trust, producing a reflexive hybrid of the two.

In this perspective, trust cannot be viewed solely either as a phenomenon at the psychological level or at the institutional (systemic) level (Lewis & Weigert, 1985). It should be considered as mediating both perspectives and adding a third: the actual actions/gestures of the social worker. Put another way, the social worker is positioned between the ethics of rights and the ethics of care in which his or her relationship with the child must be mediated through trust and trustworthiness based on agency. A theoretical refinement of the concept of trust must resolve this difference in levels of analysis.

> [...] Only trust in the capacity for self-presentation to be reflected contains a guarantee for suitable continuity of behaviour under difficult, changing conditions. Only this form of trust regards the other person's characteristics. Only this form of trust regards the other person truly as free – and not merely as a being with certain constant characteristics. Only this form of trust can make itself conscious of the function of trust, the function of the reduction of complexity in the face of freedom of the other person, and in this knowledge find an orientation. And conversely, a functional theory of trust such as is here being attempted is only meaningful if, and insofar as, a social order is in a position to make trust in reflected presentations psychologically possible and, in social terms, to institutionalize it.
>
> (Luhmann, 1979: 62)

In other words, the core perspective in an analysis of trust in the relationship between social workers and children at risk, seen from the social workers' perspective, is one that enables an exploration of how social workers talk about trust, how they regard trust, what they do in order to produce reflexive self-representations and whether and how the contextual institutional formal/informal frames hinder or facilitate such tactical behaviour. By doing this, we can address the above-mentioned challenge of conceptualising the trust learning process and the strength of trust/distrust relations. However, one last issue remains to be discussed, namely the distinction between trust and distrust.

Trust and distrust

Luhmann differentiates between trust and distrust as functional equivalents. They are not just each other's opposite, and there is no normative distinction identifying one as better than the other. Both serve the same purpose – to reduce complexity. However, choosing between the two has different implications. Whereas choosing trust simplifies life by accepting risk, choosing distrust implies suspicion and the anticipation of various negative consequences. Distrust calls for strategic defensive action and defines the other as an enemy rather than a collaborator (Luhmann, 2005). Psychologically speaking, it is therefore much harder to choose distrust than trust, since risk is still present whichever one chooses. A person who distrusts must anticipate consequences to a larger extent than a person who trusts another person to carry out something risky. In order to define a situation in terms that allow rational action and by the same token adequate self-representation, various counterstrategies need to be implemented by the person choosing distrust. Again, Goffman's considerations about proper action in specific situations offer powerful tools to explain role play in interactions between social workers and children at risk.[6] One has trust when one assumes that the other's behaviour can be positively incorporated into one's own perspective and, by contrast, one chooses distrust when this is not the case (Luhmann, 2005).

Conclusion: The opening quotations revisited

As suggested in the chapter outline, it *is* possible to achieve children's participation on a level that resembles the eighth rung of Hart's Ladder of Participation, but such participation is potentially challenged by institutional demands posed by the very system whose purpose it is to help the children. The social workers' views cited earlier in the chapter illustrate the municipality's struggles to achieve external system validity through various control mechanisms. For instance, the girl in quotation 1 expresses the desire to be listened to because of her prior experience of *not* being listened to: 'Those who have something to do with foster children should be better at listening to the children, because they often have experiences from life that enable them to take a great deal of responsibility for their own lives' (Quotation 1). Conversely, quotations 2 and 3 reflect the dominant social work practice of focusing on the dark side of the ethics of rights. They emphasise procedure and documentation and are thereby examples of how the system goes about seeking external juridical legitimacy. But quotations 2 and 3 also tell us that social workers' perception of what constitutes social work practice conflicts with the municipality's efforts to achieve system internal and external validity. 'But I do love my job, even though I'm constantly being checked up on, I still love it – I think I can make a difference' (Quotation 2) and 'If new social worker students knew how much time we spend on citizens [face-to-face relations] and documentation, writing, meetings etc. they would run away screaming – I know I would' (Quotation 3). The institutional struggles stem from the challenges involved in at once ensuring internal control of the social work, enforcing the child's rights externally and reconciling both these activities with discourses of standardisation and homogeneity (the generalised other).

As the girl in quotation 4 notes, although she has experienced various efforts to help her, none of the people she has been in contact with have listened to her. Her experience of the relationship is characterised by over-ruling, patronising and 'know it all' attitudes and her frustration is clear in the quotation. Seen from a Luhmannian perspective, the girl is situated within an immensely complex system which she has no chance of comprehending and hence she puts her trust in the social worker in order to relieve her frustration. The social worker effectively reduces complexity in two ways. First of all, by establishing a trusting relationship to the girl through her statement that '[...] If anyone thinks they can decide over you, they're wrong. You make the decisions' (Quotation 4). The social worker thus reinstates the girl in a powerful position. Secondly, the social worker reduces complexity by assuming the risk and responsibility herself: '[...] if you're not sure what to do, you come to me. If others have a problem with that then they answer to me, not to you. I'm glad you called me so we can sort this misunderstanding out' (Quotation 4). By saying this, the social worker positions herself in between the system and the girl, even though she is in fact a representative of the system. By displaying trustworthy behaviour (through spoken as well as symbolic gestures), she steps out of her role as a system representative offering a specific package of care and takes up a new position as a co-player with the girl, a quite different role from the other system representatives towards whom the girl feels little (or no) trust. She does this by insisting that other system representatives must answer to her, but also by displaying a trusting attitude towards the girl. In doing this, the social worker points towards future actions and thereby reshapes the girl's past experiences, thereby also reducing future risk.

Through this brief analysis of a few illustrative quotations, we can see how the Luhmannian concept of trust offers a nuanced approach to the situated position of the social worker and simultaneously enables a focus that is sensitive to the dynamics of the ethics of care and the ethics of rights. I also demonstrate the importance of trust as a device for enabling children's participation in their own cases (both in the sense of the right to participate actively in their own cases, but also in the sense of the right to be taken care of). By taking my point of departure in the specific situated position of the social worker, and by combining the trust ethic of care and rights, it becomes possible to reflect upon the character of social work, how it is conducted and how the institutional framework hinders or facilitates trust relations between the social worker and the specific child. This enables a critical perspective on social work, social workers and the social worker-child at risk relationship. This analytical perspective thus provides a foundation for reflecting upon the institutional framing of social work and upon how the practice and institutional framing of social work can be adjusted towards a more trusting environment. However, in certain respects the concept needs to be developed, nuanced and strengthened – especially in the following two ways:

1) Luhmann is quite unclear about how trust as a learning process is embedded in some kind of natural processes in early childhood (Luhmann, 2005: 66). If the concept of trust is to be meaningfully incorporated in an analysis of trust perceptions and the role played by trust in the social worker-child at risk relationship, it is necessary to take into account the potentially negative (or absent) trust learning process experienced by the child. Here, the issue of asymmetrical power relations also enters into play. This is not to say that every child at risk has *a priori* experienced negative trust learning processes. However, the mere possibility that the child may have experienced distrust from a social worker makes it prudent to take into account. The notion of potentially negative trust experiences should also include considerations about the individual social worker's potentially negative trust experiences; hence the trust relationship is reciprocal. Here one can find inspiration in Warming's discussion of trust, recognition and power (Warming, Chapter 1).

2) Although trust in a Luhmannian perspective encapsulates both *structure* and *process* – and thereby the notion of time – the *strength* and *borders* of trust/distrust relationships are almost absent in Luhmann's work on trust. One rather obvious reason for this is that what constitutes trustworthy action is to some extent a subjective perception. However, it is also because the concept of trust is not normative. Since the social worker-child at risk relationship is not fixed in time or reduced to a single meeting, we need to focus on the temporal dimension of trust (which could also be labelled as some kind of process (Möllering, 2006)) and supplement this with a methodological trust-distrust continuum which can be deployed in an analysis of social workers' perceptions of trust and distrust.

Notes

1 However, the first quotation comes from the text: 'Har andre plejebørn det som mig?' ('Do other foster children feel the same way I do?') (Warming, 2005: 149).

2 As a consequence of Luhmann's inattention to the difference between trust and confidence at this stage of his career, what he is actually talking about in the opening lines is confidence. However, for the moment the implications of this conceptual confusion are minor. The distinction between trust and confidence will be further developed later in the chapter.

3 However, this Parsons inspired approach makes my reading of Luhmann somewhat different than one might do when dealing with the late Luhmann. For instance, I focus on communication, actions, agency and cognitive aspects of trust. If I had used the 'late' Luhmann I would have focused on psychological systems, social systems and the surrounding environment. Additionally I would solely have concentrated my research on communication and how the communications about children at risk constitute the autopoiesis of the social system.

4 For a differentiation between confidence, faith, hope, familiarity and symbolic gestures see Luhmann (1988).

5 See for instance Baier (1986), Hardin (1996) or Mullin (2005) for nuanced discussions of the subjective/normative aspects of trustworthiness.

6 See for instance Schwalbe's (1993) notion of self-representation and agency, based on a Goffmanian perspective.

Bibliography

Baier, A. (1986) 'Trust and antitrust', *Ethics*, 96(2): 231–60.

Carey, M. (2003) 'Anatomy of a care manager', *Work, Employment & Society*, 17: 121–34.

Cockburn, T. (2005) 'Children and the feminist ethic of care', *Childhood*, 12(1): 71–89.

Dalrymple, J. (2003) 'Professional advocacy as a force for resistance in child welfare', *British Journal of Social Work*, 33(8): 1043–62.

Dickens, J. (2006) 'Care, control and change in child care proceedings: Dilemmas for social workers, managers and lawyers', *Child and Family Social Work*, 11: 23–32.

Deutsch, M. (1958) 'Trust and suspicion', *The Journal of Conflict Resolution*, 2(4): 265–79.

Gaskell, C. (2010) '"If the social worker had called at least it would show they cared". Young care leavers' perspectives on the importance of care', *Children & Society*, 24: 136–47.

Goffman, E. (1983) 'The interaction order', *American Sociological Review*, 48(1): 1–17.

Grover, S. (2004) 'Why won't they listen to us? On giving power and voice to children participating in social research', *Childhood*, 11(1): 81–93.

Hardin, R. (1996) 'Trustworthiness', *Ethics*, 107(1): 26–42.

Hart, R. A. (1992) *Children's Participation from Tokenism to Citizenship*, Florence, Italy: UNICEF International Child Development Centre, Spedale degli Innocenti.

Jalava, J. (2003) 'From norms to trust – The Luhmannian connections between trust and system', *European Journal of Social Theory*, 6(2): 173–90.

James, A., C. Jenks & A. Prout (1998) *Theorizing Childhood*, Cambridge, UK: Polity Press, Blackwell Publishers Ltd.

Knudsen, M. (2001) '…*Man bliver helt mør i hovedet – Den vanskelige samtale*', UFC Børn og familier, Formidlingscentret i Aabenraa med støtte fra Socialministeriet, Aabenraa: Vizuel A/S.

Lee, N. (1999) 'The challenge of childhood. Distributions of childhood's ambiguity in adult institutions', *Childhood*, 6: 455–74.

Leeson, C. (2007) 'My life in care: Experiences of non-participation in decision-making processes', *Child and Family Social Work*, 12: 268–77.

Lewis, D. J. & L. Weigert (1985) 'Trust as a social reality', *Social Forces*, 63(4): 967–85.

Luhmann, N. (1988) 'Familiarity, confidence, trust: Problems and alternatives' in D. Gambetta (ed.) *Trust: Making and Breaking Cooperative Relations*, Padstow, Cornwall: Basil Blackwell Ltd., pp. 94–107.

Luhmann, N. (2000/1984) *Sociale Systemer – grundrids til en almen teori*, København: Hans Reitzels Forlag.

Luhmann, N. (2005/1968) *Tillid – en mekanisme til reduktion af social kompleksitet*, København: Hans Reitzels Forlag.

Luhmann, N. (1979) *Trust and Power*, Avon, UK: UMI, Pitman Press.

Meagher, G. & N. Parton (2004) 'Modernising social work and the ethics of care', *Social Work and Society*, 2(1): 10–27.

Mik-Meyer, N. (2001) 'Moderne management-teoris indmarch på socialområdet', *Uden for Nummer*, 2(2): 4–13.

Misztal, B. A. (1996) *Trust in Modern Societies*, UK: Polity Press, Blackwell Publishers Ltd.

Misztal, B. A. (2001) 'Trust and cooperation: The democratic public sphere', *Journal of Sociology*, 37: 371–86.

Möllering, G. (2001) 'The nature of trust: From Georg Simmel to a theory of expectation, interpretation and suspension', *Sociology*, 35(2): 403–20.

Möllering, G. (2006) *Trust: Reason, Reflexivity*, Amsterdam: Elsevir Ltd.

Mullin, A. (2005) 'Trust, social norms, and motherhood', *Journal of Social Philosophy*, 36(3): 316–30.

Orme, J. (2002) 'Social work: Gender, care and justice', *British Journal of Social Work*, 32(6): 799–814.

Parton, N. (1998) 'Risk, advances liberalism and child welfare: The need to re-discover uncertainty and ambiguity', *British Journal of Social Work*, 28: 5–27.

Ruch, G. (2005) 'Relationship-based practice and reflective practice: Holistic approaches to contemporary child care social work', *Child and Family Social Work*, 10: 111–23.

Satka, M. & G. B. Eydal (2004) 'The history of Nordic welfare policies for children' in H. Brembeck, B. Johansson & J. Kampmann (eds) *Beyond the Competent Child*, Roskilde Universitet: Samfundslitteratur, pp. 33–62.

Schwalbe, M. L. (1993) 'Goffman against postmodernism: Emotion and the reality of the self', *Symbolic Interaction*, 16(4): 333–50.

Sehested, K. (2002) 'How new public management reforms challenge the roles of professionals', *International Journal of Public Administration*, 25(12): 1513–37.

Seligman, A. B. (1998) 'Trust and sociability: On the limits of confidence and role expectation', *American Journal of Economics and Sociology, Inc.*, 57(4): 391–404.

Smith, C. (1997) 'Children's rights: Have carers abandoned values?', *Children and Society*, 11: 3–15.

Smith, C. (2001) 'Trust and confidence: Possibilities for social work in "high modernity"', *British Journal of Social Work*, 31: 287–305.

Qvortrup, J., M. Bardy, G. Sgritta & H. Wintersberger (eds) (1994) *Childhood Matters – Social Theory, Practice and Politics*, Avebury, UK: Ashgate Publishing Company.

Warming, H. (2005) *'Har andre plejebørn det som mig?'*, Pozkal, Polen: Frydenlund.

7
Trust and Facilitation in Educational Interactions

Claudio Baraldi and Federico Farini

This chapter explores the building of trust in interactions within the education system. Moving away from the distinction between confidence and trust, which highlights their differentiated and complementary functions in modern society, the analysis focuses on the controversial importance of expertise and interpersonal closeness in building trust in education and in conditions of distrust. The chapter presents an empirical analysis of videotaped interactions in the context of peace education activities with international groups of adolescents, in order to examine the design of facilitators' actions that can promote a trusting commitment. In particular, the analysis highlights the cultural presuppositions which can support adolescents' trusting commitment in relationships with facilitators. The chapter offers both a theoretical contribution and examples of practices of trust building in educational situations in which facilitation of communication processes substitutes teaching of knowledge and norms.

The function of trust

In a sociological perspective, trust may be observed for its function in society, which is a way of dealing with the disappointment of expectations (Giddens, 1990, 1991; Luhmann, 1968, 1988) in communication systems (Luhmann, 1984).[1] In the accomplishment of this function, trust is different from confidence. Both confidence and trust accomplish this function when unfamiliar experiences arise, which imply changes and therefore potential disappointment of expectations in communication systems. In these situations, the function of confidence is to enable the unproblematic continuation of communication, taking for granted that expectations will not be disappointed; confidence means taking for granted that, for instance, today I will not be fired from my workplace or I will not be abandoned by my beloved spouse. On the contrary, the function of trust is to deal with the *risk* of disappointment of expectations.

In today's society, all social actions, such as political decisions, investments, funding and efforts of scientific research, choices of schools and universities, marriages, are observed as risky (Giddens, 1990; Luhmann, 1991), and can disappoint established expectations. Trust deals with this risk of disappointment as a consequence of actions engaged in social relationships. It implies the decision of engaging in social relationships that could be disappointing; it implies the choice of risky alternatives, the choice of 'one action in preference to others in spite of the possibility of being disappointed by the action of others' (Luhmann, 1988: 97). Confidence turns into trust when alternatives to an established social relationship become evident: for example, confidence in a lifelong marriage turns into trust in a contingent affective relationship with the partner (Giddens, 1992).[2]

The structure of modern society (Luhmann, 1997) requires both confidence as a prerequisite for participation in communication and trust as a condition for specific opportunities of action. Confidence makes opportunities for participation available and trust mobilises specific engagement, 'extending the range and degree of participation' (Luhmann, 1988: 99; see also Pinkney, Chapter 5). Confidence is a prerequisite for the reproduction of the most important social systems in society, such as the economy, politics, law, science, education, families and medicine, while trust assures the reproduction of the specific social relationships that are included in these systems. On the one hand, those who participate in communication inside these systems must be confident in the reproduction of the economy, politics, law, science, education, families and medicine; the reproduction of these social systems maintains the structure of society and the hypothesis of its failure is not considered. From this perspective, social participation is an unavoidable necessity. On the other hand, participants must trust specific activities, in specific communication processes with specific partners, such as classroom interactions in education, business meetings in the economic field, negotiations between parties in politics and doctor-patient interactions in healthcare settings.[3]

In a social system, confidence is not menaced by lack of trust in specific interactions. However, lack of trust in these activities can affect confidence in the system, as withdrawal from specific activities and social relationships reduces the range of possible actions and therefore participation. While individuals cannot retreat from participating in communication in the system, lack of trust can reduce confidence in its effectiveness, thus eventually jeopardising the function of the specific system in society and consequently its reproduction. Lack of trust means lack of alternatives, which creates alienation, prevents commitment and leaves the floor to disappointment of expectations. Social systems generate conditions of risk and corresponding necessities of trust; therefore, confidence becomes dependent on trust, just as trust is dependent on confidence. Without trust social systems 'cannot stimulate supportive activities in situations of uncertainty and risk' (Luhmann, 1988: 103). Only encouragement of *risk of trust* can avoid risks for the reproduction of confidence.

Necessity of trust regards specific interactions among specific partners, who can affect the reproduction of social systems, especially those where interactions are of the greatest importance, such as families, education or medicine. Encouraging risk of trust provides opportunities for participants' trusting commitment in these interactions. Therefore, for maintaining confidence in the social systems, trusting commitment in specific interactions with parents, teachers or doctors is vital for the reproduction of families, education and medicine. Building trust means creating effective conditions for trusting commitment, it does not mean reduction or elimination of risky alternatives of action and engagement, which would transform trust into confidence. This would be a paradoxical process in that building trust would turn out to be elimination of trust. Building conditions of trusting commitment means promoting the production of risky alternatives of action in social systems.

Building trust in education

The distinction between confidence and trust is useful to understand children's commitment in the interaction with adults, in particular in institutional interactions that are included in social systems such as education.

Children's commitment seems to be exclusively or primarily connected with their confidence in adults' expert guidance. Children must be confident in school education because they cannot avoid participating in it: withdrawal is impossible in its first mandatory phase and is strongly discouraged in the following phases, which are considered fundamental for individual career prospects in society. Confidence in education should support acceptance of teaching, requests of learning and evaluation (Mehan, 1979; Parsons, 1959; Walsh, 2011). The expectations concerning teachers and students as roles are established in the education system, and the disappointment of these expectations disables the function of education. Dropping out is normatively treated as a consequence of institutional processes (evaluation of learning) rather than of distrust.

Childhood studies (Hengst & Zeiher, 2005; James et al., 1998; Jenks, 1996) challenge this representation of the relationship between children and adults. According to these studies, children cannot be considered passive recipients of adults' information and command; on the contrary, they are social agents who actively participate in the construction of social systems (Baraldi & Iervese, 2012). This approach enables meaningful connections to the concept of trust (Warming, Chapter 1). In particular, we can state that children take the same risks of action as adults and social attention moves towards children's trusting commitment alongside the necessity of building trust in their relationships with adults.

In fact, education involves children's confidence as well as children's trust. Children can distrust specific educational activities that involve certain partners, particularly, although not only, teachers. Distrust in interactions with specific teachers can determine children's marginalisation or self-marginalisation in the education system, including 'slantwise actions' (Pantea, Chapter 8), with possible drop-out and consequent reduction of effectiveness of education in society. If children do not risk trust in educational activities, their marginalisation can reduce the alternatives of action in the education system. Consequently, the lowered risk of trust activates a vicious circle: it implies loosing opportunities of children's action, reducing their preparation to risk trust, and activating anxiety and suspicion for educators' actions.

During the last two decades there has been a growing perception that children's distrust can involve and undermine the educational system, if not the whole society (Goleman, 1995). In this situation, reflection on education has elaborated new strategies of building trust. According to Giddens (1990, 1991), modern societies have two options for building trust.

Firstly, trust can be built through expertise, which guarantees basic presuppositions of action and relationships. This way of building trust, however, is considered weak in motivating commitment and can easily fail when expertise proves ineffective in facing risks (for example environmental, medical, political and economic risks). Secondly, trust can be achieved through interpersonal affective relationships, which mobilise it through a process of mutual disclosure. In this second case, trusting commitment concerns the relationship in itself, a pure relationship (Giddens, 1991), and trust results in a demand for intimacy. Interpersonal affective relationships seem to be much more motivating than expertise (see also Ule, Chapter 9). However, in many social systems actions can only be based on expertise; for example, trust in scientific or medical expertise seems to be unavoidable.

Within the educational system, trust is primarily based on teachers' expertise: teachers are held to be the experts who must be trusted for their knowledge and competence. The typical Initiation, Reply, Evaluation (IRE) sequence in teacher-students interactions (Mehan, 1979) presupposes the teacher's expertise in Initiating and, above all, Evaluating students' Replies. The reproduction of the interaction is assured through students' trust in teachers' expertise as initiators and evaluators. However, critical pedagogy and childhood studies have questioned the effectiveness of teachers' expertise in promoting students' trusting commitment. According to childhood studies, in education, children's opportunities of participation are strongly reduced 'by curricular and behavioural rules and structures' (Wyness, 1999: 356), and the education system is not interested in children's agency (James & James, 2004), that is it shows distrust in children's agency.[4] Therefore, the educators' expertise is often ineffective in motivating children to engage in the activities proposed. Students' replies are considered passive alignments that do not demonstrate students' trusting commitment, which can only be demonstrated through expressions of agency.

The success of person-centred approaches in critical pedagogy demonstrates this change of perspective in education. Rogers (1951) suggests that teachers should risk interpersonal affective relationships with students, listening to their personal expressions and supporting them empathically. In other words, teachers should understand that children are social agents who can and must tackle important issues: acknowledging and addressing the complexity of their feelings in order to 'recognise' them (Pantea, Chapter 8). These ideas have inspired the development of important pedagogical movements (Goleman, 1995) and theories (Hicks, 1996; Mercer & Littleton, 2007). In this perspective, adults' facilitation is the most effective way of promoting children's agency (Hill et al., 2004). Facilitation means supporting children's self-expression, taking their views into account, consulting them, involving them in decision-making processes, sharing power and responsibility for decision-making with them (Matthews, 2003; Shier, 2001). Children can only trust facilitators who 'dance' with them (Holdsworth, 2005: 150), those who show sensitivity towards their personal expressions. Therefore, children's trusting commitment requires affective conditions.

Against this backdrop, interpersonal affective relationships seem to guarantee children's trusting commitment. However, trusting commitment in interpersonal affective relationships can fail and leave the floor to strong disappointment and great difficulties (see Grosse & Warming, Chapter 3; Turton, Chapter 4). Affective relationships cannot eliminate risky alternatives. Children's trusting commitment should not be expected to coincide with adults' expectations, even if these are affective, and 'adult society must accept that there will be complexities when children express views that do not coincide with those of adults' (Holland & O'Neill, 2006: 96).

Building working trust in case of confidence in distrust

Kelman (2005) highlights the problems in building trust under conditions of affective facilitation. He analyses facilitated interactions in workshops that involve Israeli and Palestinian representatives trying to reach peaceful agreements (Kelman, 2005). These group interactions are different from those involving students in classrooms; their analysis, however, leads to some insightful suggestions about facilitation of trusting commitment in cases of confidence in distrust.

According to Luhmann (1968, 1984), while trust enlarges the range of possible actions in a social system, distrust restricts this range, meaning that it requires additional premises for social relationships that protect participants from a disappointment considered highly probable (see also Christensen, Chapter 6). When distrust is established, trust building appears very difficult. Kelman analyses the difficulty of building trust when mutual distrust is the basis of the interaction. In these cases, the interaction is permeated by confidence in distrust; furthermore the unavoidable interdependencies between the parties prevent them from withdrawing from interaction.

Confidence in distrust is not compatible with the reproduction of social systems; it can be considered an extreme condition of conflict. In this condition, a peace process 'becomes possible when the parties conclude that it is in their own best interest to negotiate an end to the conflict – in effect, to enter into an exchange relationship' (Kelman, 2005: 641). However confidence in distrust creates an entrapping dilemma: 'The parties cannot enter a peace process without some degree of mutual trust, but they cannot build trust without entering a peace process' (Ibid.). Trust can be built through successive approximations of increasing degrees of commitment, starting from the building of a feeble trust that does not commit participants to anything relevant. Therefore, trust does not presuppose sympathy, friendship or interpersonal closeness. It can be built only on self-interest, enhancing mutually acceptable accommodation and the joint solution of specific problems, thus becoming *working trust*. Self-interest is contrasted with interest in the other, which is the basis of interpersonal affective relationships. Working trust and interpersonal relationships (self-interest and interest in the other) can merge, but only at a later stage of the interaction. Interpersonal closeness is not the basis of trusting commitment and may only be created after working trust has been built.

Kelman agrees that trust can be built through facilitation. Facilitation, however, regards interactive problem-solving activities and means that a third party (the facilitator) has the task 'to create the conditions that allow ideas for resolving the conflict to emerge out of the interactions between the parties themselves' (Kelman, 2005: 642). Facilitators set rules for the discussion and monitor their respect, helping participants to create constructive and non-adversarial debates. They do not participate in the actual discussion, do not offer their own perspectives or solutions, nor evaluate the parties' ideas. Facilitators must be the repository of trust, 'bridging the gap of mutual distrust that divides the parties and enabling them to enter into a process of direct communication' (Kelman, 2005: 645). Ultimately, facilitation establishes the preconditions for mutual trust that is mutual reassurance, based on acknowledgement of participants' needs and fears and on responsiveness to them. Both parties must show trusting commitment in the interaction with the facilitator, who can be considered trustworthy because he or she shows commitment to his or her role, and in this way acts in favour of the reproduction of the social system (see Christensen, Chapter 6).

In the next few sections we will analyse building trust in international groups of adolescents dealing with peace education. The analysis aims to understand if, and in which ways, facilitation is effective in enabling adolescents to communicate, creating conditions of working trust, mutual reassurance, mutual recognition of needs and trustworthiness of facilitators. In particular, it focuses on the relationship between working trust and interpersonal closeness in the specific educational situations examined. These are not extremely conflictive; however they involve activities in which: 1) conditions of interaction are unfamiliar (see also Christensen, Chapter 6); 2) adolescents come from different cultural traditions that are not shared and are sometimes conflicting; 3) trust building cannot be based on previous interpersonal contacts. In this situation, facilitators are assigned the task of creating working trust during the activities and trustworthiness is based on actions that can promote trust building in communication both *among* adolescents and *with* adolescents.

Observing trust building in adult-children interactions

Our analysis aims to understand the strategies of building trust through facilitation in adult-adolescents group activities that are defined as educational. More specifically, we aim to explore the ways in which facilitators' actions create the conditions of adolescents' trusting commitment and to enhance a reflection on the relationship between education, facilitation and building trust.

The analysis regards two international summer camps promoted by the School of Peace of Monte Sole, established in the Province of Bologna, Italy, in the place where in 1944 a Nazi assault killed almost 800 children, women and old people. Each camp was attended by four delegations of ten adolescents coming from different countries, two of which were always Italy and Germany, to symbolise peaceful resolution of extreme conflict. The camps aim to promote adolescents' learning through interpersonal relationships, fostering their ability in conflict resolution, their interest in peaceful relationships and their respect for different perspectives, while reducing their prejudices and stereotypes. English is normally used as a *lingua franca* during the activities.

The activities are not part of a school programme which can satisfy adolescents' self-interest enhancing their individual careers. Adolescents' voluntary participation is based on personal motivation. However, voluntary participation does not assure the success of peace education, because the nature and details of peaceful relationships are unknown to the participants and are created only in group interactions. Participants do not share ideas, values or principles but at least some of them share the perspective of unavoidable differences and conflicts. Since self-interest is not a precondition and peace is far from being a common practice in adolescents' social environment, the risk of distrust cannot be avoided and trust must be built in the interaction. Under these conditions, facilitation is considered primarily important in promoting adolescents' trusting commitment, enabling their participation in communication and assuring their mutual reassurance and responsiveness. By increasing the possibilities of adolescents' active participation or agency and by reducing their anxiety and suspicion for interlocutors, facilitation can prepare adolescents to risk trust.

In the next section, trust building will be analysed in specific interactions that involve facilitators and adolescents. In analysing these interactions we will follow the basic methodology of Conversation Analysis (Hutchby & Wooffitt, 1998), which consists in working on naturally occurring interactions and more specifically on the contribution of single turns or actions to the ongoing sequence, with reference to the context (Drew & Heritage, 1992). Actions are considered context shaped as well as context renewing; every current action contributes to the context-ual framework in terms of which next action(s) it projects. Following Gumperz (1992), context implies cultural presuppositions, which are pat-terns of expectations created in social systems, such as the education system, working as premises of communication processes (Luhmann, 1984, 1997) by enabling the selection of ways of organising specific interactions.

This analysis conducted here concerns: 1) the design of turns (actions) produced in the interaction, in particular facilitators' turns; 2) the organ-isation of the sequences in which facilitators' and adolescents' turns are intertwined; 3) the cultural presuppositions of turn design and sequence organisation. Cultural presuppositions are particularly important, in that they establish the meanings of turn design and organisation of sequences, defining expectations that concern guiding values or coding (Luhmann, 1984); positioning (Harré & van Langenhove, 1999) of participants' actions as role performances and/or personal expressions; and type of results deriving from the interaction (cognitive, normative, affective). In this way, cultural presuppositions define the meaning of trust building; there-fore we analyse trust building not only looking at turn design and organ-isational sequences, but also identifying its cultural presuppositions. Our analysis highlights the linguistic cues for these cultural presuppositions as shown in specific turns and in the organisation of sequences of turns in the interaction.

In particular, the analysis focuses on two kinds of sequences: 1) facil-itators' risky actions, which open alternatives in the interaction, down-grading facilitators' authority and upgrading adolescents' authority through active participation (Farini, 2009; Heritage & Raymond, 2005); 2) adolescents' risky actions, which demonstrate choices among alter-natives, agency and authority. In this analysis, we observe trust as based on a communicative process, constructing participants as trustworthy. This process requires that one party displays trust, inviting the other party's co-authorship, and the other party displays commitment in co-authoring the process (Warming, Chapter 1). This analysis highlights the degree of mutual accommodation, joint solution of problems, inter-personal closeness, reassurance, responsiveness to needs as well as the trustworthiness of facilitators.

The interactions were videotaped and transcribed, enabling the researcher to view and analyse them in detail and repeatedly. The analysis is based on recordings collected in two camps, each of them lasting two weeks.

These camps involved delegations of adolescents from Italy and Germany (both camps), Serbian and Albanian Kosovo (first camp), France and Poland (second camp). During these camps, daily group activities involving adolescents were recorded, for a total of 52 hours.

Group activities concerned the interpretation of the meaning of objects, facts and events related to peace, by means of the workshop materials, visits, games and discussions. This kind of activity requires the building of working trust to deal with problems arising from different interpretations and to promote mutual accommodation and mutual responsiveness. Our analysis moves from the design of facilitators' turns that proved to be effective in building trust, demonstrating their trust-worthiness, opening alternative directions in the interaction and upgrading adolescents' authority in expressing interpretations. The turns analysed are: 1) promotional questions, which open alternatives for adolescents' actions, demonstrating facilitators' trust in their agency and active participation; 2) feedback questions, which verify and explore the understanding of adolescents' interpretations, thus demonstrating attentiveness to their needs; 3) formulations, which both demonstrate responsiveness to adolescents' needs and open alternative possibilities for adolescents' actions. These kind of turns promoted adolescents' trusting commitment, enhancing their mutual accommodation.

Promoting trusting commitment in peace

In this section, we will analyse three excerpts from group interactions in which interpretation of meanings related to peace (negative behaviours, separation/connection among human beings, human rights) were discussed and which required the building of working trust and facilitators' trustworthiness. These three excerpts should not be considered completely representative of the tendencies in the camps where we observed situations in which facilitation did not work successfully in building trust. However, the chosen excerpts reflect our interest in highlighting successful facilitation in trust building.

Excerpt 1 (first camp) is taken from a discussion following a guided tour to the location of the 1944 slaughter. The discussion is about the Nazi behaviour, which is compared to behaviours in contemporary conflicts and involves adolescents from Kosovo. In turn 1, Erica initiates the interaction formulating two questions which had been raised by Marcin and Victor during the guided tour. Formulation identifies the gist of the previous turn (Heritage, 1985) and is important in building trust as it both demonstrates responsiveness to the interlocutors' perspective and sustains its further development (Baraldi, 2009; Baraldi & Gavioli, 2007). The formulation in turn 1 opens with an acknowledgement of the previous turns ('ok') and a discourse marker ('so'), which stresses that the current turn is developing the previous one (Hutchby, 2007). These two lexical elements indicate responsiveness to the adolescents' agency; the core of Erica's formulation shows responsiveness because it takes the adolescents' agency seriously and enables its continuation. Erica concludes her turn with a promotional question, which projects possible alternative interpretations and an upgrading of the adolescents' authority, while downgrading her own.

Through his response, Victor upgrades his authority, thus contradicting Erica's formulation. In doing this, however, he proposes an explanation of the Nazi behaviour which seems to legitimise it (turns 2 and 4), although his difficulties in speaking English hamper a clear understanding of his interpretation. At this point, in an educational perspective, the facilitators could evaluate Victor's action as cognitively incorrect or normatively unacceptable. On the contrary, in this situation facilitators risk trust supporting Victor's agency. After Boris' linguistic help has supported Victor's self-expression (turn 3), in turn 5, Erica's new 'so-prefaced' promotional question stresses the relevance of Victor's turn in the interaction. Not surprisingly, in this environment Marcin can risk trust in her action, by self-selecting as next speaker and expressing her interpretation, without being explicitly invited by the facilitators to do so (turn 6). Victor reacts to Marcin's interpretation promoting its continuation (turn 7), without waiting for the facilitators' appreciation of its relevance to the interaction. Responding to Victor's acknowledgement of her authority, Marcin accounts for the behaviour of Nazi soldiers, leaving aside any moral judgement, although in a different and contrasting way (turn 9).

Excerpt 1

1. Erica (F): ok, so let's continue, just to summarise, we have two things on the table, one the problem Marcin suggested, I describe you the situation in Fallujah, from a military point of view, it was almost the same as in Monte Sole, but Marcin asked, it's different? Partisans here, what else over there, terrorists or civil population or army, what's there, ok let me summarise a bit and then, the other question on the table is Victor question: how was possible that Nazi troops came here killing all these people, looking for partisans and

		because they weren't able to catch them they came back to the villages and killed all the civil population. It's like this?
2.	Victor:	ehm, no it's not why they, if they want to hunt the partisans, they said it was *berufung*
3.	Boris (F):	mission
4.	Victor:	a mission and they see the partisans troops to partisan and then, they don't follow them, they went back and why is their mission to shoot them or they could killed other people
5.	Erica (F):	so, why not follow partisans up to the hill but kill other people who were not their target
6.	Marcin:	I can suggest, alright, I give an example of the soviet forces are trying to spring the communist regime all over the Europe in nineteen twenty and first of all they attack Poland and they came to Warsaw, they fall, they fell at the battle of Warsaw, in nineteen twenty then the eastern part of Poland was destroyed, burnt, so it was a total war, I think that in the Second World War when the Nazi commanders order to provide a total war to destroy all enemy target in order to, to frighten the civilian people
7.	Victor:	do you think they attacked because frightening the civil population of a country
8.	Marcin:	maybe but there is there's another thing I that I feel: maybe it was not the initiative from the high headquarter, the soldiers maybe afraid, this soldiers who were fighting in Italy at the Nazi service, they were also human, men and they could be afraid for their life and maybe it was the reaction of it, I don't know

Excerpt 2 (second camp) regards an activity called 'borders and bridges': adolescents are asked to take pictures of objects which represent either *borders*, as symbols of separation, or *bridges*, as symbols of contact, and to interpret these pictures in the group discussion. The excerpt concerns the phase of group discussion which is coordinated by the facilitators. The task consists in elaborating and clarifying differences between separations and connections.

In turn 1, Federica's question ('bridge or border?') concerns an object which was photographed. In educational settings, this kind of question is generally understood as Initiation of the IRE sequence, which continues with Reply and Evaluation. In this case, however, Federica's question does not project expectations of 'correct reply', which should match predetermined knowledge, but is a promotional question that projects possible alternative interpretations, demonstrating Federica's trust in the adolescents' agency and an open development of the interaction. As a consequence, in the third and following turns, after Luca's response, there are no evaluations; in turn 3 we find linguistic help ('age') and in turn 5 we find Alain's echo of Luca's take-up (turn 4), which confirms its meaningfulness. After this double echo, Marek's statement in turn 6 ('it is a bridge') could be interpreted as a correction of Luca's interpretation with Leni cooperating in its design in turn 10. However Alain's coordination of this exchange among the facilitators downgrades their authority as experts and upgrades the adolescents' interpretation; with his lexical choices ('for him/her'), Alain introduces the facilitators' interpretation as hypothetical (turn 9: 'for Marek is a bridge'; turn 11: 'for Leni too'), thus putting forward the legitimacy of different interpretations. Furthermore, in turn 11 Alain deals with this interpretation as subject to the adolescents' authority. After a long pause, which indicates the expectation of new interpretations in the group, he involves the adolescents through a promotional question ('and for you, boys and girls?'). This promotional question indicates his trust in the adolescents' agency and suggests that as facilitators they have the right to produce interpretations.

In turn 12, Matthias' response introduces new opportunities for interpretation. In turn 13, Federica formulates Matthias' turn, highlighting the interactional relevance of his action, while encouraging new action on his part. The formulation is followed by a new promotional question ('it can be also?'), which gives Matthias the opportunity to promote alternatives for next actions. Matthias ambiguous alignment ('in some way') projects a new question (turn 15), which is prefaced by a sequential marker ('and') that stresses continuity with the previous turn (Heritage & Sorjonen, 1994). This is a feedback question whereby Federica explores the meanings of Matthias' interpretation, as expressed in turns 12 and 14, showing attentiveness to it and treating it as relevant to the interaction, therefore upgrading Matthias' authority in interpretation. Matthias' hesitation in turn 16 projects Federica's initiation of a suggestion (turn 17), but Luca immediately self-selects as interlocutor, expanding on Matthias' interpretation (turn 18). On the one hand, Luca's self-selection shows that the interaction has successfully opened alternatives for new actions and expansions; on the other hand, it shows he is risking trust in the facilitator's interest for the adolescents' interpretations.

Excerpt 2

1. Federica (F): bridge or border?
2. Luca: eh, yeah a border? a border between the new age and the old age, the epoca come si dice *(epoca, how do you say it)*
3. Maria (F): age
4. Luca: age
5. Alain (F): age
6. Marek (F): it's a bridge
7. Alain (F): what
8. Marek (F): it's a bridge
9. Alain (F): for Marek is a bridge
10. Leni (F): for me too
11. Alain (F): for Leni too (3.0) and for you, boys and girls?
12. Matthias: for me is also a bridge because this picture (not understandable) two times and doesn't divide
13. Federica (F): so, you mean that a border is always dividing two things or maybe then, it can be also?
14. Matthias: yeah, in some way, yes
15. Federica (F): and what do you mean for the border or the bridge?
16. Matthias: mm
17. Federica (F): because there are two differences
18. Luca: I don't know because I think that a border is a line where two things are near, nearby

Excerpt 3 (second camp) regards the interpretation of gay marriage during a discussion on human rights. In turn 1, Maria refers to Alessandro's interpretation (not shown in the excerpt) without evaluating it. By suggesting that different participants can express different opinions, Maria does not select some correct knowledge to learn and opens up alternatives for action. However, the adolescents seem to be unwilling to participate in the discussion. Maria's encouragement is followed by a four-second silence, and when she selects a specific next speaker to move the interaction forward ('eh, Luca?'), the candidate speaker first is hesitant and does not seem to understand the question (turn 2), then he shows very low enthusiasm for his involvement (turn 4: 'boh' an expression for 'I really don't know'), and finally he refuses to express his opinion (turn 6). Nevertheless, Maria insistently promotes Luca's participation asking him questions, clarifying their meaning (turns 3, 5, 9), and echoing Luca's previous turn

(turn 7). Echoing is a kind of action that shows attentiveness and involvement in the perspective of the interlocutor (Baraldi & Gavioli, 2007). After being repeatedly invited to risk trust, Luca finally expresses his interpretation (turn 10). Maria supports his action through a continuer (Gardner, 2001) that is a short turn that communicates attentiveness and invites continuation (turn 11). The insistence of the facilitator creates new opportunities for action.

In turn 13, Alessandro refers his action to Luca's previous one; his self-selection as current speaker is accepted by Maria who ratifies the relevance of his turn by echoing it (turn 14). In turn 15, Luca aligns with this echo and with Alessandro's turn. This interactively-constructed joint authorship produces meanings with the active contributions of both the adolescents and the facilitator. In turn 16, however, Alessandro's highly depreciative lexical choice ('faggots', 'froci' in Italian) results in the inclusion of gay people in a negatively-connoted 'Them', projecting an ethnocentric form of communication (Pearce, 1989) that contradicts the cultural presuppositions of peace education. Therefore, it seems that Maria's decision to risk trust in promoting adolescents' participation is producing undesired consequences. She reacts to this risk initiating a correction (turn 17), which is completed by Alessandro (turn 18) and which she confirms in the third turn (turn 19). Maria's reaction projects a hierarchical form of communication between the facilitator and the adolescent, which parallels the ethnocentric form projected by Alessandro. Furthermore, the joint switch to the Italian language builds a side sequence that excludes most participants from the interaction.

In turn 21, Maria switches back to English with a formulation of Luca's and Alessandro's interpretation of the topic. This formulation projects the adolescents' interpretations as starting point for a new course of actions; the contingently produced hierarchical form is dissolved and substituted by a promotional one. This is demonstrated by the fact that Emilio immediately self-selects as speaker, expressing his perspective (turn 22), which refers to Luca's, Alessandro's and Maria's actions, introducing a cultural interpretation of the dichotomy acceptance/non-acceptance of gay people. Luca's and Alessandro's actions, supported by Maria's facilitation, have opened new opportunities for action, promoting a new risk of trust, which is visible in Emilio's appreciation. Emilio's action partially contradicts the meanings cooperatively produced by Maria, Luca and Alessandro and projects Maria's formulation (turn 23), which in its turn proposes Emilio's action as a topic for discussion, thus supporting Emilio's agency. Rather than presenting her formulation as a synthesis produced by an expert, Maria projects an expectation of possible revision ('if I understood well eh; block me if do not') that is the expectation of the adolescent's agency.

Excerpt 3

1. Maria (F):		I 'm talking with everybody because, probably, I don't know, you have different opinion from Alessandro, or the same, one thing to-, say something more about it (4.0) eh Luca?
2. Luca:		eh, mm?
3. Maria (F):		you wanted to say something more?
4. Luca:		boh
5. Maria (F):		or you have different opinion, what do you think about it?
6. Luca:		no, it's a difficult subject
7. Maria (F):		it's a difficult subject
8. Luca:		yes
9. Maria (F):		why?
10. Luca:		because if she were in Spain, she would be accepted
11. Maria (F):		mhm
12. Luca:		but in England no, she doesn't
13. Alessandro:		depend on the state, on the law of a state
14. Maria (F):		it depends from the state
15. Luca:		yes
16. Alessandro:		tipo in Spagna li fanno sposare i froci, mentre in Inghilterra no *(like in Spain faggots can get married, while in England they can't)*
17. Maria (F):		non si dice *(don't use that word)*
18. Alessandro:		eh, gli omosessuali *(eh, homosexual people)*
19. Maria (F):		mh va beh *(mh, that's fine)*
20. Alessandro:		se li fanno sposare non vuol dire che *(if they are allowed to get married it doesn't mean)*
21. Maria (F):		sorry, sorry, sorry, the other don't, so, Luca is saying it depends, if you live in Spain, you are accepted, if you live in England no why Spain and England, sorry? and then Alessandro was saying it depends from the state, for example in Spain it's possible for them to marry
22. Emilio:		for me, the possibility in Spain to get married it doesn't mean be accepted by the people, I think in English

	and Spain look homosexual in the same way other people do another way
23. Maria (F):	ok, Emilio then is saying it doesn't really depend on the laws, if I understood well eh, block me if do not, if it doesn't really depend on laws because it can be that it depends also from the people, that live in a country, probably in Spain and in England you can have both behaviour

Excerpts 1–3 show that, through promotional and feedback questions, formulations and also linguistic help, facilitators can promote adolescents' trusting commitment in the interaction, supporting their agency and avoiding evaluations of their interpretations. Facilitators are able to build trust projecting affective expectations, which are expectations of adolescents' self-expression as a result of the interaction (Baraldi, 2009). Therefore trust building is enhanced by facilitators' turns that project affective expectations, promoting mutual accommodation, responsiveness and production of alternatives, that is adolescents' risk of trust. In these interactions, the building of working trust does not presuppose interpersonal relationships and closeness but it is based on contingently produced affective expectations in the course of interaction, which are projected through the positioning of facilitators.[5]

Two different ways of promoting working trust through facilitation are observable. In excerpt 1, facilitation promotes trust in the direct interaction between adolescents who cooperate in constructing a joint narrative. In this case, facilitation seems to be in line with Kelman's observations and suggestions about facilitation as coordination of the parties' autonomous solutions. In excerpts 2 and 3, facilitators act as mediators (Baraldi, 2010) of contacts among adolescents, promoting their alternate participation in the interaction in triadic exchanges. In these cases, trust is based on a specific form of facilitation in which the third party actively intervenes in its construction.

Conclusions

In this chapter we have discussed the function of trust with reference to risks of disappointment of expectations. We have dealt with trusting commitment in interaction as a basis for social relationships, which allows the reproduction of confidence in social systems. We have explored the ways in which trust is built in specific group interactions involving adolescents and facilitators.

Facilitation is an effective way of building trust in group interaction in educational situations and in situations of distrust and conflict. Trustworthiness of facilitators is a crucial starting point for trust building. However, the meaning of facilitation is controversial. On the one hand, studies on child-adult relationships stress that facilitation enhances interpersonal affective relationships and closeness. Therefore, facilitation is understood as active promotion of interlocutors' agency and support of their self-expression; trusting commitment requires commitment in building its affective conditions. On the other hand, studies on situations of distrust stress that facilitation is not based on interpersonal relationships, as the main aspect of trust building concerns mutual accommodation and joint solution of problems, based on self-interest (working trust). Therefore, facilitation creates the conditions for effective direct interactions between the parties, avoiding the introduction of facilitators' perspectives.

Both these positions seem to attach great importance to sharing and avoiding risks. On the one hand, affectivity reduces risky alternatives. On the other hand, mutual accommodation and joint solution of problems reduce differences of perspectives. However, building trusting commitment means promoting risky alternatives of action. What clearly emerges in both perspectives is that facilitators and other participants *must* in fact risk trust, choosing among alternative lines of action.

The topics of trust commitment and trust building can be applied to interactions between adults and children because the attention of scholars and social planners has shifted to children's social agency and changes in adults' roles in the interaction with children. In this chapter we have analysed some ways of building trust in international groups of adolescents in which adults acted as facilitators to promote peace education. The aim was to understand if and in what ways this facilitation was effective in building trust. In the situations analysed, interactional conditions were unfamiliar, adolescents came from non-shared cultural traditions and trust building was not based on previous interpersonal relationships. Our analysis explored facilitators' actions promoting adolescents' trusting commitment. These actions are: promotional questions that open alternatives for adolescents' actions and highlight adults' trust in their agency; feedback questions that verify and explore the meanings of adolescents' interpretations; formulations that both demonstrate responsiveness to adolescents' needs and open alternatives for their actions. These kinds of actions promoted trust building, upgrading adolescents' authority in interpretations.

These turns contain linguistic cues for a form of facilitation. This form of facilitation can be considered a cultural presupposition of trust building and is based on the following patterns of expectations: 1) the interaction is coded as promotional, that is it is guided by the value of promotion as opposed to control; 2) facilitators' trustworthy positioning consists in personal commitment which permeates their role performances; 3) the main expectations about results are neither cognitive nor normative, but affective. Given its features, this form of facilitation is frequently also a form of mediation (Baraldi, 2010), facilitators' questioning and formulating do not simply sustain direct interactions between the parties; they actively *coordinate* these interactions with promotional effects. The representation of facilitation in studies on adult-children interactions seems closer to these results than the representation in studies on building working trust.

This does not mean that we need to abandon the concept of working trust. Working trust seems to be essential in all institutional situations in which trusting commitment must be built without interpersonal premises. In institutional interactions, affective closeness is neither the starting point nor a probable final result. However, the mere reference to roles and cognitive or normative expectations works badly in adult-children interactions. Rather than the merging between working trust and interpersonal relationships (Kelman, 2005), we have observed in our data a contingent construction of affective expectations, which works from the very beginning in supporting working trust. This combination of affective expectations and working trust allows mutual accommodation, which is based on the opening of risky alternatives in action and interpretation. The production of risky alternatives in the interaction seems to be the most effective result of this form of facilitation, and a genuine way of building trust. This means that a joint solution of problems is not the most probable result of facilitation, nor does this seem a particularly important feature of trust building. A further consequence is that self-interest is not so important in this form of facilitation. Self-interest is linked to an individualistic representation of institutional engagement. We do not deny its importance in modern society but we think that it cannot be the basis of social relationships where affective expectations, although contingently constructed, are the basis of trust building. Affective expectations highlight personal commitment – not self-interest – and contrast individualistic approaches to social relationships.

Finally, this form of facilitation can change educational interactions. It substitutes both teaching and evaluating and their function in building trust, going beyond person-centred approaches, in that facilitators' actions strongly influence the interaction and primary cognitive expectations are excluded. The analysis of this form of facilitation, in empirical interactions, demonstrates that the new paradigm, asserting the possibility and opportunity of children's agency in their interactions with adults, can be practiced, in at least some areas of education (see also Baraldi, 2008, 2009; Baraldi & Farini, 2011; Baraldi & Iervese, 2010, 2012; Baraldi & Rossi, 2011). How far this form of facilitation can get along with education in different contexts can be the object of further, broader research.

Notes

1   Our analysis, which focuses primarily on Luhmann's theory, is coherent with Christensen's conceptual approach in Chapter 6, and Warming's analysis of Luhmann's contribution to the field in Chapter 1. As Luhmann's theory has evolved in the years, we shall draw mainly on his last theorisation (1988), which starts from the guiding-distinction between trust and confidence, rather than that between personal trust and system trust (1968), and is directly connected with his final theoretical elaborations of risk (1991), autopoietic social systems (1984) and society (1997).
2   For a different concept of trust, relying on 'positive expectations', 'predictability', and 'social integration', rather than opening of risky alternatives, see Pantea, Chapter 8; Pinkney, Chapter 5; Ule, Chapter 9.
3   There is a claim that institutional conditions may not be sufficient to ensure trust in specific interactive settings (see Christensen, Chapter 6; Pinkney, Chapter 5; Ule, Chapter 9). This suggests that, in some social systems, such as social assistance, there could be a basic problem of confidence.
4   The same conditions of distrust in children's agency can be seen in welfare politics and social assistance, which should protect them (Pantea, Chapter 8; Pinkney, Chapter 5; Turton, Chapter 4). These may be seen as conditions of 'institutionalised mistrust', based on power structures that are imposed by adults (Warming, Chapter 1).
5   Contingency seems insufficient in the case of social work, where trust involves time and continuity in the relationship (Pinkney, Chapter 5). Adopting a developmental approach, Ule (Chapter 9) claims that past experiences of trustworthiness are necessary to ensure trust, and Christensen (Chapter 6) underlines the necessity of taking into account past experience. The problem is that individuals' past experiences cannot predict the form of a communication system, which is produced only through communication.

Bibliography

Baraldi, C. (2008) 'Promoting self-expression in classroom interactions', *Childhood*, 15(2): 239–57.
Baraldi, C. (ed.) (2009) *Dialogue in Intercultural Communities. From an Educational Point of View*, Amsterdam: John Benjamins.

Baraldi, C. (2010) 'Is cross-cultural mediation a technique? Theoretical/methodological frameworks and empirical evidence from interaction' in D. Busch, C. H. Mayer & C. M. Boness (eds) *International and Regional Perspectives on Cross-Cultural Mediation*, Frankfurt am Main: Peter Lang.

Baraldi, C. & F. Farini (2011) 'Dialogic mediation in international groups of adolescents', *Language and Dialogue*, 1(2): 207–32.

Baraldi, C. & L. Gavioli (2007) 'Dialogue interpreting as intercultural mediation: An analysis in healthcare multicultural settings' in M. Grein & E. Weigand (eds) *Dialogue and Cultures*, Amsterdam: John Benjamins, pp. 155–75.

Baraldi, C. & V. Iervese (2010) 'Dialogic mediation in conflict resolution education', *Conflict Resolution Quarterly*, 27(4): 423–45.

Baraldi, C. & V. Iervese (eds) (2012) *Participation, Facilitation, and Mediation. Children and Young People in Their Social Contexts*, London, New York: Routledge.

Baraldi, C. & E. Rossi (2011) 'Promotion of participation and mediation in multicultural classrooms', *Irish Educational Studies*, 30(3): 383–401.

Drew, P. & J. Heritage (eds) (1992) *Talk at Work: Interaction in Institutional Settings*, Cambridge: Cambridge University Press.

Farini, F. (2009) 'Activities 2: Coordinating reflection' in C. Baraldi (ed.) *Dialogue in Intercultural Communities. From an Educational Point of View*, Amsterdam: John Benjamins, pp. 155–72.

Gardner, R. (2001) *When Listeners Talk: Response Tokens and Listeners Stance*, Amsterdam: John Benjamins.

Giddens, A. (1990) *The Consequences of Modernity*, Cambridge: Polity Press.

Giddens, A. (1991) *Modernity and Self-Identity. Self and Society in the Late Modern Age*, Cambridge: Polity Press.

Giddens, A. (1992) *The Transformation of Intimacy*, Cambridge: Polity Press.

Goleman, D. (1995) *Emotional Intelligence*, New York: Bantam Books.

Gumperz, J. (1992) 'Contextualization and understanding' in A. Duranti & C. Goodwin (eds) *Rethinking Context: Language as an Interactive Phenomenon*, Cambridge: Cambridge University Press, pp. 229–53.

Harré, R. & van L. Langenhove (eds) (1999) *Positioning Theory*, Oxford: Blackwell.

Hengst, H. & H. Zeiher (eds) (2005) *Kindheit soziologisch*, Wiesbaden: VS Verlag für Sozialwissenschaften.

Heritage, J. (1985) 'Analysing news interviews: Aspects of the production of talk for an overhearing audience' in T. Van Dijk (ed.) *Handbook of Discourse Analysis, Vol. 3. Discourse and Dialogue*, London: Academic Press, pp. 95–117.

Heritage, J. & G. Raymond (2005) 'The terms of agreement: Indexing epistemic authority and subordination in talk-in-interaction', *Social Psychology Quarterly*, 68(1): 15–38.

Heritage, J. & L. Sorjonen (1994) 'Constituting and maintaining activities across sequences: And-prefacing as a feature of question design', *Language in Society*, 23: 1–29.

Hicks, D. (ed.) (1996) *Discourse, Learning, and Schooling*, Cambridge: Cambridge University Press.

Hill, M., J. Davis, A. Prout & K. Tisdall (2004) 'Moving the participation agenda forward', *Children & Society*, 18: 77–96.

Holdsworth, R. (2005) 'Taking young people seriously means giving them serious things to do' in J. Mason & T. Fattore (eds) *Children Taken Seriously. In Theory, Policy and Practice*, London: Jessica Kingsley Publishers, pp. 139–50.

Holland, S. & S. O'Neill (2006) 'We had to be there to make sure it was what we wanted. Enabling children's participation in family decision–making through the family group conference', *Childhood*, 13(1): 91–111.

Hutchby, I. (2007) *The Discourse of Child Counseling*, Amsterdam: John Benjamins.

Hutchby, I. & R. Wooffitt (1998) *Conversation Analysis*, Cambridge: Polity Press.

James, A. & A. L. James (2004) *Constructing Childhood. Theory, Policy and Social Practice*, Houndmills: Palgrave.

James, A., C. Jenks & A. Prout (1998) *Theorizing Childhood*, Oxford: Polity Press.

Jenks, C. (1996) *Childhood*, London: Routledge.

Kelman, H. (2005) 'Building trust among enemies: The central challenge for international conflict resolution', *International Journal of Intercultural Relations*, 29: 639–50.

Luhmann, N. (1968) *Vertrauen. Ein mechanismus der reduktion sozialer komplexität*, Stuttgart: Enke.

Luhmann, N. (1984) *Soziale Systeme*, Frankfurt am Main: Suhrkamp.

Luhmann, N. (1988) 'Familiarity, confidence, trust: Problems and alternatives' in D. Gambetta (ed.) *Trust: Making and Breaking Cooperative Relations*, Oxford: Department of Sociology, University of Oxford, pp. 94–107.

Luhmann, N. (1991) *Soziologie des Risikos*, Berlin: De Gruyter.

Luhmann, N. (1997) *Die Gesellschaft der gesellschaft*, Frankfurt am Main: Suhrkamp.

Matthews, H. (2003) 'Children and regeneration: Setting and agenda for community participation and integration', *Children & Society*, 17: 264–76.

Mehan, H. (1979) *Learning Lessons*, Cambridge, Massachusetts: Harvard University Press.

Mercer, N. & K. Littleton (2007) *Dialogue and Development of Children's Thinking*, London: Routledge.

Parsons, T. (1959) 'The school class as a social system: Some of its functions in American society', *Harvard Educational Review*, 29: 297–318.

Pearce, W. B. (1989) *Communication and the Human Condition*, Carbondale: Southern Illinois University Press.

Rogers, C. (1951) *Client-centred Therapy: Its Current Practice, Implications and Theory*, Boston: Houghton Mifflin.

Shier, H. (2001) 'Pathways to participation: Openings, opportunities and obligations', *Children & Society*, 15: 107–17.

Walsh, S. (2011) *Exploring Classroom Discourse. Language in Action*, London: Routledge.

Wyness, M. G. (1999) 'Childhood, agency and education reform', *Childhood*, 6(3): 353–68.

8
Negotiating 'Children's Best Interests' in the Context of Parental Migration

Maria-Carmen Pantea

The chapter explores how children and young people[1] with migrant parents internalise a citizenship identity shaped by a discourse focused on victimisation, uncertainty and institutional mistrust. It is built on the idea that citizenship is a learning process sustained by individual and collective narratives and consists of memories, shared values and experiences (Somers, 1995 cited in Delanty, 2003: 602). The chapter revisits the axis domination-resistance and the dichotomy trust-mistrust by taking into account children's strategies that avoid this binary. It suggests a more sensitive discussion of the dichotomy between trust and mistrust and argues that seeing children's reactions to governance in exclusively deliberately and confrontational ways (for example trust vs. mistrust) is providing an unrefined understanding of their experiences which are not necessarily antagonistic. In order to overcome this crude reflection of children's experiences in relation to power, the concept of slantwise actions is being proposed.

Originally developed by Campbell and Heyman (2007), the notion of slantwise actions denotes the unstructured experiences of coping or 'getting along'. The chapter is suggesting the consideration of the unintentional and accidental actions that are slantwise to power (not explicitly confrontational, but which may ultimately shape the power) in the interpretation of children and young people's reactions to governance.

This research suggests that the narrative model of victimisation cultivated by media and welfare institutions, shapes children's early learning of citizenship. The image of ideal childhood, based on bi-parental care, renders migration insensitive to children's 'real needs'. Ultimately, this approach is reifying the notion of ideal childhood as protected and free from adult-specific responsibilities and behaviours. Children and young people with migrant parents are being seen as victims with little control over their own lives or, on the contrary, uncontrollable, incompetent in taking care of themselves and their siblings in the absence of 'qualified adults'.

On the one hand, children and young people's relationships with state institutions such as school authorities and the Child Protection Agency may be experienced as mistrustful, disempowering, domineering or imagined as such. On the other hand, children and young people are not passive in the process of institution-provided governance and search for escape routes to resist interference in their everyday lives. Children and young people who pose barriers when interacting with state representatives are reciprocating the institutional mistrust. They internalise a sense of being different, marginal and subjected to institutional interference as part of their notion of citizenship.

Informed by public discourses and institutional practices based on mistrust, young people develop avoidant strategies of disengagement. They resonate with the concept of slantwise actions developed by Campbell and Heyman (2007). This rules out the potential risks and benefits of interacting with institutions. The slantwise actions become part of the way young people learn to relate outside their immediate circle characterised by a highly particularised trust. Transnational families, also, do not challenge the institutional narrative. Their response is for intimacy across borders and self-sufficiency. Avoidant strategies become a model which transnational families at large use 'to interpret their place in [society] and to act' (Delanty, 2003: 602).

This chapter suggests that by looking into the escape routes of children's interactions with institutions, new ways of understanding the dynamics of trust are likely to emerge. These are able to broaden the exclusionary either/or view of trust and to see slantwise actions not as expressions of a lack of citizenship, but as symptomatic of an institutional mode of governance.

Context of the research

The study is located in Romania, the home of half of the European children with migrant parents: 350,000 children out of 700,000 (AAS and UNICEF, 2008). Parents' migration needs to be conceptualised by considering its underpinning structural factors, namely: the prolonged and erratic economic transition, underemployment, the ambivalent function of the state as labour exporter, the local cultures of migration not related to poverty, as well as the Western consumption models and the demand for migrant labour force. Whether migration is in children's best interest is subject to various interpretations. This is also the case in terms of what damages children from transnational families. Debates on the care of children with migrant parents have invariably been met with anxiety at all levels, from the individual children and parents, to extended families, institutions and policy-makers. A possible reason is that, arguably, all actors have 'an interest in migration to work'[2] (Isaksen et al., 2008: 402). Under these circumstances, the issue of care is politically silenced and delegated to individuals to resolve, in a logic of self-governance. As argued later, the approach toward children with migrant parents fails to account for the structural context that generate migration, and instead, is turned into a personal matter of distress to be resolved individually. In the terms of Marston and McDonald (2006), this silenced governmental policy is itself a social artefact with its own trajectory. Keeping silence on migration, but potentially on other issues perceived as socially sensitive, is a political statement on self-governance. It is a policy situation in which taking no action means in fact, 'action'.

In such a general context, families secure their own private arrangements for navigating transnational life, with young people lacking trust in big institutions. The reverse also holds true as welfare institutions do not trust children's capacity to take care of themselves or their siblings, nor their capacity to participate in decision-making about their own lives. A narrative on 'children left behind' informs children's construction of citizenship identity in ways that are mistrustful to institutions.

By looking into the modes of governance exerted upon this group of children largely defined as vulnerable, this chapter examines their responses in ways that reflect the institutional mistrust, but also shows the search for alternative escape routes. The chapter also speaks about the intergenerational reproduction of the low institutional trust in former totalitarian societies, where the ethos of non-participation persists.

The chapter explores the intersection between migration and children/young people's governance at the structural level (legislation, media and social services), in a need to respond to the following questions: Which are the forms of citizenship that are being shaped by existing discourses on children with migrant parents? What are children and young people's responses to governance able to tell about their notion of citizenship and participation? More generally, to what extent is the dichotomy trust vs. mistrust instrumental in understanding children and young people's reactions to power?

Conceptual framework

Trust has been characterised by two elements, the first one being positive expectations, which denote that another's action will be beneficial rather than detrimental (Robinson, 1996: 576). The second element is the risk taking suggesting that where trust begins rational prediction ends (Luhmann, 1979: 25). This chapter will use an early sociological conceptualisation of trust as a 'collective attribute [...] applicable to the relations among people rather than to their psychological states taken individually' (Lewis & Weigert, 1985: 968). Trust is dynamic; it is built, increases, stabilises, enters dissolution (Rousseau et al., 1998) and is multidimensional. There are degrees and levels of trust. Interpersonal trust is the trust between people; institutional trust or system trust, refers to the trust in the functioning of organisational, institutional and social systems (Bijlsma-Frankema & Costa, 2005).

It has been argued that power attracted two lines of understanding: the structural, repressive and monolithic forms (Marx, Parsons, Durkheim) that characterise political and economic systems, and the more dynamic conception of power, as embedded in human relations (Gramsci, Foucault, Giddens). According to these last authors, power is not an intrinsic propriety of individuals but is inherent in human relations, like those between parents and their children (Groves & Chang, 1999). In a Foucauldian sense, power is not always repressive and one of its critical forms is the way people are made subjects of (self)-government.[3]

Children and young people's reactions to the power exerted by adults and adult-centred institutions have been generally understood as situated on an axis that starts with domination and ends with resistance. Naturalised domination denotes '"differentials of power [that] come already embodied in culture", in which "power appears natural, inevitable, even god-given" in domains such as gender, kinship, race, nation and class' (Yanagisako & Delaney, 1995 cited in Campbell & Heyman, 2007: 5).

Together with naturalised domination, resistance is a reaction to power and one of the most prevalent concepts embraced by the sociological literature on childhood, which tends to overlook that other options are also possible. One major characteristic of resistance is its intentional character. Initially theorised by Gramsci, everyday resistance refers to the small, seemingly trivial daily acts through which subordinate individuals or groups undermine, rather than overthrow, oppressive relations of power (Gramsci, 1971 cited in Groves & Chang, 1999: 235). Importantly, resistance 'is reserved for actions and meanings actors themselves understand to be defiant' and should be distinguished from accidental defiance and avoidance (Campbell & Heyman, 2007: 4).

As the paper will show, children and young people's reactions to power cannot be seen exclusively on a resistance-domination axis. According to Campbell and Heyman (2007), slantwise actions is a concept able to describe the category of unintentional responses, unstructured experiences used by children for coping or 'getting along'. They include accidental reactions that are not reducible to intentional resistance or internalised domination. Such actions that do not fit the resistance vs. internalised domination axis are to be understood as the best solutions at hand for dealing with crisis situations and are unintentional, neither explicitly resisting, nor dominated by adult governance. In its initial interpretation, the concept was used for reflecting the housing arrangements developed by illegal immigrants at the US border (Campbell & Heyman, 2007).

The concept of slantwise actions is able to facilitate our understanding of the complex ways children and young people rely on persons and institutions, beyond trust and mistrust. It has been said that one can either trust or not trust a person, institution and so on (Hardin, 1992). Also, it is by now common place that trust functions as a way of 'reducing the complexity' (Luhmann, 1979: 418). This chapter suggests that the responses to the complexity of social interactions are more intricate than the dichotomy trust vs. mistrust, even acknowledging the multidimensionality of trust. As this chapter demonstrates, children and young people initiate a variety of responses that include, beyond trust and mistrust, the unstructured avoidant strategies of disengagement. It involves spontaneous refusal to deal with the complexity of potential consequences of both trusting and mistrusting, when other escape routes are available.

Children's understanding of and responses to power can be incorporated into the notion of citizenship. Traditionally, its definitions excluded children. Yet, alternative conceptualisations of citizenship have been proposed. One of them is the notion of cultural citizenship. According to Delanty (2003), unlike normative, disciplinary citizenship, cultural citizenship does not refer to rights or memberships, but is an ongoing process conducted in communicative links. It entails 'the learning of a capacity for action and for responsibility but, essentially, it is about the learning of the self and of the relationship of self and other' (Delanty, 2003: 602). Thus, central to cultural citizenship are language, discourses and cultural models people use to make sense of their society, to interpret their place in it, and to act (Delanty, 2003).

Methodology

The chapter is based mainly on secondary sources involving an unsystematic literature review that included research papers, media articles on migration archived in a UNICEF Daily Press catalogue, NGO reports and legislation. For the empirical work, we undertook 16 in-depth interviews with 14 children and young people from Romania experiencing the migration of at least one parent. The discussion does not embark in a detailed account on the information collected, which has been described elsewhere (Pantea, 2011). In this discussion, only the instances able to inform a better understanding of young people's trust, governance and citizenship are included.

The age of interviewees ranged from 14 to 19, with an average of 17. They experienced different patterns of parental migration, from migration in the context of family dissolution and quasi-abandonment, to cyclical migration of one or both parents. At the time of interviewing, all participants had at least one parent abroad. The fieldwork included the interviewing of seven parents and five social workers from communities with high incidence of migration. Unrecorded notes were coded successively in Nvivo8. The identity of research participants is protected by anonymity.

Discourses and policies on children with migrant parents

According to Foucault, discourses are groups of regular and systematic statements that are either spoken or written, articulated rules, roles and procedures.[4] They are produced by and through institutions (Danaher et al., 2000). Discourses on children with migrant parents are mainly a product of legislation, media and social services. Ultimately, families themselves articulate their own beliefs and values that legitimise or reprove migration. In a move of 'constant readjustment' (King, 1999 cited in Piper, 2005: 8), certain sets of assumptions are being shared and circulate between media, law, social services and families.

Discourses on migration do matter, as they provide the framework of actions and identity work and thus enable children to learn a particular model of cultural citizenship. As the chapter maintains, the narratives and commonly held beliefs on migration shape the way cultural citizenship is being learned and exercised by children and young people in transnational families (Delanty, 2003). Also, the understanding of children's best interests constitutes a key aspect in the governance of childhood. The following part will examine the discourses that shape the way children learn citizenship and the understanding of their best interests.

State policies and the invisibility of children with migrant parents

There has not been much debate on family life in post-communist Romania. Migration opened up the private area of family and generated contested notions of proper parenting. Work abroad started as a short-term solution for families in the 1990s and as a strategy for the state that later organised recruitment campaigns for temporary employment in the EU. Whether migrants had children did not seem to enter either state or media interest at the time.

It was not until 2006 that authorities acknowledged the issue and required migrants to make legal the guardianship of the children 'left behind'. Notoriously unsuccessful, with only 7 per cent of the migrant parents officially entrusting their children to members of the extended family (AAS & UNICEF, 2008), the requirement became a binding law in 2011 with apparently not much change following. With all its shortcomings, the law on guardianship remains the only official space for acknowledging *children with* migrant parents, although the way of doing so is by focusing on *migrants with* children.

The law does not seem to be sensitive to the actual circumstances of migration, which are mainly temporary and circular, in the grey economy, and it has a repressive character.[5] Also, the requirements of guardianship are hard to meet.[6] Besides being unknown to migrants, the legal conditions are sometimes difficult to be met even by local administration, for example psychological testing of the proposed guardian. If registered, the person providing the care, usually a grandparent, will be qualified to represent the child in its relations with institutions, including schools, medical settings and police.

In a Foucauldian understanding, by virtue of direct governmental control, both young people and their parents are being made subjects of state governance. The law regards young people as dependants and is exclusively directed at their parents who seem to resent leaving a door open for state interventionism in family life, or do not meet the intricate criteria for registering the caregiver. However, even if the law is focused on children, there is no stipulation for their participation in the decision on guardianship that is definitely influencing their lives. There seems to be no consistent policies for creating the enabling circumstances for parents to meet the same economic goals without leaving their children against their will, or migrating together. In

2007 the government attempted unsuccessfully to encourage voluntary repatriation by organising labour fairs abroad. The reasons for the lack of uptake of the scheme were exclusively economic.

The sociopolitical assumptions of the law on parental responsibility for children are not new, but the social and political willingness to blame parents for various social ills is recent (Piper, 2005: 252). Its resulting norm is the tendency of the state to reduce expenditure on social welfare, in this case by reinforcing migrant parents' responsibility for their children. This choice is far from being politically innocent. It echoes the Foucauldian concept of responsibilisation, a governance procedure for 'the making of' social subjects; parents (as citizens) are called to be responsible for themselves and their children, so that state institutions do not have to intervene. This ubiquitous strategy can be read as a regulatory 'technology of citizenship and self-government' (Cruikshank, 1991 cited in Mckee, 2009: 469), by which the government tacitly finds its way into transnational families.

The high fines for breaking the law are associated with a low level of trust in parents' capacity 'to govern' their children. Conversely, these repressive regulations further weaken parents' trust in social services, manifested by the low percentage of those actually legalising the situation of children at home. Resenting a communist legacy of state intrusiveness in family life, migrants and children pose barriers to state intervention and secure their own arrangements for navigating a transnational livelihood.

A proposal advanced in an electoral campaign considered forbidding both parents to migrate simultaneously (Filimon, 2010). The main argument was that 'money obtained abroad does not justify the abandonment of children at critical ages' (Minca cited in Filimon, 2010). Whilst the proposal was meant to protect children's interests, it would definitely limit parents' right to travel to find work. The idea attracted high criticism as it recalled communist repressive practices of state interference in family life and an unrealistic view of the economic constrains that push parents to migrate in the first place.

On the whole, children with migrant parents have only recently become of interest to the state as a problem which is hard to resolve because of mutual mistrust. Whilst the considerable migrant remittances received a sensible level of public acknowledgement, the responsibility for children is delegated, in a logic of self-governance, to individual families liable to secure their private solutions for childcare.

Media: Children with migrant parents and the notion of risk

The state policies followed media interest in migration. Transnational families are portrayed as endorsing deviations from the normative childhood. Instances of child suicides, accidental injuries and death as a consequence of neglect have become recurrent themes.

Media attitudes go from reinforcing a sacrificial model, toward implied contestations of parenthood. Both approaches endorse the conventional gender roles, with media higher propensity to identify instances of children at risk following mothers' migration. In this context, migration is implicitly defined as a problem and children, its victims. This discourse frames an understanding of the children 'left behind' as marginalised and deficient.

More recently, instances of children with migrant parents have been portrayed as autonomous and uncontrollable adding to the previous notions of 'deserted' children. A common theme is the pattern of excessive consumption, as co-modification of parental care. Yet, concerns over school truancy, dropout, aggressive behaviour, delinquency, teen pregnancy and drug use have also attracted the attention of the media. The anti-social behaviour of some young people is attributed to the diminished effectiveness of parents from afar and increased distrust as the only mechanism of governance available to them.

Parents' migration becomes a common interpretative grid for explaining young people's negative agency,[7] although 'one shouldn't hold parents accountable for everything. Some young people will act out with or without their parents being at home' (Olivia, 18 years old). Anti-social behaviour turns young people with migrant parents into eligible candidates for increased disciplining efforts by the state that, conversely, weakens their institutional trust.

Ultimately, all these behaviours are not presented as deviations from the logic of victimisation, or expressions of agency, but can be interpreted as children's defensive mechanisms or coping strategies to the dysfunctional family processes. They actually confirm the idea of children as dominated by processes of family separation. Paraphrasing Jenks (1996), in such rather crude way, children from transnational families are seen 'either dangerous or in danger' (Jenks, 1996 cited in Gallacher & Gallagher, 2008: 499). This resonates with a broader anxiety over children and young people in general and, by using this rhetoric, media also activates vague notions of class.[8]

Overall, media discourses tend to ignore the potential differences between the experiences of children and young people. Whilst half of those with both parents abroad are below ten years old (AAS & UNICEF, 2008), the other half are above this age and may tend to think of themselves in terms of agency. The dichotomy children vs. adults constructs children as passive, helpless, dependent and leaves no specific room for young people as a social group (Davidson, 2005 cited in Smette et al., 2009: 369). This process is responsible for the lack of a parallel discourse on the young people 'left behind'.

Thus, their roles in care provision do not receive the due acknowledgement. On the contrary, the law requiring the guardian to be at least 18 years older than those being cared for, increases the mistrust and isolation of the young people who do engage in caring relationships with siblings or grandparents. Informed by these regulatory discourses, young people internalise the ambivalent and cautious feeling that their participation is, in fact, sanctionable and should be safeguarded from institutional intrusion.

Furthermore, media prioritises the notion of individual choice at the expense of making explicit the structural forces that surround migration. This de-contextualisation of migration leaves the space open for the assumed culpability of parents and for the de-politicisation of migration. Issues like unemployment, poverty and the International Monetary Fund shock programme to Romania remain more or less silenced. Young people's participation in the reproduction of care is a private, potentially sanctionable matter of self-governance. Besides, by framing migration in terms of children's needs and less in structural terms, media and parents reinforce children's sense of culpability.

Seen as victims or as actors with negative agency, with little control over their own lives, or on the contrary, uncontrollable, incompetent in taking care of themselves and their siblings in the absence of 'qualified adults', children and young people internalise marginal notions of citizenship. This is based on a sense of being atypical, vulnerable, in the mistrustful position of always questioning the quality of their family relations when weighed against the normative notion of 'functional family'. Overall, the discourses on the 'children left behind' reify the categories of children 'at risk' and improper parenting.

Social services: From 'fixing' children to seeing the positive side of migration

As a former totalitarian state, Romania has a legacy of state interventionism in family life. In recent years, state interventionism is being legitimised only in extreme situations. However, the recent legislation regards all children with migrant parents as being at risk and thus eligible for some sort of professional intervention. Migrant parents and their children fit the profile of the 'open textured' families (Ruddick,

1982 cited in Moosa-Mitha, 2005: 384) who are more deliberately surveyed and regulated by state institutions.

Following media, victimisation of children from transnational families became the prevalent approach in social services. The basis for intervention is often local and informed by an understanding of migration and its potentially negative effects upon development. The social work institutions fail in acknowledging that migration is a social reality far more intricate, uncertain and ambiguous. With rare exceptions, interventions addressing children with migrant parents have been delegated (in an alleged ethic of care) to the (feminised) NGO sector. It may also be that children with migrant parents represent such a 'sensitive matter', and are such a diverse group, that a governmental policy able to attract a high level of endorsement is from the very beginning hazardous.

NGOs tend to embrace a victimising approach of children with migrant parents. Their interventions employ a passive view of children and tend to focus on crisis situations and cases of *de facto* abandonment, ignoring the potential benefits of migration (Piperno, 2011). The unit of reference is the family, with no aim at generating awareness at the structural context in which migration takes place. Frequently grounded in a psychological understanding of the consequences of migration, NGOs tend to employ clinical approaches, which focus on the destabilising effects of migration on the social-emotional development of children. This includes introversion, social anxiety, isolation, disruptive behaviours as defence mechanisms and suicidal thoughts. Children with migrant parents are thus defined as groups at risk, in need for psychological assistance if not rehabilitation. 'Fixing children' in order to enable them to cope with migration has become the NGO conventional approach.

Impelled by practical reasons, institutions, NGOs included, apply a reductionist perspective over the experiences of living in transnational families. However, young people's attitudes are more complex, intricate and fluid, including sometimes conflicting combinations of solidarity with the migrant, empathy, care giving and a sense of sacrifice but also a commodification of love, uncertainties, mistrust and blame. As this complexity of feelings does not receive due acknowledgement, one could describe young people's relation within the social services as being grounded in an 'absence of recognition' (Delanty, 2003: 603). This further weakens young people's institutional trust.

However, in rural areas where NGOs are less active, if not totally absent, local authorities perceive migration as a solution. In large villages from the North[9] where employment is scarce, migration is seen as a solution and there does not seem to be a problem in having children being cared for by the extended families, usually grandparents. Concepts of abandonment and neglect, largely circulated by media and NGOs, are perceived as improper. It is argued that the needs of children with migrant parents are being met by the extended family and through remittances, whilst the absence of migration is actually making the most vulnerable dependent on means-tested state provisions. This position may be read as an alienating consequence of scarcity or of an economically driven notion of community. A stronger sense of social capital may be able to attenuate the social route which reinforces an unforeseen division between deserving and undeserving young people.

Children and young people's responses to governance

Generally, children and young people's responses to governance went through a rather dichotomous understanding, according to which they either trust or do not trust the institutions meant to assist them, or either submit or resist to the power exerted by adults or adult-centred institutions. Previous scholarship on children's relation to power tended to overemphasise resistance: either in its manifest, or in its more subtle forms of challenging the adult exertion of power (the so called 'everyday resistance'). Resistance is an expression of mistrust.

Although a discourse on children's resistance to adult governance might sound appealing to the growing research on children's agency and resistance, their experience in the context of parental migration cannot be read exclusively through these confrontational lenses. Neither is trust vs. mistrust a dichotomy able to capture the complex ways children and young people relate to institutions.

This chapter argues that resistance in all its forms, either understood as intentional reactions to power or based on mistrust,[10] is not the only way of relying to power.[11] The main argument is that not all children's reactions to power are intentional and meant to undermine, contest or suppress the power represented by adults and institutions. Recent research advises that reactions to power are more complex and go beyond the dichotomy of resistance versus domination and arguably, also beyond trust versus mistrust. There are other more complex models of nonintentional reactions to power, like accidental defiance, improvisation or avoidance. In the previous literature, these were erroneously forced into resistance and arguably mistrust, despite not having meanings defined as defiant by actors themselves (Campbell & Heyman, 2007).

Campbell and Heyman's concept of slantwise actions was initially applied to interpreting the housing arrangements developed by illegal immigrants at the US border. Understood as an ideal type, slantwise action does not replace resistance or internalised domination, but is a useful tool in understanding unintentional actions like 'getting by'. In Campbell and Heyman's understanding, slantwise is an 'outside-observer-based (ethic) category' (Campbell & Heyman, 2007: 4). According to its authors, the concept comes at a time when 'the binary conceptualization of resistance versus domination, while productive, has entered its mature phase and increasingly shows its limitations as ethnographers try heavy-handedly to label diverse phenomena as either resistance or domination' (Campbell & Heyman, 2007: 26–7).

In the logic of slantwise actions, children and young people with migrant parents try to navigate parental absence in ways that are neither subversive, nor self-victimising, and which minimise the risks involved in trust. They develop a close understanding of migration both by trusting their parents' choices and by trying to make ends meet in sometimes-hostile environments. As these experiences are not spectacular, they risk escaping the media and the ethnographic accounts which are often informed by a scholarship on mistrust, or the one of resistance vs. internalised domination.

As interviews demonstrate, children and young people's stories are not necessarily confrontational. For instance, Mona, a girl of 15 who was left in charge of her younger sister of seven, claimed their parents are 'at work in the afternoon shift' when she attended parents' meetings at school or when she accompanied her sick sister to the emergency room. Her action was not intentionally aimed at resisting or submitting to the institutional governance over children in her situation. Mona did not trust institutions to deliver anything by virtue of being 'a child left behind'. Her parents abroad, she was happy for institutions to leave her alone and sort her own problems out. In Hardin's terms, her behaviour also activates an element of class, as young people who are socioeconomically deprived are thought to be more distrustful than others (Hardin, 1992).

In situations like the above, inside the family, the care provided by a child to another was considered a sensible solution to parental migration. It is in the larger institutional area that children are regarded as recipients of care and where such situations are regarded as 'dysfunctional' and 'false maturity' (Frank, 1995 cited in Cockburn, 2005: 82). In Mona's frame of reference, stating that parents are on the afternoon shift is making sense. She does not understand her statement as defiant or mistrustful, and does not aim at implicitly challenging the institutional power exerted upon her. Mona did not interpret her action as either resistant or compliant, either trustful nor mistrustful. She learned practically, through her everyday actions, the institutional narratives of migration, and acted accordingly. In Campbell and Heyman terms, her behaviour would 'not fit neatly into the domination-resistance axis' (Campbell & Heyman, 2007: 3) and, arguably, neither in the trust vs. mistrust dichotomy. In Grounded Theory logic, Mona's slantwise action is to be understood as the best solution at hand for dealing with a crisis situation in parents' absence. This may involve unintentional actions and escape routes that are neither explicitly resisting, distrustful nor dominated by adult governance.

In such situations, young people anticipate a low level of structural trust from institutions. Schools, hospitals, welfare agencies are potentially unreceptive, complex and thus an investment of trust is unlikely to bring any gains. Consequently, the response is for disengagement from what Baraldi and Farini (Chapter 7) called 'adults' expert guidance'. Yet, this situation may not totally exclude a trustful relation with an atypical adult, working in the very same institutional structure (for example, a teacher who is very familiar with the situation). Yet, as shown in Warming (2011), such adults are themselves marginal and powerless in shaping what Hayward (2010) called 'the institutionalization of identity stories' (Hayward, 2010: 659). Institutions remain stable in their dominant narratives, while young people may opt for avoidant slantwise strategies.

Flavia, 16 years old, having troubles at school, is faced with other parents' accusations directed against her allegedly careless migrant mother. With a long history of parental absence, she is now able to describe the situation as tragic-comical: 'I didn't know whether to cry or to laugh'. This type of reaction, neither resistance nor domination, has been instrumental in Flavia's psychological escape from the otherwise intrusive situation. It can enter the category of slantwise action, unintentional and relevant in another frame of reference. Here, Flavia's detachment is displayed differently from the commonly assumed dramas of children with migrant parents. This is simultaneously a silenced statement of disengagement from any trust-based relation. This option is the most practical solution in her economy of relations with persons and institutions outside her immediate cycle.

Such avoidant behaviours seem to be informed by high interpersonal trust – or strong ties to similar others – and a certain uneasiness when relating to institutions. They are not necessarily informed and purposeful expressions of institutional mistrust, but rather options for avoidance, enabled by the high value attached to strong ties. Interviewed young people with migrant parents seemed more likely to rely upon traditional, informal sources of support to navigate parental absence and did not seem to be aware of the eventual institutional assistance. These responses fit the model of slantwise reaction.

Implications for children's participation and citizenship

According to Delanty (2003), citizenship is a learning process that begins early in life. It 'takes place in communicative situations arising out of quite ordinary life experiences, but it can also arise out of major crises and catastrophes such as the experience of victimhood or injustice' (Delanty, 2003: 603). A central dimension of the cognitive experience of citizenship appears to be 'the way in which individual life stories are connected with wider cultural discourses' (Delanty, 2003: 603). How is the reciprocal lack of trust between children with migrant parents and institutions likely to impact their experience of citizenship? What are the slantwise actions able to tell about children's notion of participation?

This research suggests that discourses on children with migrant parents as victims or as uncontrollable agents function as a narrative that shapes their perception, judgement, choices and, ultimately, their notion of citizenship. Whilst legal and media discourses are gaining legitimisation, children's perspectives remain out of sight. The law on guardianship, informed by a lack of trust in both migrants and their children, does not require children's participation in a decision that will influence their life. Also, those who improved their lives following parent's migration or who are coping well with their absence are not represented in the discourse of child welfare services. In this way, an ideology on transnational families is being created: 'when an account is constructed, inserting a ruling conceptual frame and suppressing the experience of the "subject" of the lived actuality that the account claims to be about, the account is said to be ideological' (Campbell, 2001: 243).

The official discourse of the law, the media and ultimately the family seem to emphasise the rhetoric of children as objects of care and of parents acting on their behalf. From the ubiquitous discourse on 'children left behind', young people internalise a sense of marginality, an idea of exclusion from a commonly accepted notion of family, a sense of parental powerlessness in dealing with more structural limitations and disconnection from the institutional networks. Young people's distress ultimately brought about by social and economic processes is turned into a personal pathology. Social services are in the position to assist at individual level and less to question the very structure that perpetuates the patterns of migration as an individual solution to a structural lack of choices. It is not by chance that the option of families and children is to retreat from institutional interactions from which they appear disconnected anyway. In the web of institutions, these families remain inaccessible and children help maintain the distance by reciprocating mistrust or by the escape routes of slantwise actions.

This chapter calls for a more refined understanding of children's age when discussing migration. Both media and social services tend to assume the legal definition of the child as a person below 18, an approach not always sensitive to the situation of those who may not regard themselves as children when arrangements on migration are being made. A hypothetical discourse on 'youth left behind' would not attract the same victimising discourses and need for control, either from the state, its institutions or from families. By acknowledging the large variety of transnational families, more informed policy approaches addressing children and young people alike could be advanced.

A condition for children's participation and citizenship requires more integrative discourses and mutual trust between children or families and the welfare institutions. This is indeed a challenge, as the current discourses are objectified and institutionalised. In Hayward's terms, the current narrative on 'children left behind' is one of the 'bad stories' that cannot simply be radically changed, as 'the institutionalisation of identity stories lends them resilience in the face of challenge and critique' (Hayward, 2010: 659). The solution would be to change the very institutions: rules, law and policies, which are the moulds into which children's alienation, stigmatisation and exclusion have been built.

Conclusion

The social construction of children with migrant parents fluctuates from children being seen as i) victims of economic transition, of poor state policy and consumption-driven parenting, ii) objects of care in an official self-governing policy of delegating the responsibility for childcare to families, or iii) invisible and under-recognised participants in the transnational dynamics of labour. This situation tends to confirm the argument that 'the more one is in a position to make decisions for children, to speak on their behalf, the more one is able to silence their voices' (Lee, 2001: 10). The corollary of this 'absence of recognition' (Delanty, 2003: 603) is the lack of trust.

It has been argued that in Eastern Europe in general, children and young people do not seem to trust any big institutions. This was largely linked with the political past (Roberts, 2009; Vladimirov et al., 1999 cited in Ådnanes, 2007; Growiec & Growiec, 2010). The current research suggests that the opposite is also true: institutions do not trust young people, they are subjected to control, regulation and condescending attitudes. Research on social work with children in foster care in Denmark also highlights children's experiences of control, disciplining and blame instead of involvement, listening and responsive support (Warming, 2011).

Do children resist the governance exerted upon them in the context of parental migration and mistrust, or do they submit to the power exerted upon them by adults and institutions? The response is problematic, if at all possible. Interviews with young people identifies experiences of resistance and internalised domination as extreme instances in the exercise of power and trust dynamics. Children with migrant parents do try to resist outside governance, either by apparently minor gestures of undermining adult authority or through confrontational reactions. Also, at times, they may accept the power exerted upon them by institutions, caregivers or parents. Whilst children with migrant parents do display reactions that are overtly resistant and mistrustful or, on the contrary, submissive to the adult exerted governance, their responses are not always situated on this axis. This research suggests that in their various degrees, trust and mistrust are not able to cover the whole spectrum of possible ways young people relate to governance.

Sociology of childhood advanced the understanding that responses to adult governance are either based on resistance or internalised domination. Governance of children and young people is grounded in a semantic area of power, control, resistance, trust and mistrust. However, seeing children's reactions to the governance exerted upon them in exclusively deliberate and confrontational ways provides an unrefined understanding of children's experiences that are not necessarily antagonistic.

This chapter has shown that the dichotomies of resistance vs. domination and trust vs. mistrust are unable to describe children's reactions to power that are not always intentional. It suggested that the concept of slantwise actions initially developed by Campbell and Heyman (2007) can be used for explaining children's accidental and unintentional reactions to power and for refining the dichotomy trust vs. mistrust. When faced with situations liable to destabilise the sometimes precarious *status quo*, children and young people with migrant parents may opt for escape routes. These simultaneously cancel out the perceived costs of investing trust and avoid the potential losses of mistrust. Any potential benefits are also annulled in what appears to be an option for autonomy.[12]

Ultimately, classifying children's reactions to the power exerted upon them as being based on trust or mistrust, carries political meaning and is able to mobilise or prevent interventions. When the notion that children invariably trust institutions is assumed, potentially adultocratic solutions for the management of their best interest are likely to follow. Alternatively, categorising young people as mistrustful makes them subjected to disciplining measures. By including the option of slantwise actions, or avoidant escape routes that reject the engagement in either trustful or mistrustful relations, questions about the role of institutions are likely to follow.

Although in its proposed conceptualisation in Campbell and Heyman (2007) the notion is more complex, its value for the sociology of childhood can be highlighted in at least two directions. First, it is able to be a more accurate reflection of children and young people's experiences, which cannot always be integrated on the resistance vs. internalised domination axis or into the trust vs. mistrust dichotomy. Second, the examination of slantwise actions is able to contribute to the debate on rights vs. welfare policy approaches, while informing the two discourses by a more nuanced understanding of children's experiences. The main limitation of this chapter is being only able to indicate the existence of actions that do not fit in the pre-existent axis resistance vs. domination or trust vs. mistrust, without further expansion of the concept. As the value of looking into the slantwise actions and reactions is manifold, it may be applied to other areas of inquiry as for example children's responses to parental separation, displacement and foster care.

Notes

1 During the paper, interchangeable reference will be made to the terms 'children/ young people', as although technically many participants can be considered 'children', they do not identify themselves with the term.
2 Reasons may range from the high value of remittances (between 3–5 per cent of GDP), to higher consumption at home and employment prospects abroad.
3 Here, *government* is to be understood as 'the conduct of conduct'.
4 According to Hayward (2010), they are not always reproduced in discursive forms, but also learned practically, through everyday actions in institutional contexts.
5 It involves, for instance, high fines for not registering a guardian and impromptu visits from the social workers when registering.

6 They stipulate that the guardian has to be a relative with at least the minimum income guaranteed and at least 18 years older than the child to be cared for, full physical and psychological capacity, no disabling conditions or previous parenting convictions, no more than three other children in care.

7 According to Dominelli (2002, cited in Moosa-Mitha, 2005: 386), agency implies an 'active self' that can be used in either positive or negative ways.

8 See, for instance, the depreciatory terms used in Romanian media in order to denote migrant parents as 'strawberry pickers'.

9 Situation documented in Romania's North region of Maramures and in villages with large non-migrant Roma populations. For similar findings, see also AAS and UNICEF, 2008 and SFR, 2007.

10 According to Hardin (1992), trust (in its various degrees) is a precondition for action.

11 Nevertheless, the paper does not oppose the idea that power is embedded in children's lives, that children are living in a condition of 'naturalised domination' (Yanagisako & Delaney, 1995 cited in Campbell & Heyman, 2007: 5) or that ultimately, childhood is 'a state of oppression' (Kitzinger, 2006: 182).

12 Sometimes sustained by pre-existent interpersonal trust.

Bibliography

Ådnanes, M. (2007) 'Social transitions and anomie among post-communist Bulgarian youth', *Young*, 15(1): 49–69.

Asociatia Alternative Sociale (AAS) & UNICEF (2008) *Analiza la nivel national asupra fenomenului copiilor ramasi acasa prin plecarea parintilor la munca in strainatate*, Bucharest: UNICEF.

Bijlsma-Frankema, K. & A. Costa (2005) 'Understanding the trust-control nexus', *International Sociology*, 20(3): 259–82.

Campbell, H. & J. Heyman (2007) 'Slantwise. Beyond domination and resistance on the border', *Journal of Contemporary Ethnography*, 36(1): 3–30.

Campbell, M. (2001) 'Textual accounts, ruling action: The intersection of knowledge and power in the routine conduct of community nursing work', *Culture and Organization*, 7(2): 231–50.

Cockburn, T. (2005) 'Children and the feminist ethic of care', *Childhood*, 12(1): 71–89.

Danaher, G., T. Schirato & J. Webb (2000) *Understanding Foucault*, London: Sage Publications.

Delanty, G. (2003) 'Citizenship as a learning process: Disciplinary citizenship versus cultural citizenship', *International Journal of Lifelong Education*, 22(6): 597–605.

Filimon, S. (2010) 'Liliana Minca vrea sa interzica plecarea la munca in strainatate a ambilor parinti', *7est*, Bucharest, 20 April 2010, http://www.ziare.com/articole/minca+parinti+strainatate, date accessed November 2011.

Gallacher, L. & M. Gallagher (2008) 'Methodological immaturity in childhood research? Thinking through "participatory methods"', *Childhood*, 15(4): 499–516.

Groves, J. & K. Chang (1999) 'Romancing resistance and resisting romance ethnography and the construction of power in the Filipina domestic worker community in Hong Kong', *Journal of Contemporary Ethnography*, 28(3): 235–65.

Growiec, K. & J. Growiec (2010) 'Trusting only whom you know, knowing only whom you trust: The joint impact of social capital and trust on individuals' economic performance and well-being in CEE countries', *MPRA Paper No. 23350*, Warsaw: Institute for Structural Research.

Hardin, R. (1992) 'The street-level epistemology of trust', *Analyse und Kritik*, 14: 152–76.

Hayward, C. (2010) 'Bad stories: Narrative, identity, and the state's materialist pedagogy', *Citizenship Studies*, 14(6): 651–66.

Isaksen, L. W., S. Uma Devi & A. Hochschild (2008) 'Global care crisis. A problem of capital, care chain, or commons?', *American Behavioral Scientist*, 52(3): 405–25.

Kitzinger, J. (2006) 'Who are you kidding? Children, power and the struggle against sexual abuse' in A. James & A. Prout (eds) *Constructing and Reconstructing Childhood: Contemporary Issues in the Sociological Study of Childhood*, London: Routledge, pp. 165–89.

Lee, N. (2001) *Childhood and Society. Growing Up in an Age of Uncertainty*, London: Open University Press.

Lewis, J. D. & A. Weigert (1985) 'Trust as a social reality', *Social Forces*, 63(4): 967–85.

Luhmann, N. (1979) *Trust and Power*, Chichester: Wiley.

Marston, G. & C. McDonald (2006) 'Introduction: Reframing social policy analysis' in G. Marston & C. McDonald (eds) *Analysing Social Policy: A Governmental Approach*, Albingdon: Edward Elgar, pp. 1–15.

Mckee, K. (2009) 'Post-Foucauldian governmentality: What does it offer critical social policy analysis?', *Critical Social Policy*, 29(3): 465–86.

Moosa-Mitha, M. (2005) 'A difference-centred alternative to theorization of children's citizenship rights', *Citizenship Studies*, 9(4): 369–88.

Pantea, M. (2011) 'Young people's perspectives on changing families' dynamics of power in the context of parental migration', *Young*, 19(4): 375–95.

Piper, C. (2005) 'Moral campaigns for children's welfare in the nineteenth century' in H. Hendrick (ed.) *Child Welfare and Social Policy*, London: Routledge, pp. 7–13.

Piperno, F. (2011) 'The impact of female emigration on families and the welfare state in countries of origin: The case of Romania', *Migration Studies*, iFirst.

Roberts, K. (2009) *Youth in Transition. Eastern Europe and the West*, London: Palgrave Macmillan.

Robinson, S. L. (1996) 'Trust and breach of the psychological contract', *Administrative Science Quarterly*, 41: 574–99.

Rousseau, D., Sitkin & Burt (1998) 'Introduction to special topic forum. Not so different after all: A crossdiscipline view of trust', *Academy of Management Review*, 23(3): 393–404.

Smette, I., K. Stefansen & S. Mossige (2009) 'Responsible victims? Young people's understandings of agency and responsibility in sexual situations involving underage girls', *Young*, 17(4): 351–73.

Soros Foundation Romania (SFR) (2007) *Effects of Migration: Children Left at Home*, Bucharest: SFR.

UNICEF (2008) *Peste 8% din copiii României au p_rin_ii pleca_i la munc_ în str_in_tate*, www.unicef.org/romania/ro/media_8657.html, date accessed November 2011.

Warming, H. (2011) 'Children's participation and citizenship in a global age: Empowerment, tokenism or discriminatory disciplining?', *Social Work & Society*, 9(1): 119–34.

9
'I trust my mom the most': Trust Patterns of Contemporary Youth

Mirjana Ule

This chapter examines the effects of changed social relations during the period of transition on the extent and structure of trust among young people in Slovenia.[1] We proceed from the assumption that a high level of generalised trust is of crucial importance in motivating young people to participation and civility. Yet at the same time we find a low level of generalised trust among young people in Slovenia and a contraction of trust confined to people from the personal sphere. We discuss the negative consequences which these circumstances have on young people's ability to cope with the hyper-complex social conditions of the modern world and for their social and political citizenship.

The life experience of young people in modern industrial societies has undergone fundamental changes over the past two decades. These changes are partly due to circumstances which transcend national borders, such as the restructuring of the labour market and the increasing demand for a new, highly specialised, flexible and educated labour force, as well as social policy measures which have just about everywhere extended the period of dependence of young people on their families. Some of these changes are specific to the so-called 'transition countries', which moved rapidly from socialism to a market economy and parliamentary democracy (Ule, 2010).

The central concepts developed by social scientists over the last two decades to explain the structural changes in growing up and life courses are the individualisation, de-standardisation and deregulation of growing up (Heinz, 1997). These concepts are used to cover new institutions for the socialisation of individuals, the pluralisation of life conditions, patterns and styles of growing up and life courses (Beck & Beck-Gernsheim, 2002). These are not normative concepts which would lead people towards a more independent way of life, but rather a theoretical description of factors which shape both the socially structural as well as subjective level of changes in modern societies. It encompasses the ambivalence of social and psychological processes and structures produced by this new phase of modernisation.

One of the definitive signs of the process of individualisation is that it also implies the shifting of social demands, responsibility, supervision and organisation onto individuals. However, this does not mean that people for this reason become independent of external control and social restrictions. On the contrary, individuals remain dependent in a multitude of ways on the labour market, educational and social institutions, consumption, legal codes, traffic regulations, urban planning codes, fashion, and on medical, psychological and educational advice (Beck & Beck-Gernsheim, 2002). Thus, individualisation does not necessarily mean an increase in individual choice and decision-making, but rather primarily a change in how social control is exerted (Beck, 1997). Individualisation is thus a hidden force stimulating the production, shaping and scripting of not only our own biographies, but also of our social ties and networks in various phases of our life course, concomitant with ongoing negotiation with others and the demands of the labour market, educational system and market offerings.

This contemporary blend of coercive forces and freedoms is manifested today at two structural levels: *in changes in the valuation of institutions*, which are of central importance for the individual, from mid-level 'community' institutions (class, family, local community) towards global social institutions (the labour market, social insurance, educational system, consumption) and in *the change in demands of these institutions towards individuals*; from the precise standardising of individual behaviour to an increasingly lax provision of limiting conditions and demands that each person take responsibility for their lives into their own hands (Heinz, 2003).

This is the framework within which the social and political reconstruction of youth has taken place. The majority of the changes took place over a relatively short period of time, which caused the weakening of the old, stable frames of reference that used to ensure a fairly reliable and predictable transition to adulthood; these transitions have now become uncertain and vague. A key factor and indicator of the social integration of young people is the degree and extent of their trust in other people and institutions. That these changes have powerfully affected the changed nature of growing up is shown by empirical data. Research on youth in the last two decades in Europe has found 'tectonic shifts' in the life orientations and structures of trust among young people. There has been a pronounced shift away from big issues; from the public, and especially the political, to the everyday world of immediate life, the personal, family, partners and friends. This trend is universal, having been found in Scandinavian, Central European, Mediterranean and Eastern European countries (Leccardi & Ruspini, 2006; Brannen et al., 2002; Biggart & Kovacheva, 2006).

In this chapter I analyse changes and transformations in the life orientations and structures of trust of young people in Slovenia that have occurred during the transitional period of the past two decades. It is true that young people are now liberating themselves from traditional ties and dependencies, but they are also becoming more and more subjected to the pressures of other social institutions upon which they have very little or no influence. These institutions are the labour market, the educational system, systems of social care and protection, and systems of social security and health. Youth, which used to be a privileged societal group in the socialist period, has become the 'weakest link' of the transitional period in Slovenia (Ule, 2010).

In the first section I analyse the role of trust in social integrations in modern European societies and emphasise the importance of generalised trust, and trust in loose ties for the development of civility, tolerance and sociability in young people. I draw attention to the reduction of generalised trust in former transition countries compared to other European countries. In the second section I analyse some data on the extent and structure of trust among young people in Slovenia which indicate a critical level of generalised trust and trust in institutions in particular. I present a focus group analysis of trust among young people in Slovenia. In the concluding section I summarise the findings and observe a connection between the growing distrust of young people in social and political institutions and the social exclusion of young people. The growing social exclusion of young people is in opposition to the demands for increasingly earlier responsibility of the young for their own biographies and social integration. I conclude that in the absence of changes in key social, economic and political relationships' which keep young people in positions of social, economic and political dependence, there will be no major changes in the participation and citizenship of children and youth.

The role of trust in social integration and participation of young people

In the course of growing up, children and youth develop different forms of sociability which form the basis for their admission into social and political citizenship. Classical authors like Piaget and Kohlberg have already observed that people acquire the fundamental elements of social capital, such as norms of reciprocity and generalised trust, in their early periods of life, and that these remain fairly stable through later life (Piaget, 1965; Kohlberg, 1981). Longitudinal studies on the effects of investing in the social capital of young people show that the presence of strong social capital resources, especially participation in extracurricular activities in one's youth, is importantly related to the political and civic behaviour of the individual as an adult (Smith, 1999). It is interesting that only a few studies have been devoted to the process of generating social capital in childhood and youth. In their study of the roots of social capital, Stolle and Hooghe found '[...] that generalised trust can be seen as a relatively stable characteristic in one's life: trust levels at age 17 are strongly related to trust levels at age 34, which means that in order to fully understand adults' social capital, we need to shift our attention to the study of youth [...]' (Stolle & Hooghe, 2004: 414).

Trust is an important component of social capital, which I understand as a property of social life that allows participants to be more effective in their efforts to achieve goals shared with others (Putnam, 2000). However, any form of cooperation requires a certain measure of trust in the form of expectations of the behaviour of others in uncertain circumstances. Trust and the stabilisation of expectations enable stable social relations. Cooperation can arise from a clearly felt sense of collective belonging and solidarity towards others who share the same collective identity (Cozzolino, 2011). It can also develop as a result of recurrent mutual contacts (Simmel, 1908), in the course of which norms of mutuality and trust gradually take shape. Trust is thus manifested as being based mainly on past interactions which have the effect of demonstrating that others are trustworthy (Hardin, 2006). Such cooperation can be found in smaller, cohesive communities in which expectations regarding the cooperatively-oriented behaviour of others are a consequence of effective social control and sanctions. Cooperation is also tied to the values system and social norms of the actors, who prioritise socially responsible behaviour.

Of course, the social environment and the actor's assessment of the extent to which this environment is worthy of his trust also have a major influence. In this case we refer to trust in advance (Hardin, 2006), when the trust is based on the expectation (expressed in terms of probability) of the future behaviour of others. Since our knowledge about the future behaviour of others is more than often not perfect, we have to trust them. Trust is a mechanism for the reduction of uncertainty which arises as a consequence of system complexity, inadequate information and the free will of actors. The decision to trust or not is the result of a more or less rational reflection done in a specific situation. The degree of trust in society is thus in the first instance a response to the behaviour of others, to whether they are worthy of our trust or not. Readiness to trust is connected significantly with the actors themselves, especially with their values and positive attitude towards life in general. A lack of trust towards others can also be reflected through their opportunistic behaviour. Individuals who do not trust others because they believe them to be untrustworthy often behave in ways which abuse the trust placed in them by others. There is a high correlation between trust and trustworthy behaviour at the aggregate as well as at the individual levels (Yamagishi & Yamagishi, 1994: 140).

There are also no grounds for arguing that trust should be identical at the macro, mezzo and micro levels. The macro level characterises relations among people who do not know one another and who are not members of the same social networks, hence it does not concern existing social ties, but rather anonymous or potential ties. The mezzo level is represented by ties with co-workers, neighbours and members of interest groups, located in the space between strong and weak social ties. Social capital at the mezzo level is crucial for mobilising people to collective action in the workplace and in local communities, and for coordinating joint projects. At the other end of the continuum, at the micro level, it is the strong social ties among people who have known each other for a long time, meet frequently, are in intimate relationships and are included in intensive relationships of social support (Iglič, 2004). It is an inner circle of social networks formed by individuals in accordance with their interpersonal identities. Trust and cooperation at the micro level contribute to the more successful resolution of everyday crises and to the feeling of belonging and security. At the micro level, social capital is expressed through inclusion in close-knit networks and the activation of these ties in social support processes. Cooperation and trust at the macro level have an important influence on the tolerance of a society and its ability to resolve conflicts between different social groups, on the functioning of public institutions and on political democracy (Hardin, 2006). A default trust in other people contributes to the faster change from possible to actual social ties and to a solidarity which transcends the borders of existing networks.

The most commonly used indicators of social capital at the macro level are generalised trust in people and collective identity, understood as a sense of belonging and attachment to a certain collectivity. Generalised trust is a measure of the degree of trust in anonymous others and is linked with the value orientations and ethnic identity of the person who trusts. It arises from altruistic trust (Mansbridge, 1999) and optimistic trust (Uslaner, 2003; Hardin, 2006). Empathy and altruistic trust include well-intentioned behaviour towards others. They differ only in the view of the intention and with respect to the free will of the actor. In the case of altruistic trust, the actor decides to trust despite the associated risk. At the same time, altruistic trust and empathy are difficult to separate from what Hardin (2006) calls optimistic trust and Yamagishi and Yamagishi (1994) call cognitive error. In the case of cognitive error, people trust more than what would be expected based on an objective assessment of risk. Thus, altruistic trust such as optimism and empathy lead to trust where it would not be expected: it is first of all just a character trait (empathy), secondly a more or less stable attitude of people towards their social environment (optimism) and thirdly conscious behaviour (altruistic trust).

Optimism takes shape in important ways in the early years and accompanies the individual throughout life. Later events and experiences can change it in a small degree only. For this reason trust, which is closely connected with an optimistic view of life, is also a relatively stable individual trait. Longitudinal studies of trust are rare, but one has shown that over a period of 17 years, 70 per cent of the population studied remained in the same category of trust or lack of trust (Uslaner, 2003: 56). Greater fluctuations at the national level are a reflection of the change of generations with different experiences. On the other hand, when there are major changes in trust over the course of a period of adulthood, this change is not individual but collective, in the sense of a collective response to an important change in the environment. A decrease in the degree of optimistic trust within a given generation or society in general is usually associated with important political events and a reduction in prosperity, which imbues citizens with the feeling that things are taking a turn for the worse and their life opportunities are worse than before. Thus, Uslaner (2003) shows that the factors behind the decrease in the level of trust in the USA over the past four decades are not just generational changes, as asserted by Putnam (2000), but that this generational change has been accompanied by growing inequality. We can assume something similar is happening in the case of a decrease in trust in Slovenia.

Trust represents one of the most important mechanisms for stabilising expectations, especially in conditions where there is a normative vacuum. In societies of the late modern, this trust acquires a crucial role: not only does it fill in social, political and cultural voids, it also appears as a social binder which attempts to make up for the loss of traditional social ties, norms and values. The comparative advantage of particular societies should be in the willingness and ability of actors to function as agents of this linkage (Iglič, 2004). But this opens up an important dilemma of how to increase the space for the autonomous functioning and networking of individuals, and to achieve synergistic effects of their common operation without opening the doors wide to particularism and clientelism. It seems that the burden of resolving this dilemma rests primarily on the actors themselves. It is expected of them that in conditions of greater autonomy they will resolve the conflicting expectations placed before them by multiple networks to the best of their ability.

Trust in open, loosely knit networks is thus different from trust in close-knit networks of strong ties, particularly in the view of expectations that actors cultivate towards one another. In each case, trust is understood in the sense of expectations of the behaviour of others. An important difference is in how high the expectations are set. In closed networks expectations are high, sometimes even so high that they obligate another person to perform self-sacrificing and heroic acts. In open networks expectations are more limited. Actors are not expected to act in good faith if this requires sacrificing their convictions and interests or violating social and legal norms. They are expected to act in good faith in a weaker sense in situations where the interests of others are not encroached on as a result. In situations where the interests of actors are in conflict, then the good intentions of others are expressed in respect for the principle of procedural equality and impartiality.

The extent of trust in others and tolerance toward others is extremely important for the formation of social cohesiveness. Or, as the classical philosopher and sociologist Georg Simmel proposed, '[...] trust is one of the most important synthetic forces within society [...]' (Simmel, 1968: 326). What is more, Simmel assumed that trust does not require personal acquaintance, and thereby enables social interaction and cooperation with strangers. Or, as Sztompka wrote much later, '[...] trust begets trust, and trust is usually mutual [...]' (Stzompka, 1997: 14).

Cooperation which operates through weak ties takes place without high expectations of the benevolence of others, since this is restricted significantly by the morality of universalism, rational reflection, the interests of other participants and the threat of sanctions. Only under this condition can interpersonal networks and the sociability encompassed within them serve to promote rather than impede development. In contrast, the encouragement of cohesiveness and integration based on strong, close ties increases social divisions and decreases social integration.

It is these expectations, which are based on fairness in the sense of equal treatment for all, that enable the generalisation of trust. Social networks and informal exchanges and interactions, no matter how strong they are, can be counterproductive for social capital if they are not based on expectations as understood in the weak sense, since only these enable civility in the sense of positive treatment of those whom we do not know personally. As Shils (in (Iglič, 2004: 154) notes in his lecture on the virtue of civil society, the civility of civil society is not an insignificant thing – whereas the concept of civil society encompasses social networks, the participation of citizens and their interaction with the state, civility is directed at the quality of relationships and how citizens treat one another. Civility implies inclusion in a common moral universe by means of which it contributes to greater social integration and along with that the stabilisation of liberal democracy.

The characteristic of post-socialist societies is namely this lack of trust in open networks of loosely knit ties. As with confidence in key institutions of the polity, post-socialist countries also lag well behind Western democracies in trust in other people (see Figure 9.1).

Figure 9.1 Differences in the degree of generalised trust (confidence in the political system and trust in people) in EU countries (on a scale of 1–10)

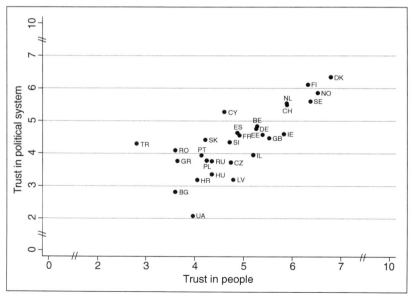

Source: European Social Survey, 2008.

In answer to the question 'do you think we can trust most people, or is it necessary to be cautious?', in Slovenia there was a strong tendency towards 'it is necessary to be very cautious'. This situation was in contrast to the situation in Scandinavian countries, which taken as an aggregate tend to be most strongly oriented towards the position 'most people can be trusted' (Miheljak, 2002). Many researchers consider this low level of trust in open, loosely knit networks in institutions and people in general in Eastern European countries as a fundamental problem of the post-socialist consolidation of democracy (Sztompka, 1997).

A crucial problem of post-socialist Eastern Europe is the problem of ownership transformations and the related emergence of new owners. This is not only a moral problem but even more a social and psychological one: a problem of values and identity, which Eastern European countries still feel after two decades of ownership transformation. The processes of transforming property ownership are not excessive but an entirely normal and legally legitimate practice. The problem is that the existing legal vacuum opens up a manoeuvring space for various other forms of semi-legal operations. The result of these processes, in the absence of stable legal norms, is corrupt activity. Slovenia, whose typically Central European values had been fairly resistant to corruptive phenomena, was also unprepared for this. As a result, people were unaccustomed to these practices and reacted with a loss of generalised trust in the system and national institutions.

Whom do young people in Slovenia trust the most?

A comparison of data on young people in Slovenia and data from public opinion surveys of the general population indicates that where trust among the general population is low, it is even lower among young people (Ule, 2010). Different studies of representative samples of the youth population during different time periods indicate that trust in the personal sphere (parents, friends) has increased over the last decade while generalised and institutional trust has decreased (Ule & Kuhar, 2008; see Table 9.1).

Slovenia is a country characterised by strong family ties, which places it in the Southern European (Mediterranean) cultural model (Ule, 2004). The centre of gravity for young people is already by definition limited to the family and private sphere and not the public sphere and workplace. The development of the culture and leisure industry relies on this fact. It is not just a question of the ideology of the personal, but also the real process and realistic possibility for shaping one's life situation (Ule,

Table 9.1 Responses of young people in Slovenia in 1995, 2000 and 2008 to the question: 'How much do you trust the following?' (per cent of respondents in Slovenia that trust 'a lot' or 'completely')

	Youth 1995		Youth 2000		Youth 2008	
	Not at all	*Completely*	*Not at all*	*Completely*	*Not at all*	*Completely*
Parents	0.9	33.7	1.1	45.8	0.0	55.6
Siblings	5.6	26.2	3.7	38.6	2.8	28.9
Schools, educational institutions	9.1	1.3	5.8	2.2	4.5	4.3
Political parties	32.2	0.0	51.2	0.2	42.2	0.0
Leading politicians	29.6	0.1	45.6	0.7	31.1	0.0
Media (newspapers, TV)	7.8	0.9	18.7	2.8	17.8	1.1
Friends	0.3	27.8	0.5	41.2	0.0	28.9
Priests and church	36.1	2.1	37.9	5.3	68.9	2.2
Courts of law	8.2	2.8	2.9	13.1	8.9	0.0

Source: Ule, 1995, 2010.

1998). This process began in the second half of the twentieth century with the transformation of patriarchal family models into permissive models in family life. Today the family serves as a place of refuge and shelter from the stresses of the wider world, which in highly competitive societies are surely not small. Long-term upbringing becomes possible since there is no longer a need for authoritarian control and the constant monitoring and maintenance of generational rules. This is the result of changing the family into a leisure time and consumer unit in a society of services (Ule, 2004). Parents thus devote themselves increasingly to the specific personality, emotional and cognitive traits of their children, and less and less to attempts to adjust the child to the characteristics of the local environment (An-Magritt & McKee, 2003; Maccoby & Martin, 1983; Wyness, 2000).

To highlight subjective experiences about trust dynamics among young people in Slovenia, we used the qualitative method of focus groups. Focus groups are more sensitive than quantitative methods, since they uncover people's feelings, beliefs, experiences and reactions in a manner not possible using questionnaire surveys. Focus groups enable us to see young persons as *actors* who are in charge of giving meaning to their lives. They are particularly good at discovering the assumptions underlying participants' attitudes, of which the participants may not be aware until they discuss a topic with others. They are often forced to reflect on their standpoints and elaborate on their answers. Focus groups offer a unique research advantage because they stimulate everyday interpersonal conversation that tends to make participants more comfortable with the research process.

The study was carried out in 2010. The young people who took part in our focus groups came from different target environments: the capital of Slovenia, suburbs of the capital and two non-urban regions. We chose four different environments to maximise the differences among the target population, hoping to stimulate the full range of attitudes towards trust. Altogether there were 15 focus groups with 79 participants. 36.5 per cent of the participants were male, 63.5 per cent were female. The participants were between 21 and 25 years old.

The questions that guided the focus group were as follows:

1. What does trust mean for you? Do you think that you trust people in general?
2. Who is the most trustworthy person for you? Why this person in particular?
3. To what extent do you trust public institutions, for example, educational, medical, social, political, media?

4. What is happening today with trust, does it seem to you that it is changing?

The main findings of the qualitative study were as follows:

Trust is defined by young people as a virtue and value and it is linked to interpersonal relations. Trust is associated with security and inter-dependence;

> 'Trust for me is a value based on the knowledge that another person will take you seriously, treat you with respect and without prejudice, and always try to do what's best for you.' (Female 12[2])

> 'It's important since it gives you a sense of security and the feeling that you're not alone.' (Female 1)

> 'It seems to me that if you don't trust people and society, society excludes you for being different.' (Male 15)

These statements indicate that young people expect that trust in others will bring them greater social security and enable social inclusion, which is also a basic condition for their participation in civil society and for their seeing and feeling themselves to be citizens with, in a democratic society at least, the same rights and responsibilities as every other citizen. Young people strongly associate trust with self-confidence;

> 'I think trust is a very important virtue. But I would say that people first have to have trust in themselves.' (Female 11)

For the majority of interviewees the most trustworthy figures are parents, especially mothers;

> 'My parents are the most trustworthy people for me, especially my mom.' (Female 9)

> 'I also trust my mom the most. She's always helped me and I think she always will, in all areas.' (Female 11)

> 'Definitely my mom. Because she has demonstrated that she's worthy of my trust.' (Male 18)

In particular, young people emphasise the unconditional help from their mothers;

> 'Mom, I'd say ... she just knows the best way to help and I can tell her a lot of things.' (Female 37)

> 'Sure, that's true, mom is always there and always ready to help, even when something may not be to her liking, I can always count on her.' (Male 8)

The family is clearly a strong supportive and empathic environment for young people. The family remains a well-placed institution for building relationships of trust since it can offer a nurturing atmosphere of caring which allows for partners' mutual disclosure, a necessary condition for trust (Gonzales-Mena & Eyer, 2004). Parents and especially mothers are the only people that young people can defy without losing their love and trust (Misztal, 1998). The intimate sphere can enable above all the building of basic trust, a feeling of ontological security for the individual, trust in the continuity of our personal identity and the predictability of everyday interactions.

As part of the qualitative study we also conducted five focus groups with the mothers of the young people surveyed and asked them what they thought about the trust placed in them and the longer period of dependence on parents by young people.

What does children's trust mean to mothers?

> 'Having your child's trust is definitely a sign that you're doing the right thing. I'm sometimes worried that my child will not turn to me for help.' (Mom 7)

> 'It means a lot if they trust me, it's the best thing that can happen ...' (Mom 15)

> 'I like having their trust, it's a good feeling if children trust you, you have the feeling that you know what is going on in their lives.' (Mom 21)

To what extent did mothers trust their own parents when they were young, has it changed?

> 'No, I never placed a lot of trust in mine and I never confided in them.' (Mom 2)

> 'We were different; the times were also different, less stressful.' (Mom 3)

> 'I never talked about problems with my parents. I had much more supervision and a lot fewer choices, I had significantly less freedom.' (Mom 10)

Based on these responses we could conclude that mothers do not see the great trust placed in them by their children as a problem; on the contrary, they are proud of it and are thus willing to share even more of their resources (emotional, time, material) with their children. Mothers of the current generation of youth belong to the generation of women who were the first to enrol in large numbers in university studies and who wanted to become independent as quickly as possible. They usually left home with clear ideas of what they wanted to achieve in life. But today they feel that conditions for their children are different, and that growing up is riskier. They also believe that young people today are more fragile psychologically than they were themselves, with less life experience than that which young people had in their time. They consider them less capable of solving financial and other difficulties, and hence they support their children when the latter decide to continue living at home. They interpret this desire as a strategy to reduce external risks. For this reason they also support the independence of young people in the family. We find similar reasoning elsewhere in Europe (Leccardi & Ruspini, 2006).

How do young participants in the focus group justify the observation that people in general are not to be trusted?

In the opinion of young people, trustworthiness must be demonstrated;

> 'I think it's increasingly difficult to trust in today's world and society. So it's important to find that person you can tell everything to, and know that they will not disappoint you or take advantage of your trust.' (Male 5)

Young people refer to the bad intentions of the system's institutions or to the selfishness and greed of people, often in connection with the nature of society as a whole;

> 'I also don't trust anyone. It seems to me that everyone just looks after their own interests, not the public good.' (Male 22)

> 'Less and less, definitely! Because even public agencies are increasingly subordinated to capital and losing their primary mission. I don't trust them much at all, when you see what's happening it really makes you think.' (Male 26)

The belief prevails that today's society is rife with various fraudsters and scammers;

> 'I don't even get involved in politics anymore, I think all politicians are greedy and thieving, I have a little more trust in educational institutions.' (Female 11)

> 'Sure, in a capitalist society we've all become individualists and materialists ... and we're less trusting of everything we hear.' (Female 12)

Institutional and generalised trust has a very low value;

> 'I don't trust politicians at all; they only work for their own benefit. For that reason I also don't bother to vote.' (Female 6)

> 'I have practically no confidence in them, since they all always have some interests of their own and in most cases they just work to advance their own welfare and not the welfare of others.' (Male 3)

These statements are a reflection of the fairly widespread mistrust of young people towards politics. This is also shown by data from other studies in Slovenia (Kuhar, 2005). For as long as this attitude towards politics remains unreflective upon, it represents a reason for their political passivity and renouncement of their rights and duties of citizenship, for example voting. They draw attention to negative experience as a reason for a lack of trust; this can also be the experience of associated people, for example parents.

> 'No institution, not even ones for social welfare, serves only its (original) purpose, they all serve themselves, that's why I don't trust them.' (Female 12)

The level of trust in advance and in general is thus quite low among young people in Slovenia. Trust is particular and based on experience, requiring a process of demonstration. Latent social critiques which are expressed in the statements provided are not sufficiently articulated and present in public to be a mobilising factor for youth. Since there is no significant youth civil society movement in Slovenia which would offer the opportunity for at least alternative political activation of young people, there is a danger of social and political isolation of youth and a change of social criticism into pre-political forms of public activity (chauvinism, interethnic intolerance, hate speech in public). This situation is not good for the development of a democratic society since it opens the door to dangerous forms of political populism and totalitarianism. In *The Origins of Totalitarianism* (1962), Hanne Arendt equated political isolation with '[...] impotence insofar as power always comes from men acting together, "acting in concert" (Burke); isolated men are powerless by definition' (Arendt, 1962: 474).

One of the main reasons for the absence of generalised trust in Slovenia as well as in other Eastern European countries is definitely the set of negative perceptions of the processes of modernisation and transition. Some call this the negative experience of transition. This is the conviction that people have internalised the materialist orientation of contemporary society and that selfishness has become a basic operating principle for most people. For this reason people are not to be trusted since the expectation is that their goal is to advance their own interests even or indeed primarily at the expense of others' interests. The experience of transition, both personally and socially from socialism to postsocialism, causes a strong increase in the amount of uncertainty on the one hand and the quantity of experience on the other. It is the perception of new types of risk in the face of which the individual does not feel sufficiently protected (Ilišin, 2007; Ule, 2010). If the thesis regarding the transition effect holds, then the low level of trust in these spaces might be of a transitional nature, but it is not clear how long this transition or period of adjustment will last. Trust or lack thereof is a fairly stable trait of individuals, and any change is usually associated with the collective dynamics of the degree of trust, for example a consequence of an increase or decrease in general social welfare.

Conclusion: The absence of generalised trust as a response of young people to hyper-complex social conditions

Research on youth in Slovenia shows a low level of generalised trust and trust in the fundamental institutions of modern societies and states (Ule & Rener, 2001). The immediate environment of life, in particular the family, is the only world which is truly important to young people and which they trust. The personal sphere is increasingly becoming a place of self-realisation for children and young people and not a place of duties and obligations. For this reason trust in the personal also has a sociopolitical significance for young people. But this is a phenomenon with ambiguous effects. The accessibility or absence of a family support network reproduces social inequality and creates a gap between those who are well equipped and those who are not. For this reason one of the most important factors of social differentiation of young people today is the existence of family support.

A turning inward to the personal sphere and the family is also supported by contemporary neoconservative ideologies and national policies. This trend most likely has its background also in the crisis of welfare societies in Western Europe and in the transition processes in Eastern Europe (Spannring et al., 2008). However, external factors would not have this strong effect were it not for the attractiveness of the family and the personal for youth. The reasons for this shift should be sought in the changed contractual relationships between parents and children. This is shown in the liberalisation of parenting styles and in increasingly informal and personal relationships between adults and youth. Parents have less and less need for a formal demonstration of authority. Very early on, a relationship of partnership is established between parents and their growing children. Parents become confidants and counsellors for their children when the latter have psychological or financial difficulties, as well as strong advocates for their children in the public sphere and institutions (Ule, 2004; Maccoby & Martin, 1983). Here we have organised lobbying in mind in which parents as a group apply pressure to cultural and educational institutions from outside in order to improve opportunities for their children. Whereas youth in the 1970s and 1980s rejected this conceptual world as a space of control and coercion, today it seems they accept it with open arms. The difference is that parents have achieved a kind of contractual relationship in which children fulfil their desires for social advancement without resisting much. Parents must protect and support their offspring long past the period of psychosocial maturity. Today parents are perhaps even more dependent on their children than the other way around, since the self-image of many parents is closely linked to the success in life of their children (Beck, 1997; Ziehe, 1991; Ule, 1998).

The changed life circumstances of youth in the late modern society are thus hyper-complex, and hard to perceive and unmanageable for young people. The growing uncertainty of transitions to adulthood is a common denominator of youth across Europe (Walther, 2006). State and public support systems do not always operate in accordance with the needs and concerns of all young people. Strategies of systemic inclusion have lost legitimacy. The loss of security, which was once inseparably connected to institutional paths and transitions, means that the risk of mistaken strategies can appear even when a young person follows tried and tested institutional paths, for example by finishing their schooling, but then finding that their education and training do not suit the actual needs of the labour market. It is only a short step from uncertainty regarding the achievement of social inclusion to the question of what it even is. The same factors can affect the course of life in a restrictive or a liberating way. Besides the standard factors such as social and national origin and gender, the importance of nonstandard factors, such as sociocultural capital, communicative skills and emotional stability, is growing.

This development has a distinctly dark side; (young) people are becoming increasingly overwhelmed by social conflicts and contradictions, and feeling them more directly, without the protection of social buffers provided by intermediate institutions of earlier periods of modernisation such as peers, subculture, class consciousness and belonging. The response of most young people to hyper-complex life situations is an implosion into the personal and a policy of reducing risk in life choices. The changed attitude towards the public and the private is a common social phenomenon characteristic of all modern youth. When competitiveness and selective admission to prestigious schools and suitable employment become increasingly stronger, family emotional support and family social networks are crucially important (Baethge, 1996; Ule & Rener, 2001).

In the struggle for at least temporary success in this strongly unequal encounter of young people with the hyper-complex systems of capital and social power, participation in decision-making and social influence is critical. In democratic societies the institution of citizenship takes care of this. The concept of citizenship has become an analytical instrument for understanding the position of exclusion and marginalisation in recent decades. In accordance with modern concepts we distinguish among political, civil and social citizenship. In the view of Wallace and Jones (1992) only indirect political and social citizenship, tied to the economic dependence on parents and the absence of political action, is possible for youth. If young people as a heterogeneous social group have anything in common, it is this impeded or prohibited access to full citizenship. When social exclusion of youth is systemic and not random; when responsibility for one's biography must be taken increasingly earlier in childhood and children must be mature enough for important decisions; this impeded access or exclusion of young people from rights of citizenship implies arrogance and cynicism. This is destructive for citizenship identity and the sense of belonging.

It is also in direct contradiction to the demand of the late modern that each individual is reflexively in charge of his or her own biographical project as early as possible, which requires sociopolitical responsibility and accountability: this is impossible to achieve if the individual lacks the necessary citizenship rights and obligations. For this reason, it is meaningless to talk about how young people should again become social subjects and how we can help them in addressing their problems and risks. First we need a change in the conditions that keep young people in a position of social, economic and political dependence, and which today perhaps even more than in traditional societies impose social immaturity and prolonged dependency on young people.

Notes

1 In this contribution we will use the term trust throughout the text, although some distinctions could be made between trust and confidence in terms of Luhmann's proposal. For a discussion on this distinction please see Chapter 1 and Chapter 7 in this book.
2 The interviewees are denoted by the numbers.

Bibliography

An-Magritt, J. & L. McKee (eds) (2003) *Children and the Changing Family: Between Transformation and Negotiation*, Oxford: Routledge.

Arendt, H. (1962) *The Origins of Totalitarianism*, Cleveland: The World Publishing Company.

Baethge, M. (1996) 'Individualization as hope and disaster' in J. Hurrelmann (ed.) *The Social World of Adolescents*, Berlin: W. de Gruyter, pp. 27–41.

Beck, U. (ed.) (1997) *Kinder der Freiheit*, Frankfurt am Main: Suhrkamp.

Beck, U. & E. Beck-Gernsheim (2002) *Individualization: Institutionalized Individualism and its Social and Political Consequences*, London: Sage.

Biggart, A. & S. Kovacheva (2006) *Social Change, Family Support and Young Adults in Europe*, San Francisco: Wiley.

Brannen, J., S. Lewis, A. Nilsen & J. Smithson (2002) *Young Europeans, Work and Family*, London: Routledge.

Cozzolino, P. J. (2011) 'Trust, cooperation and equality: A psychological analysis of the formation of social capital', *Social Psychology*, 50(2): 302–20.

European Social Survey (2008) Round 4 Data (Data file edition 3.0), Bergen, Norway: Norwegian Social Science Data Services.

Gonzales-Mena, J. & W. D. Eyer (2004) *Infants, Toddlers, and Caregivers: A Curriculum of Respectful, Responsive Care and Education*, 6th edn, Boston: McGraw Hill.

Hardin, R. (2006) *Trust*, Malden, Massachusetts: Polity Press.

Heinz, M. (2003) *Widerhaken der 'Individualisierung'*, Institut für Gesellschaftspolitik, http://www.hfph.mwn.de/igp/res/beck.htm, date accessed 25 May 2011.

Heinz, W. R. (ed.) (1997) *Theoretical Advances in Life Course Research*, Weinheim: Deutscher Studien Verlag.

(Iglič, H. (2004) 'Dejavniki nizke stopnje zaupanja v Sloveniji', *Družboslovne razprave*, XX(46/47), pp. 149–75.

Ilišin, V. (ed.) (2007) *Croatian Youth and European Integration*, Zagreb: Institute for Social Research.

Kohlberg, L. (1981) *The Philosophy of Moral Development*, San Francisco: Joss-Bassey.

Kuhar, M. (2005) 'Youth and politics in Slovenia: A pre-political group in a post-political age' in J. Forbig (ed.) *Revisiting Youth Political Participation: Challenges for Research and Democratic Practice in Europe*, Brussels: Council of Europe, pp. 53–60.

Leccardi, C. & E. Ruspini (2006) *A New Youth. Young People, Generations and Family Life*, Aldershot: Ashgate.

Maccoby, E. E. & J. A. Martin (1983) 'Socialization in the context of the family: Parent–child interaction' in P. Mussen & E. M. Hetherington (eds) *Handbook of Child Psychology, Vol. IV: Socialization, Personality, and Social Development*, New York: Wiley, pp. 1–101.

Mansbridge, J. (1999) 'Altruistic truth' in M. E. Warren (ed.) *Democracy and Trust*, Cambridge: Cambridge University Press, pp. 290–309.

Miheljak, V. (ed.) (2002) *Mladina 2000. Slovenska mladina na prehodu v tretje tiso letje*, Maribor: Aristej.

Misztal, B. A. (1998) *Trust in Modern Societies. The Search for the Bases of Social Order*, Cambridge: Polity Press.

Piaget, J. (1965) *The Moral Judgment of the Child*, New York: The Free Press.

Putnam, R. D. (2000) *Bowling Alone*, New York: Simon & Schuster.

Simmel, G. (1908/1968) 'Exkurs über den Fremden' in G. Simmel (ed.) *Soziologie. Untersuchungen über die Formen der Vergesellschaftung*, Berlin: Duncker & Humblot, pp. 509–12.

Smith, E. S. (1999) 'The effects of investments in the social capital of youth on political and civic behavior in young adulthood: A longitudinal analysis', *Political Psychology*, 20(3): 553–80.

Spannring, R., G. Ogris & W. Gaiser (eds) (2008*) Youth and Political Participation in Europe*, Opladen: Barbara Budrich Publ.

Stolle, D. & M. Hooghe (2004) 'The roots of social capital: Attitudinal and network mechanisms in the relation between youth and adult indicators of social capital', *Acta Politica*, 39: 422–41.

Sztompka, P. (1997) *Trust, Distrust and the Paradox of Democracy*, Berlin: Papers des Wissenschaftszentrums Berlin.

Ule, M. (1995) 'Growing up and social change in Slovenia' in L. Chisholm (ed.) *Growing Up in Europe: Contemporary Horizons in Childhood and Youth Studies*, Berlin: De Gruyter, pp. 161–70.

Ule, M. (1998) 'The life world of young people' in M. Ule & T. Rener (eds) *Youth in Slovenia: New Perspectives from the Nineties*, Ljubljana: Youth Department, pp. 173–203.

Ule, M. (2004) 'Changes in family life courses in Slovenia' in M. Robila (ed.) *Families in Eastern Europe*, Amsterdam: Elsevier, pp. 87–101.

Ule, M. (2010) 'Fragments on young people in Slovenia: The end of utopias in the era of transitions', *Annales, Series Historia et Sociologia*, 20(1): 57–70.

Ule, M. & M. Kuhar (2008) 'Orientations of young adults in Slovenia toward the family formation', *Young*, 16(2): 153–83.

Ule, M. & T. Rener (2001) 'The deconstruction of youth' in A. Furlong & I. Guidikova (eds) *Transitions of Youth Citizenship in Europe: Culture, Subculture and Identity*, Strasbourg: Council of Europe, pp. 271–88.

Uslaner, E. (2003) 'Trust and civic engagement in East and West' in G. Badescu & E. Uslaner (eds) *Social Capital and the Transition to Democracy*, London: Routledge.

Wallace, C. & J. Jones (1992) *Youth, Family and Citizenship*, Buckingham-Philadelphia: Open University Press.

Walther, A. (2006) 'Regimes of youth transitions', *Young. Nordic Journal of Youth Research*, 14(2): 119–39.

Wyness, M. G. (2000) *Contesting Childhood*, London: Falmer Press.

Yamagishi, T. & M. Yamagishi (1994) 'Trust and commitment in the United States and Japan', *Motivation and Emotion*, 18: 129–66.

Ziehe, T. (1991) *Zeitvergleiche. Jugend in kulturellen Modernisierungen*, München: Juventa.

Conclusion: Potentials, Challenges and Limitations of the Trust Approach

Hanne Warming

The ambition of this book was to explore how the concept of trust can contribute to the analysis and theoretical conceptualisation of children's participation, citizenship and life quality. This ambition has been fulfilled through a collection of chapters, which provides a range of diversity both concerning the theoretical conceptualisation of trust, and with regard to national contexts and subsystem types (see Introduction and Bronfenbrenner, 1979, 1994), that is analysed. Although this diversity indeed was intended, it also presents something of a challenge when it comes to drawing general conclusions from the book. I shall nevertheless venture to draw a three-pronged overall conclusion from the research presented in the foregoing chapters. First, we may conclude that trust dynamics are spatially[1] contextualised. Second, the chapters clearly show that the concept of trust is potentially extremely valuable in analysing and theorising about children's participation, citizenship and life quality. However, it also has a number of limitations and requires further theoretical development. Third, both the potential of the trust concept, as well as its limitations and the need for further theoretical development, are a result of the many theoretical definitions of trust that exist and of the spatial contextualisation of trust dynamics.

In the Introduction, I referred to a literature review of articles dealing with trust in childhood research journals, which revealed that trust and related concepts tend to be very vaguely defined and often not explicitly conceptualised (Christensen, forthcoming). This finding is quite surprising, given that scientific articles are usually required to provide clear definitions of key concepts. It may be that researchers and reviewers take for granted that everybody knows what trust is. Indeed, most people are familiar with the term 'trust', and often use it in everyday life. However, Chapter 3 by Grosse and Warming and Chapter 9 by Ule show that the everyday usage of the word covers a wide range of different meanings. These include: inner security, a feeling of safety (absence of fear or anxiety), confidence, familiarity, positive expectations, predictability and a moral attitude. Theories of trust mirror this diversity, but they do this by prioritising one or only a few everyday meanings rather than engaging with the complexity of meanings surrounding the term. Luhmann's theorising is, to some extent, an exception, as he covers all of these dimensions apart from the notion of trust as a moral attitude (due to his functionalistic approach). However, in his theorising, not all these dimensions are conceptualised as trust, but rather as different, though related, phenomena. In addition, he introduces another quite different definition of trust as the 'opening of risk alternatives' (Baraldi & Farini, Chapter 7; Luhmann, 1988, 1991). Thus, it is possible to make a distinction between theoretical definitions of trust, which reflect the diverse everyday usage of the term, and Luhmann's approach in which trust is explicitly defined as involving risk acknowledgement and acceptance, distinguishing it from confidence and familiarity (Luhmann, 1988). Connected to this, a further distinction is evident between on the one hand psychological concepts of trust, and on the other hand micro- and macro-sociological concepts of trust. It is primarily the former that have informed everyday understandings and usages of the term.

The collection of chapters in this book together illustrate the usefulness both of the more familiar everyday understandings of trust, and the Luhmannian definitions. They further show that this abundance of definitions enables analysis of the different dimensions of, and dynamics shaping, children's participation, citizenship and life quality.

Trust as an inner feeling

Many of the theories which reflect everyday meanings address trust as an inner feeling. This includes the theory of basic trust (Erikson, 1950), the theory of attachment patterns and inner security (Ainsworth et al., 1978) and – when empirically investigated – the distinction between 'particularised trust' and 'general trust' (Uslaner, 2002).

Contributions from psychology on trust as an inner feeling

The theory of basic trust, and the theory of attachment patterns which may be regarded as a more developed version of the former, have been especially influential in much research on trust dynamics in children's lives. This includes Chapters 1, 3, 4 and 5 in this book, however these chapters are also critical of the traditional developmental psychological perspective which regards children as passive objects of adults' agency, and overlooks the impact of the historical and cultural context.

These theories suggest that basic trust is essential to the child's well-being and resilience, which is his or her capacity to act and to overcome risk factors (Schaffer, 1992; Clauss-Ehler, 2004), including the late modern threat against ontological security (Giddens, 1990). According to the theory of attachment patterns, the development of this protective and empowering feeling of inner security is determined by early attachment patterns (Ainsworth et al., 1978; Koester & McCray, 2011). This empirically well documented theory (see Chapter 3) provides important insights into the development and significant role of basic trust in children's lives; however, this book highlights the need to move beyond the prevailing individualistic and familial approaches in order to replace this view of children as passive objects of adult agency with an understanding of the child as an agent. In Chapter 1, I point to these limits of the theory as seen from an ontological position within the new childhood studies. These points are then substantiated and exemplified through the empirical analyses in Chapters 3, 4, 5, 6 and 8.

Psychological dynamics of trust as spatially contextualised

Ule (see Chapter 9) points to a correlation between historical changes in discourses on appropriate parenting styles which have, in turn, shaped intra-family intergenerational power relations; and generational differences in young people's confidence in their parents. This finding suggests that the development of basic trust is influenced by the historically shaped discursive context for parenting and intergenerational power relations, and is thus spatially contextualised. Likewise, Turton argues in Chapter 4 that although family abuse in itself violates the development of basic trust, a discursive context which excommunicates such experiences and thereby renders them unintelligible and guilt infested, exacerbates this trust violation.

Yet the social context can also play a protective role. Based on data from Sweden, Grosse and Warming describe in Chapter 3 how the historical normalisation of divorce has meant that in these countries this event no longer harms the development of basic trust, as seemed to be the case earlier and still may be in other countries. Social norms about what is 'normal', 'acceptable' and 'desirable' influence parents' ways of parenting as well as children's perceptions of their life situation, including their relationship to their parents and their opportunities for agency and by extension for developing basic trust.

Another example of a protective societal context is one which other supportive and caring adults offer the child the security and trust it needs in cases where its parents do not. This can occur, for instance, in communities characterised by high levels of social capital, where neighbours, teachers, adult friends and/or extended family members play a supportive role. It may also occur in contexts where a child-friendly and responsive welfare system exists. Grosse and Warming provide empirical examples of such protective contexts, revealing how they enable the child's agency by providing it with a feeling of security.

Chapters 5 and 6 by Pinkney and Christensen, respectively, reveal how New Public Management, which has many different manifestations despite being a global trend across the developed world (Pollitt & Bouchaert, 2011), hampers social workers' ability to offer children this important support. This is due, in particular, to two features of New Public Management: 1) power relations which disempower children (see Chapter 1 by Warming and Chapter 2 by Moran-Ellis & Sünker), and 2) the fact that under the New Public Management, time with clients becomes a scarce resource due to institutional logics that force system representatives to focus on other issues (see Chapter 5 by Pinkney and Chapter 6 by Christensen). These dynamics are detrimental to the social space of social work with children because they undermine trust, which is based on choice and mutuality and takes time to be built up. We will return to these points shortly.

Directions for future research on trust as an inner feeling

Over 20 years ago, Giddens (1991) highlighted that people's need for basic trust as a precondition for wellbeing and agency is historically and geographically specific, inasmuch as it is connected to the late modern challenge to individuals' ontological security. However, the empirical analyses in this book also show that the development of basic trust is spatially contextualised. Thus, in terms of future research, we see a pressing need for empirical studies on the development of basic trust as a spatially contextualised phenomenon. This includes investigating how politics, organisational and institutional structures, power relations and discourses shape children's development of basic trust and feelings of security.

Although the finding that the development of trust – including basic trust, particularised trust and trust dispositions – is spatially contextualised should not be revolutionary to sociologists, the relationship between trust, space and place is nevertheless seriously under-theorised. Possible pathways for such theorising include Bronfrenbrenner's ecological system theory (Bronfrenbrenner, 1979, 1994), which inspired the structure of this book (see Introduction); and Bourdieu's relational theory of practice, including his concept of habitus (Bourdieu, 1985, 1989; Bourdieu & Wacquant, 1992; Bourdieu et al., 1999), as suggested in Chapter 1. Here, it is crucial to acknowledge the impact of the generational order, both as a discursive construction of child-adult relations (exemplified by Ule in Chapter 9) and as institutionalised sanctioned power materialised in rights, as outlined in Chapter 2 by Moran-Ellis and Sünker, who focus on adults' trust in children.

Another fruitful avenue might be to further explore the potential of the concepts of bridging and bonding social capital (Putnam, 2000) which in empirical research are often measured using the concepts of generalised and particularised trust (Uslaner, 1999). Unlike the concept of basic trust, these concepts are based on a sociological approach to trust as 'a property of collective units', as suggested by Lewis and Weigert (1985: 986), although when studied empirically they are often measured as an inner feeling 'that another can be trusted'. This inner feeling reflects Fukuyama's definition of trust as socially (re)produced: 'the expectation that arises within a community of regular, cooperative behavior, based on commonly shared norms' (Poulsen & Svendsen, 2005: 2; see also Fukuyama, 1995). Thus, these concepts help us move the concept of trust as an inner feeling towards a more sociological understanding. Moreover, empirical research suggests that levels of generalised trust are significantly higher in social democratic than in conservative and liberal welfare regimes (Larsen, 2007: 84),[2] suggesting that the development of generalised trust depends on social redistribution mechanisms (see also Chapter 9 by Ule). This statistical correlation calls for qualitative studies and theories that can help us understand the mechanisms behind it.

A processual approach to trust

The concept of basic trust, and the distinction between particularised and generalised trust, view trust as a 'state', either in term of a personal structure developed during the first years of a child's life, or as a societal feature. However, several of the chapters in this book document the analytical power of a processual approach to trust in conceptualising children's life quality, participation and citizenship.

Trust building: Facilitation and relation specific trust

The analytical power of a processual approach is documented in Baraldi and Farinis' analysis in Chapter 7, which provides an in-depth, communicative analysis of the trust building process in an educational context, from a Luhmannian perspective. This analysis illustrates how trust building can facilitate children's engaged and empowered participation. The chapter also shows that it is possible to move from a state of distrust and conflict towards an atmosphere of trust and cooperation, and illustrates how this move can be promoted by personal commitment and willingness on the part of the facilitator to take the first steps in risking (communication of) trust. Based on this analysis, Baraldi and Farini suggest that the cultural precondition for trust building is that an interaction should be coded as facilitating risk, that is enabling opportunities for risk-taking rather than closing them down through assessment and control. This promotes children's engagement and willingness to take the risk to trust. More specifically, this may be done using 'questions that open alternatives for adolescents' actions and highlight adults' trust in their agency, feedback questions that verify and explore the meanings of adolescents' interpretations, and formulations that both demonstrate responsiveness to adolescents' needs and open alternatives for their actions' (Baraldi & Farini, Chapter 7). Thus, this analysis does not only demonstrate the importance of trust in facilitating children's agency, but also sheds light on how trust building can be promoted in order to empower children to participate.

Christensen, in Chapter 6, likewise illustrates the role of mediators in trust building using the example of a social worker who positions herself between the social care system and the child by displaying personal engagement and trust in the child. The social worker builds up a trusting relationship with the child which allows 'working trust' (see Baraldi & Farini, Chapter 7) between the social care system and the child, and enables the child's agency by reducing the complexity of the social system. In this example, working trust, and the resulting reduction of complexity, is only possible due to the mediating role played by the social worker. This is, first of all, because the child only trusts the specific social worker in question, not the social care system as such. Second, the child is met only with trust, since the mediator shields the child from distrustful, patronising and controlling attitudes on the part of other system representatives and system logics. This is neither system trust bound to a specific social worker; nor personal trust bound to social care for the child, though over time it may develop into both. Instead, it must be regarded as 'relationship specific trust' bound to a specific issue: in this case social care for the child *and* a relationship between two specific persons.

Potential of and future directions for research into facilitation and relationship specific trust

Baraldi and Farini's in-depth analysis and theorising of the communicative dynamics involved in trust building as a way to facilitate children's engaged participation offers an excellent starting point for further empirical analysis of – and research based supervision of – adult facilitation of children's participation and citizenship. Such research might benefit from further theorising of the connections between trust, facilitation and citizenship by integrating theories of citizenship more explicitly. Another way to develop this approach might be to include non-verbal communication in the analysis, for example by studying how non-verbal properties of utterances interact with linguistic ones, a dimension that is often largely ignored, according to Wharton (2009).

In Chapter 6, Christensen points out the need for theoretical development to understand trust as processual, that is something built up over time, rather than as a fixed state. He argues that we need to rethink existing definitions of trust with a view to moving away from a trust – distrust dichotomy and towards a continuum. In Chapter 8, Pantea points to a further limitation of the trust approach:

> Whilst children with migrant parents do display reactions that are overtly resistant and mistrustful or, on the contrary, submissive to the adult exerted governance, their responses are not always situated on this axis. This research suggests that in their various degrees, trust and mistrust are not able to cover the whole spectrum of possible ways young people relate to governance.
>
> (Pantea, Chapter 8)

Thus, a pressing task for future research into the impact of trust building on children's lives, participation and citizenship is to develop definitions of trust in terms of a continuum, but also to theorise about how children's actions may not always be intelligible in terms of such a continuum. Regarding the latter, Pantea suggests the concept of 'slantwise actions' (Campbell & Heyman, 2007). This concept, she argues, might offer a fruitful way to theorise about children's accidental and unintentional reactions and thus to nuance the trust-mistrust dichotomy in a way which transcends such a continuum.

The finding that relationship specific trust differs from system trust and personal trust is an important dimension of the notion of trust as a continuum. Notably, it raises the important question: How and under which circumstances can relationship specific trust develop into system trust and personal trust?

Combining a processual approach with predispositions for trust: Another future direction for research into trust building

While Baraldi and Farini's analysis of trust building focuses exclusively on communication processes, Christensen argues that we need to acknowledge that what happens in the situated process of trust building is conditioned by the participants' dispositions for trust. The temporal dimension of trust – the trust building process – not only concerns the present and the future, but also the past inasmuch as it impinges upon a person's dispositions for trust. Such an understanding is in line with Pinkney's observation that children in contact with the social care system often have sound reasons to be particularly cautious about trusting adults because of their lived experiences of abuse and trust violation (Chapter 5). In such cases, she argues, the trust building process is particularly challenging, and demands more time, effort and emotional engagement from the social worker. Christensen adds that the social worker her/himself likewise can be more or less predisposed towards trust (Chapter 6). He further claims that the temporal dimension of trust, in term of a pre-disposed process of relational trust building and of becoming (system) trustful, is quite under-theorised. Moran-Ellis and Sünker (Chapter 2) emphasise that to understand adults' dispositions for (not) trusting children we need to acknowledge the intergenerational power which favours adults, and incorporate this in our theorising. Trusting children involves renouncing control of outcomes, which might not be in the adults' interest, they argue. Thus, the temporal dimension of trust as a process conditioned by predispositions must be supplemented by an analysis of power relations.

Christensen's empirical analysis in Chapter 6 documents the power of Luhmann's definition of trust for understanding the situated positions in which social workers carry out their work with children in positions at risk. Yet Luhmann's definition is inadequate with regard to the temporal dimension called for in Christensen's account, and the power perspective highlighted by Moran-Ellis and Sünker. Luhmann's shortcomings in terms of the temporal dimension are not surprising, as seen from a Luhmannian systems theoretical perspective 'individuals' past experiences cannot predict the form of a communication system, which is produced only through communication' (Baraldi & Farini, Chapter 7). Thus, theorising of the temporal dimension, as called for by Christensen, must go beyond Luhmann's approach, either by introducing an alternative definition of trust, or by re-reading the Luhmannian concept of trust in a way that detaches it from systems theory.

Regarding the former, the challenge is that trust is usually theorised as a state rather than a process, with the exception of Giddens. While the trust building process according to Luhmann is usually fragmentary (Jalava, 2001: 3), Giddens' definition of trust building emphasises continuity and facework commitments between actors who know one another, which are shaped by their personality (their degree of basic trust and ontological security) which is, in turn, grounded in early childhood (Giddens, 1990, 1991). Thus, Giddens' perspective on trust offers a potentially fruitful avenue for further theorising about the temporal dimensions of trust.

In terms of detaching the Luhmannian concept of trust from systems theory, in Chapter 1, I undertake a Bourdieu-inspired re-reading of Luhmann with a view to outlining one possible way to do this. My approach enables a critical analysis that is capable of addressing power relations, and which I believe holds great potential for theorising about the impact of intergenerational power on trust dynamics in relation to children's participation, in accordance with the theoretical challenges highlighted by Moran-Ellis and Sünker.

Critical analyses of trust building that reveal power relations

Analyses of trust and trust building that reveal power relations involve exploration of the power structures that shape social constructions of who can be regarded as trustworthy. Several analyses in this book point to how the generational order, both in itself (especially Chapter 2 by Moran-Ellis & Sünker) and in its intersections with other power relations (Chapters 1, 4, 5 and 8 by Warming, Turton, Pinkney and Pantea, respectively), constructs children, and especially certain groups of children, as untrustworthy. As a result of these constructions, children are met with distrust and control, and as 'not yet citizens', rather than with trust and recognition. This has negative consequences for children's wellbeing, participation and citizenship identity (Delanty, 2003; Hart, 2009) as pointed out in Chapter 1 by Warming, Chapter 2 by Moran-Ellis and Sünker and Chapter 8 by Pantea.

Governing through 'the community': Creating the conditions for trust and trust building

Pantea's analysis of the Romanian children left behind by parents working abroad (see Chapter 8) provides an example of such constructions, which in this case are shaped by the intersection between the generational order and the social construction of migrant families as dysfunctional. Another example is Turton's analysis in Chapter 4, in which an intersection between the generational order and the gendered construction of sexual abuse shapes stories about children abused by females as being untrustworthy. However, the mere situation of being a 'looked after child' or being discursively constructed as 'at risk' carries negative connotations that go beyond those of just being a child, as pointed to by Pinkney in Chapter 5 and in my own example in Chapter 1. These examples indicate that notions of 'who can be regarded as trustworthy' are closely linked to the governance of certain groups – what Rose has termed governing through '"the community" as a new territory for the administration of the individual and collective existence' (Rose, 1996: 331). This approach offers an alternative means of theorising about how power frames the conditions for trust and trust building.

Is trust always a normative good?

Another direction for critical analyses of trust is to address a question posed at the European Sociological Association Conference in Geneva in 2011, where we presented some key ideas from this book. The question was: 'Is trust always a normative good?'.

In most of the chapters, trust appears as 'a moral good' since it improves children's life quality, or motivates and empowers their participation and citizenship. In Chapter 1, however, I suggest that power and domination constitute 'the dark side' of system trust, since trusting a system implies accepting the power relations inherent in the system. This tallies with Moran-Ellis and Sünker's point in Chapter 2 that adults' trust in expert knowledge about children's development frames their attitudes in paternalist and patronising ways. This 'dark side' of system trust remains a lacuna in trust research in childhood studies and beyond. If we accept that power and domination constitute 'the dark side' of system trust, and at the same time that system trust supports personal trust and vice versa (a point made by Luhmann and in many chapters in this book, as we will return to below), a tricky issue arises about the relationship between personal trust on the one hand, and empowerment and domination on the other. Further research is needed to elucidate this issue.

The role of images, organisational structure and global information flows for trust and trust building

If we regard social trust building as a mutual process, then images of welfare institutions and the legal system can mitigate against the development of trust just as much as images of children and certain groups of children. This point is highlighted by Pinkney in Chapter 5, whereas Chapter 9 by Ule provides an example of how low trust and extremely negative images of the welfare institutions and the legal system affect young people's inclusion and participation. Yet Pinkney also shows how the opposite dynamic also occurs, namely that stories about victims finding support and about abuse being acknowledged can positively influence others to take the risk to trust others.

Moreover, several of this book's authors (Pinkney in Chapter 5, Christensen in Chapter 6, Baraldi & Farini in Chapter 7, Moran-Ellis & Sünker in Chapter 2 and myself in Chapter 1) suggest that organisational structures also matter for trust dynamics. Thus, Baraldi and Farini problematise the fact that the organisational set-up in schools usually demands pupils' trust in teachers' expertise (demand for system trust) instead of being based on facilitation. They argue that this organisational set-up reflects distrust in children's agency and is therefore ineffective both with regard to social trust building and in motivating children to engage in the activities proposed. Moran-Ellis and Sünker add that this is even the case with regard to School Councils, which ostensibly display trust in children, but in practice are based more on distrust as 'the terms of their remit are limited to matters which teachers are in general prepared to allow children to have power over [...] and that there is not a general sharing of power and decision making over matters central to the running of the school' (Moran-Ellis & Sünker, Chapter 2).

As shown in Chapters 1, 5 and 6, a similar organisational set up can be found in welfare institutions promoted by 'ethics of rights' (Christensen, Chapter 6) and New Public Management ideas about evidence-based practice operationalised through various standardised procedures of risk measurement and management, as well as documentation and control that oversee their implementation (Warming, Chapter 1; Pinkney, Chapter 5; Christensen, Chapter 6). Based on the Luhmannian definition of social trust as different to confidence and system trust,[3] this type of organisational set-up may be regarded as a means of containing risk through institutionalised distrust and a requirement to trust expert systems, at the expense of facilitating trust building and engaged participation by opening up risk alternatives and displaying trust in social workers as professionals, as well as in children as competent actors. System trust and institutionalised distrust – just like social trust – help to manage complexity and risk, but they do not hold the same motivational and engaging potential (Luhmann, 1988, 2005); rather, they are based on acceptance of power relations and domination (Chapters 1 and 2). Thus, such organisational set-ups are dysfunctional in terms of engaging and empowering children's participation.

Pinkney (Chapter 5) and Christensen (Chapter 6) further problematise the organisational structure based on the insight that building up social trust takes time and demands continuity. Pinkney writes:

[...] constraints on social work time and pressure of heavy caseloads often means the relationship with the child is fragmented or the time spent with the child is curtailed and has to be fitted in with many other competing priorities. The high numbers of children who do not have an allocated keyworker or social worker is testimony to the pressure on welfare services. The material conditions of labour where there are shortages of social workers, high reliance on agency and temporary contracted social work staff in field and residential care means that many distressed and hurt children will not have access to a professional who they can build trust in.

(Pinkney, Chapter 5)

Global and local dimensions of the spaces for trust building: Another direction for future research

Organisational structures, and the construction of children and certain subgroups of children as less trustworthy 'communities', shape opportunities for trust building, and thus also children's and adults' engaged collaboration to improve children's life conditions and engaged and empowered participation and citizenship. In Chapter 1, I combine Luhmann with Bourdieu and Delanty in suggesting that global tendencies to handle complexity by relying on institutionalised distrust and a search for foundational knowledge can be seen as power dynamics which shape citizenship learning as disciplinary and excluding rather than empowering and inclusive. I also pointed to another prevalent tendency in welfare organisations, namely the neoliberal responsibilisation of the individual which is a power technology that has an impact on the intertwined dynamics of trust, participation and citizenship learning. Both are global – or at least very widespread phenomena in Western societies – but their manifestations vary considerably depending on the national and local institutional context. Thus, spaces for trust building and, by extension, spaces of lived citizenship (that is citizenship as practiced, learned and experienced), are constructed in the intersection of global flows of information and communication, for example professional knowledge, governance strategies, ideas and information; and locally contextualised policies and practices. The impact of this intersection on trust building processes in children's lives, and the consequences for children's life quality, participation and citizenship have been more or less ignored, despite their acute importance for the field of childhood studies. Thus, research into how the spaces for trust building and of lived citizenship are shaped by this intersection of global flows and local policies and practices constitutes an urgent direction for future research into children's lives, participation and citizenship.

Children's lack of involvement in, and influence on, political processes

Two years ago, *A Handbook of Children and Young People's Participation* (Percy-Smith & Thomas eds., 2010) was published, containing chapters addressing real-life experiences of attempts to facilitate children's participation, as well as attempts to theorise about this. This handbook may be seen as one of many manifestations of what Hill has called a 'participatory climate which helps promote and has been fortified by the UN Convention on the Rights of the Child' (Hill, 2006: 71). Nevertheless, the handbook, and Chapter 2 by Moran-Ellis and Sünker in this book, document that there is still a long way to go. As Austin puts it:

> In many countries around the world children represent the majority of the population; globally, they represent approximately 30 per cent of the population. Yet children's voices are largely absent from political processes, and they have little influence over the development of legislation and policies and the allocation of resources to programmes that directly impact on their lives. Children's interests are often ignored by those in power; they are not regarded as full citizens, and are thus excluded from many of the political processes that would enable them to participate fully in society.
>
> (Austin, 2010: 245)

The trust approach offers a promising avenue for theorising about the disjuncture between a generally participatory climate and a reality characterised by the absence of children's voices (see for example James et al., 2007; Fitzgerald et al., 2010; Warming, 2011). Although this book was motivated by an assumption that this disjuncture needed addressing, I think that I speak on behalf of all the authors when I say that the book's findings have fuelled our enthusiasm about the potential offered by the concept of trust. The trust approach enables a dynamic understanding of the gap between a participatory climate defined and shaped by adults and a much less participatory reality and offers ideas to overcome this. This includes understanding the mutual relationship between adults' lack of recognition of children and their contributions (Aubrey & Dahl, 2006; Fitzgerald et al., 2010; Warming, 2011; Moran-Ellis & Sünker, Chapter 2), and children's wariness and ambivalence regarding participation (Thomas, 2007; Fitzgerald et al., 2010; Warming, 2012). However, the trust approach certainly also has its limitation and needs further development, not least the challenge of grasping how trust and power are intertwined, and of developing a more processual perspective. In this chapter I have outlined some directions for this further development as well as for future research that can benefit from the trust approach. The ideas outlined are intended as an invitation to engage with a crucial and urgent field of childhood research, to which I sincerely hope many scholars will respond.

Notes

1 Social-geographically approached, spatial context does not only address the place where 'things happen', but rather the 'social action situation that is more or less spatially extensive and more or less time-specific' (Simonsen, 2001: 35). This approach includes the 'space as diversity' perspective which addresses contextual power relations, as in the work of Bourdieu (1985, 1989) and, albeit in a different way in the work of Foucault (1980, 1982), and 'space as a material structure' which takes account of the physical environment, as in Foucault's analysis of the Panopticon (Foucault, 1975).
2 The question asked was: 'Generally speaking, would you say that most people can be trusted or that you can't be too careful in dealing with people'. Thus this could also be seen as a measure of trust disposition.
3 Luhmann firstly differentiates between confidence and trust. While the former (confidence) addresses the taken for granted attitude which ignores risk, trust addresses modes of acting based on reflexive choice, including acknowledgement and acceptance of a serious risk in case trust is let down. Secondly, Luhmann (2005) differentiates between social trust and system trust, that can't replace each other, but rather rely on one another. Social trust relates to self-performance and is build up in interaction, while system trust is related to the generalised communication mediums such as money (in the economic subsystem) and truth (regarding expert subsystems). Social trust is built up in a mutual process when actors expect and experience the good actions of the other, and is conversely threatened – but not necessary damaged – by disappointments.

Bibliography

Ainsworth, M., M. Blehar, E. Waters & S. Wall (1978) *Patterns of Attachment*, Hillsdale, NJ: Erlbaum.

Aubrey, C. & S. Dahl (2006) 'Views of vulnerable children on their service providers and the relevance of services they receive', *British Journal of Social Work*, 36(1): 21–39.

Austin, S. L. (2010) 'Children's participation in citizenship and governance' in B. Percy-Smith & N. Thomas (eds) *A Handbook of Children and Young People's Participation. Perspectives from Theory and Practice*, London & New York: Routledge, pp. 245–53.

Bourdieu, P. (1985) 'The space and the genesis of groups', *Theory and Society*, 14(6): 723–44.

Bourdieu, P. (1989) 'Social space and symbolic power', *Sociological Theory*, 7(1): 14–25.

Bourdieu, P. & L. Wacquant (1992) *An Invitation to Reflexive Sociology*, Cambridge and Oxford: Polity Press.

Bourdieu, P., A. Accardo, G. Balzs, S. Beaud, F. Bonvin, E. Bourdieu, P. Bourgois, S. Broccolichi, P. Champagne, R. Christin, J. Faguer, S. Garcia, R. Lenoir, F. Euvrard, M. Pialoux, L. Pinto, D. Podalydés, A. Sayad, C. Soulié & L. J. D. Wacquant (1999) *The Weight of the World. Social Suffering in Contemporary Society*, Cambridge: Polity Press.

Bronfenbrenner, U. (1979) *The Ecology of Human Development*, Cambridge, Massachusetts, US: Harvard University Press.

Bronfenbrenner, U. (1994) 'Ecological models of human development' in T. Husten & T. N. Postlethewaite (eds) *International Encyclopedia of Education*, 2nd edition, Vol. 3, New York: Elsevier Science, pp. 1643–7.

Campbell, H. & J. Heyman (2007) 'Slantwise. beyond domination and resistance on the border', *Journal of Contemporary Ethnography*, 36(1): 3–30.

Christensen, M. (forthcoming) *Tillid på trods i socialt arbejde med udsatte børn og unge – om kommunalt baserede institutionelle barrierer og facilitatorer for tillidens udfoldelse*, PhD dissertation, Roskilde University, Department of Society and Globalisation.

Clauss-Ehler, C. S. (2004) 'Re-inventing resilience. A model of "culturally-focused resilient adaptation"' in C. S. Clauss-Ehler & M. D. Weist (eds) *Community Planning to Foster Resilience in Children*, New York: Kluwer Academics, pp. 27–41.

Delanty, G. (2003) 'Citizenship as a learning process: Disciplinary citizenship versus cultural citizenship', *Lifelong Education*, 22(6): 597–605.

Erikson, E. (1950) *Childhood and Society*, New York: Norton.

Fitzgerald, R., A. Graham, A. Smith & N. Taylor (2010) 'Children's participation as a struggle over recognition: Exploring the promise of dialogue' in B. Percy-Smith & N. Thomas (eds) *A Handbook of Children and Young People's Participation. Perspectives from Theory and Practice*, London & New York: Routledge, pp. 293–305.

Foucault, M. (2002[1975]) *Overva[o]gning og straf*, Frederiksberg: Det lille forlag.

Foucault, M. (1980) *Power/Knowledge: Selected Interview & Other Writings 1972–1978*, New York: Pantheon Books.

Foucault, M. (1982) 'The subject and power', *Critical Inquiry*, 8(4): 777–95.

Fukuyama, F. (1995) *Trust. The Social Virtues and the Creation of Prosperity*, New York: Free Press.

Giddens, A. (1990) *Consequences of Modernity*, Cambridge: Polity Press.

Giddens, A. (1991) *Modernity and Self-identity. Self and Society in Late Modernity*, Cambridge: Polity Press.

Hart, S. (2009) 'The "problem" with youth: Young people, citizenship and the community', *Citizenship Studies*, 13(6): 641–57.

Hill, M. (2006) 'Children's voices on ways of hawing a voice', *Childhood*, 13(1): 69–89.

Jalava, J. (2001): *Trust or Confidence? – Comparing Luhmann's and Gidden's views of trust*. Paper presented at the 5th Conference of the European Sociological Association, 'Visions and Divisions', August 28–September 1, Helsinki, Finland.

James, A., P. Curtis & J. Birch (2007) 'Care and control in the construction of children's citizenship' in J. Williams & A. Invernizzi (eds) *Children and Citizenship*, London: Sage, pp. 85–96.

Koester, L. S. & N. McCray (2011): 'Deaf parents as sources of positive development and resilience for deaf infants' in D. H. Sand & K. J. Pierce (eds) *Resilience in Deaf Children. Adoption Through Emergence Adulthood*, New York: Springer, pp. 65–86.

Larsen, C. A. (2007) 'How welfare regimes generate and erode social capital', *Comparative Politics*, 40(1): 83–101.

Lewis, J. D. & A. Weigert (1985) 'Trust as a social reality', *Social Forces*, 63(4): 967–85.

Luhmann, N. (1988) 'Familiarity, confidence, trust: problems and alternatives' in D. Gambetta (ed.) *Trust: Making and Breaking Cooperative Relations*, Department of Sociology, University of Oxford, pp. 94–107.

Luhmann, N. (1991) *Soziologie des Risikos*, Berlin: De Gruyter.

Luhmann, N. (2005) *Tillid – en mekanisme til reduktion af social kompleksitet*, København: Hans Reitzels Forlag.

Percy-Smith, B. & N. Thomas (eds) (2010) *A Handbook of Children and Young People's Participation. Perspectives from Theory and Practice*, London & New York: Routledge.

Pollitt, C. & G. Bouchaert (2011) *Public Management Reform. A Comparative Analysis. New Public Management, Governance and the New-Weberian State*, Third edition, Oxford: Oxford University Press.

Putnam, R. D. (2000) *Bowling Alone: The Collapse and Revival of American Community*, New York: Simon & Schuster.

Poulsen, O. & G. T. Svendsen (2005) *Love Thy Neighbor: Bonding versus Bridging Trust*. Working paper 5 July, Aarhus: Department of Economics, Aarhus School of Business.

Schaffer, H. R. (1992) 'Early experience and the parent–child relationship: Genetic and environmental interactions as developmental determinants' in B. Tizard & V. Varma (eds) *Vulnerability and Resilience in Human Development*, London: Jessica Kingsley, pp. 39–65.

Rose, N. (1996) 'The death of the social? Refiguring the territory of government', *Economy and Society*, 25(3): 327–56.

Simonsen, K. (2001) 'Rum, sted, krop og køn – dimensioner af en geografi om social praksis' in K. Simonsen (ed.) *Praksis, Rum Og Mobilitet*, Roskilde Universitetsforlag, pp. 17–48.

Thomas, N. (2007) 'Towards a theory of children's participation', *International Journal of Children's Rights*, 15(2): 199–218.

Uslaner, E. M. (1999) 'Democracy and social capital' in M. E. Warren (ed.) *Democracy and Trust*, Cambridge: Cambridge University Press, pp. 121–50.

Uslaner, E. M. (2002) *The Moral Foundations of Trust*, New York: Cambridge University Press.

Warming, H. (2011) 'Children's participation and citizenship in a global age: Empowerment, tokenism or discriminatory disciplining?' *Social Work & Society*, 9(1): 119–34.

Warming, H. (2012) 'Theorizing adult's facilitation of children's participation and citizenship' in C. Baraldi & V. Iervese (eds) *Participation, Facilitation, and Mediation: Children and Young People in Their Social Contexts*, London: Routledge, pp. 30–48.

Wharton, T. (2009) *Pragmatics and Non-verbal Communication*, New York: Cambridge University Press.

Index

active citizenship, 10, 16–17, 23, 27
    and trust, 17–18, 28, 95
age, 162, 169
    and decision-making ability, 33,
        36, 99–100
    and right to protection, 21, 23
    and trust levels, 177
    voting, 41–3, 47n7
    women's voting rights, 42,
        47n10
agency, 12, 16, 28, 39–40, 45, 57,
    67, 101, 125, 136
    children's, 45, 57, 136, 151n4,
        165, 199, 204
    moral, 36
    and trust, 121–2
alienation, 24–5, 134, 169
altruistic trust, 179
appreciation, 142, 146
attachment, 178
    behaviour of social workers,
        100–1
    figure, 85–6
    and identity formation, 67
    inadequate, 59, 73, 86
    and loss, 84–6
    maternal, 84, 86
    patterns, 54–7, 67–8, 195–6
    and social behaviour, 54–7, 68
    theory of, 195–6
autopoiesis, 122

basic trust, 10–13, 15, 53, 55, 94,
    186, 195–8, 201
'becoming' perspective, 3, 52–3, 83,
    138, 176, 189–90, 201
'being' perspective, 3, 52–3
belonging, feelings of, 19, 24–5, 27,
    177–8, 190–1
Bourdieu, Pierre, 14–15, 22, 27–8, 45,
    95, 202
Bronfenbrenner, Urie, 3
bullying, 56, 65–7, 107, 109

capital
    cultural, 14
    economic, 14
    social, 3, 95, 165, 177–8, 181, 197–8
    sociocultural, 190
    symbolic, 14
care
    ethics of, 114–15, 117–18, 125, 127
    package of, 116, 127
    rights of, 114–15, 117–18, 125, 127
Care Matters, 97
childcare, 81–2, 106, 161
childhood, 11, 191
    basic trust, role of, 12–13, 15, 53–7,
        66, 94, 128, 177, 194, 203, 205
    experiences of non-standard, 39, 77
    ideal, 154
    identity formation during, 67–8
    Liza's life story, 20–1, 26
    normative, 162
    secure vs. insecure, 57–8
    sexual abuse, 82–4
    sociology of, 10, 12–13, 33, 44, 94,
        170–1
    studies, 1–2, 33, 135–6, 203, 205
Childline, 76, 88n1
children
    'becoming/being' perspective, 3,
        52–3, 83, 138, 176, 189–90, 201
    best interest, 6, 27, 34, 36, 38, 104,
        137, 156, 159–60, 171
    innocence, 82
    looked after, 93, 96, 98, 102, 106–7,
        202
    neglect, 66, 100, 106, 162
    protection, 33, 74, 77, 82, 87, 93,
        96–7, 100, 105–6, 155
    rights, 5, 43, 83, 88, 93, 96–7,
        100–4, 108, 115
    at risk, 53, 57, 114, 116, 118–19,
        122–6, 162
    sexual abuse, 33, 73–8, 81–4, 100,
        106, 202

trusting commitment, 134–7
victims, 75–8, 80–1, 83–8, 106, 155,
    162–3, 168, 203
welfare, 5, 93, 95, 103, 105–7, 110,
    168
Children Act 2004, 84, 88n9
Children's Rights Officers, 103, 107–8
chronosystems, 4
citizenship
    active, 10, 16–18, 23, 27–8, 95
    cultural, 10, 19, 24–6, 158–9
    disciplinary, 4, 19, 158, 205
    inclusive, 4, 17, 27–8, 205
civility, 174, 176, 181
Cleveland crisis, 106
Cockburn, Tom, 116
communication skills, 96
communicative acts, 13–14, 18, 21,
    25–7
complexity, 2, 16–17, 23, 28, 37, 57,
    95, 110, 118–21, 123–5, 127,
    136, 158, 164, 178, 195, 199,
    204–5
confidence *see also* trust
    children's active citizenship, 10
    distinction with trust, 16–18, 53,
        95, 121–2, 132–4, 151n3,
        207n3
    in distrust, 137–8
    family bonds and, 66–7
    in Luhmannian sense, 54, 95, 114,
        118–21, 129n2, 191n1, 195,
        204, 207n3
    participatory perspective, 32,
        36–41, 45
    in political system, 181
    secure childhood and, 57–62, 64–5
    self, 54–5, 66, 185
    social workers and, 17, 105–6,
        116–17
The Consequences of Modernity, 12
control, 6, 190, 199, 201–2, 204
    within child-parent relationships,
        36–7, 79, 83, 150, 155, 184
    governmental, 160
    participatory perspective, 34
    social, 175
    in social work, 116, 126, 163,
        168–70

and surveillance, 21, 27
in western societies, 78
cooperation, trust and, 16, 27, 177–8,
    180
critical pedagogy, 136
cues, linguistics, 140, 142, 144, 148,
    150, 200
cultural capital, 14
cultural citizenship, 10, 19, 24–6,
    158–9
cultural presupposition, 132, 140,
    146, 150

Delanty, Gerard, 4, 10–11, 18–19, 21,
    24–5, 28, 158, 168, 205
democracy, 3, 11, 17–18, 39, 43, 95,
    174, 178, 181–2
demoralisation, 25
difference-centred approach to
    citizenship, 4, 11, 18–19
disciplinary citizenship, 4, 19, 158,
    205
discourses, 4–5, 142, 197
    on the adults' narrative
        remembering process, 57–8
    on childhood, life story, 26
    of children at risk, 116
    on children with migrant parents,
        156, 159–65
    cultural, 25, 168
    of liberal professionalism, 103–5
    social work, 127, 168
    of trust in relation to children, 32
    on victimisation, 154–5, 169
    on voting rights, 42–3
    of youth in Western societies, 109
discrimination, 10, 14, 26–7
dispositions, 5, 12, 14–15
    for trust, 53–4, 60, 65, 67, 197,
        200–2, 207n2
distrust, 11–12, 27, 32, 35, 43, 46,
    58, 62, 67–8, 80, 162, 166–7,
    176, 198, 200, 202, 204
    building trust in, 137–8
    children's, in agency, 135–6,
        204
    and citizenship, 17–18, 28
    communicative act of, 21–2
    impact of, 20–1

distrust – *continued*
  institutional, 17, 19–23, 25–6, 28,
    204–5
  Luhmann's, 114, 117–23, 125–6,
    128
  in social work, 114, 117
divorce, 55–6, 63–5, 67, 196
documentation, 5, 115–16, 126, 204
domination, 14, 154, 157–8, 165–7,
    170–1, 203–4 *see also* Resistance

ecological system, 3–4, 52, 197
economic capital, 14
education to peace, 6, 132, 138–9,
    146, 149
Eight Rung Ladder of Participation, 117,
    126
empowerment, 23, 28, 203
engagement, 17, 95, 133–4, 150, 171,
    199, 201
Erikson, Erik, 11–12, 55, 94
ethics
  of care, 114–15, 117–18, 125, 127
  of rights, 114–15, 117–18, 125–7,
    204
evaluation, 54, 135, 143–4, 148
Every Child Matters, 97
exclusion (social) of youth, 191
exosystems, 4
expectations, 140, 144, 177, 179–81,
    188, 198
  affective, 148, 150
  of children 'in care', 109
  cognitive or normative, 150
  from education, 135
  insecurity and, 58
  negative, 65
  of person-to-person relations, 123
  positive, 157, 195
  in presupposition of trust building,
    150
  social, 78–9, 81, 87, 122
  trust and, 58–60, 68, 94, 119, 132–4
expertise, 39, 132 *see also* trust
  trust based on, 135–6, 204

facilitation, 132, 136–9, 141, 146,
    148–51, 198–9
familial sexual abuse, 75, 77

familiarity, 44, 54, 119, 195
*Familiarity, Confidence, Trust: Problems
    and Alternatives*, 118
family
  courts, 77
  power relations, 82, 196
  separation, 63–5, 99, 162, 171
  structure, 67, 78–9, 83, 133
  support, 59–60, 189–90, 196–7
  transnational, 155–6, 159, 161–2,
    164, 168–9
feedback questions, 141–4, 148–9, 199
fields, 1, 3, 14–15
  superior, 14–15
figure
  maternal, 74, 84
  trustworthy, 26–7, 73, 78, 185
formulations, 141–2, 144, 146–9, 199
  Parsonian, of trust, 32, 44
  of trust at interpersonal level, 37–8
functioning trust, 47n12

generalised other, 127
generalised trust, 54–6, 155, 174,
    176–8, 181–2, 187–91, 195, 198
generational order, 22–6, 28, 40, 198,
    202
Giddens, Anthony, 3, 10–13, 15–16,
    94, 106, 135, 197, 201–2
Goffman, Erving, 13, 94, 123, 126

habitus, 14–15, 117, 197
Hardin, Russel, 16, 166, 179
Harré, Rom, 10–12, 17–18
Hart, Roger, 117, 126
Hayward, Clarissa, 167, 169

identity, 4–5, 182, 186
  citizen, 27–8, 154, 156, 191, 202
  collective, 177–8
  construction of one's, 27, 67
  development in children, 68, 73
  dimension, 19
  ethnic, 179
  formation of negative, 67
  institutionalisation of, 167, 169
  social relationships and, 106
  social worker's professional, 100–1
  trust and citizen, 24–7

inadequate attachment, 86
inclusion, 21, 24, 37, 41, 66, 114,
    116, 146, 178, 181, 203
    social, 185, 190
inclusive citizenship, 4, 17, 27–8, 205
individualisation, 174–5
Initiation, Reply, Evaluation (IRE)
    sequence, 136, 143
insecurity, 52, 55, 57–8, 60, 64, 94,
    106
institutional distrust, 17, 19–23, 25–6,
    28, 204–5
institutional mistrust, 154–6, 167
institutional trust, 93, 156–7, 162,
    164, 182, 187
integration, social, 24, 175–82
intergenerational relationships, 33,
    35, 40–4, 47n12, 196, 201–2
intergenerational trust, 37
internal system trust alertness, 124
interpersonal relationship, 119,
    138–9, 148–50
isolation, political, 188

justice, social, 23, 93, 95, 97, 110

lack of trust, 60, 64, 133–4, 168–9,
    178–9, 181, 188
ladder of participation, 117, 126
life course, 5, 52–3, 174–5
linguistic cues, 140, 142, 144, 148,
    150, 200
listening, 93, 97–100, 115–16, 126,
    136, 170
looked after children, 98, 107
low staff morale, 102
Luhmann, Niklas
    concept of trust, 4
    confidence, 54, 95, 114, 118–21,
        129n2, 191n1, 195, 204, 207n3
    distrust, 114, 117–23, 125–6, 128
    trustworthy, 128

macrosystems, 4
managerialism, 103–4
maternal characteristics
    abuser, 79
    attachment, 84, 86
    figure, 74, 84

loss, 84
    role, 78, 81
meaning-making patterns, 24–6
mesosystems, 4
microsystems, 4
mistrust, 2, 4, 60–1, 65, 93–5, 106,
    109–10, 154–6, 158, 161, 163–7,
    169–71, 188, 200 *see also* distrust;
    trust
Misztal, Barbara, 1, 17, 94–5, 119
Moosa-mitha, Mehmoona, 3, 11,
    18–19
morale, low staff, 102, 104
moral trust, 54
mother *see also* maternal characteristics
    child bond, 81, 85–6
    loss of bond, 86
    mothering role, 78, 80, 84, 87
    as perpetrator, 5, 73–8, 86–7

narratives, 25–6, 46, 57–8, 62–3,
    103–4, 107, 148, 154–6, 159,
    167–9
new public management, 17, 103,
    197, 204
normative childhood, 162

Office of the Children's
    Commissioner report, 96–7
optimistic trust, 179

package of care, 116, 127
parenting, 6, 56, 61, 160, 163, 189,
    196
parents' divorce *see* divorce
Parsons, Talcott, 11, 120
participation, 160, 163, 198–9
    adolescents' voluntary, 139–41,
        146, 148
    children's, 2–3, 5–7, 10, 22, 28,
        32–45, 95–8, 117, 168–9,
        194–5, 200, 202, 204
    in decision-making processes, 108
    ladder of, 117, 126
    prerequisite in communication,
        133–4
    promotion of, 46, 149
    within scarce resource context,
        102–4

participation – *continued*
  social, 78–82
  trust and, 2–3, 15, 17–20
  of young people, 176–82
participatory rights, 34, 41
particularised trust, 54, 155, 195, 197–8
pathologies, social, 25
patterns, meaning-making, 24–6
pedagogy, critical, 136
performance, 44, 58, 104, 116, 140, 150
political isolation, 188
positioning, 37, 39, 46, 140, 148, 150
post-socialism, 181–2
power dynamics, 4, 14, 21–2, 28, 205
power relations, 10, 14–15, 20, 23, 35, 41, 43, 82, 95, 104, 128, 196–7, 201–4
power structures, 4, 14–15, 22–3, 28, 202
professionals
  collusion, 81
  denial, 41–2, 81–2, 86
  minimisation, 82, 86, 98, 106, 166
promotional questions, 141–2, 144, 149
protection, 7, 9, 20–1, 23, 33, 73–4, 77, 80, 82–4, 93, 95–7, 100, 105–6, 176, 190

questions
  feedback, 141–4, 148–9, 199
  promotional, 141–2, 144, 149

resistance, 104, 154, 157–8, 165–7, 170–1
resource shortfalls, 102
responsibilisation, 11, 27–8, 161, 205
rights
  of being a citizen, 19, 28, 41, 191
  of care, 114–15, 117–18, 125, 127
  children's, 5, 43, 83, 88, 93, 96–7, 100–4, 108, 115
  difference-centred
    conceptualisation, 19
  of free association and free
    expression, 41
  participatory, 34, 41
  relation with trust, 19–20
  voting, 41–3

risk
  children at, 53, 57, 114, 116, 118–19, 122–6, 162
  trust and, 120–1

security, 52, 67 *see also* insecurity
  feelings of, 57–8
  inner, 53, 55, 68
  ontological, 12
  social, 7, 176, 185
  through support, 59–60
self-expression, 98, 136, 142, 148–9
self-governance, 27, 156, 161, 163
self-representation, 122–5
sexual abuse
  of children, 33, 73–8, 81–4, 100, 106, 202
  familial, 75, 77, 79
social capital, 3, 95, 165, 177–8, 181, 197–8
social cohesion, 3, 15
social exclusion of youth, 191
social inclusion, 185, 190
social integration, 24, 175–82
social justice, 23, 93, 95, 97, 110
social pathologies, 25
social relations, 12, 95, 106, 122, 133, 137, 150, 174, 177
social security, 7, 176, 185
social services, 20, 99, 101–2, 121, 156, 159, 161, 163–5, 168–9
social system, 95, 116–17, 119, 122–4, 129n3, 133–8, 140, 157, 199
social trust, 17, 23, 28, 53–4, 56, 58, 61, 67, 203–4, 207n3
social work
  child protection, 96, 197
  with children in foster care, 170
  preventive and active, 68
  trust in, 2–5, 11, 17, 20, 22–3, 53, 96–7, 114–20
social worker, positioned, 5, 116, 123–7
society diagnose, 16
sociocultural capital, 190
'space as diversity' perspective, 207n1
state interference in family life, 161
superior field, 14–15
survivors, 5, 74, 76, 86, 88

symbolic capital, 14
symbolic violence, 21, 28
system internal conditions for trust,
    13–14
system trust, 12, 20, 22–3, 26–8, 45,
    53–4, 60, 66, 121, 124, 151n1,
    157, 199–200, 203–4, 207n3

time and trust, 120–1
transition countries, 174, 176
transition process, 7, 188–9
transition to adulthood, 175
transnational family, 155–6, 159,
    161–2, 164, 168–9
trust
    in advance, 177, 188
    altruistic, 179
    authoritative, 117
    based on expertise, 135–6, 204
    basic, 12–13, 197
    betrayal, 73–86
    building, 93, 96–8, 104, 106, 132,
        134–9, 141, 149–50
    childhood, role in, 12–13, 15, 53–7,
        66, 94, 128, 177, 194, 203,
        205
    as communicative act, 13–14
    correlation between trustworthy
        and, 177–8
    cultural citizenship and, 25–6
    dispositions, 197
    dynamics of, 2, 6, 11, 93, 100, 155,
        196–7, 205
    fear of, 80, 85
    finding a voice, 82–6
    functioning, 47n12
    generalised, 54–6, 155, 174, 176–8,
        181–2, 187–91, 195, 198
    generational order and, 22–4
    in globalised societies, 2–3, 27–8
    identity and, 24–7
    inability to, 73, 86
    institutional, 93, 156–7, 162, 164,
        182, 187
    lack of, 60, 64, 133–4, 168, 178–9,
        181, 188
    'leap' of, 120
    meanings of, 53–4
    moral, 54

optimistic, 179
particularised, 54, 155, 195, 197–8
personal, 6, 12, 20, 26–7, 117,
    121–3, 151n1, 199–200, 203
risk and, 120–1
social, 17, 23, 28, 53–4, 56, 58, 61,
    67, 203–4, 207n3
social constraints and, 75–8
social participation and, 78–82
system, 12, 20, 22–3, 26–8, 45,
    53–4, 60, 66, 121, 124, 151n1,
    157, 199–200, 203–4, 207n3
in system authorities, 122–3
theory, 11–18
in trust, 10, 13–14, 53–4, 60–2,
    64–8
violation/erosion, 2, 4–5, 60, 196,
    201
working, 137–8, 141, 148–50, 199
trustworthy, 14, 140, 150, 185, 202–3,
    205
adults, 75, 78, 80, 82, 87
behaviour, 122, 127, 178
correlation between trust and,
    177–8
evaluation of being, 54, 73, 122,
    138
figure, 26–7, 73, 78, 185
identity as, 26–7
insecurity and, 106
Luhmannian perspective, 128

UN Convention on the Rights of the
    Child, 19, 23, 33, 88n9, 206
Utting Report, 97

victims
    fear of trust, 80, 85
    female, 75
    male, 76, 87
    of maternal incest, 5, 73–86
    powerlessness, 83
    silencing, 86
violence, symbolic, 21, 28
vulnerability, 87, 94, 102, 107, 123

Working Together (2010), 97
working trust, 137–8, 141, 148–50,
    199